STRONGBOW

THE NORMAN INVASION OF IRELAND

Conor Kostick is a novelist and historian living in Dublin; he holds a PhD and a gold medal from Trinity College Dublin. His research into medieval history has won a number of awards, including the *Dublinia Medieval Essay Prize*, the *Marsh's Library Fellowship*, and a prestigious €100,000 European *Marie Curie* award. His other history books include *The Siege of Jerusalem: Crusade and Conquest in 1099*; *Revolution in Ireland* and – together with Lorcan Collins – *The Easter Rising: A Guide to Dublin in 1916*.

STRONG BOW

THE NORMAN INVASION OF IRELAND

CONOR KOSTICK

THE O'BRIEN PRESS
DUBLIN

First published 2013 by
The O'Brien Press Ltd,
12 Terenure Road East, Rathgar,
Dublin 6, Ireland.
Tel: +353 1 4923333; Fax: +353 1 4922777
E-mail: books@obrien.ie
Website: www.obrien.ie

ISBN: 978-1-84717-200-6

1 2 3 4 5 6 7 8
13 14 15 16 17

All quotations have been reproduced with original spelling and punctuation. Errors are author's own.

Printed and bound by CPI Group (UK) Ltd, Croydon, CR0 4YY
The paper used in this book is produced using pulp from managed forests.

PICTURE CREDITS

The author and publisher thank the following for permission to use photographs and illustrative material: front and back cover image: Cartoon Saloon; Section 1: page 1 (inset) Bibliothèque municipale de Dijon, ms 14 f 13, (E Juvin), used with permission; page 2 (top) National Library of Ireland MS700 f48r; page 3 illustration by Steve Rigby: © Worcestershire County Council, used by permission of Worcestershire Archive and Archaeology Service; page 5 (top left and right) National Library of Ireland MS700 f56r and MS700 f64r; page 5 (bottom) Emma Byrne; page 6 Copyright reserved Cambridge University Collection of Aerial Photography AHL13; page 7 top right National Library of Ireland MS700 f39r; page 7 (bottom) Welsh Government/Llywodraeth Cymru; page 8 photograph by Phil Kircher, used with permission; Section 2: page 1 two images, top, 'The Siege of Wexford' and, bottom, 'Battles in the Kingdom of Ossory', permission and copyright Ann Bernstorff; page 2 The National Gallery of Ireland NGI6315; page 3 (top and bottom) Cartsen Krieger from *Ireland: Glorious Landscapes*; page 4 Emma Byrne; page 5 Robert Vance; page 6 (bottom) National Library of Irleland MS700 75v; page 7 (top) Carsten Krieger from *Ireland: Glorious Landscapes*; page 7 (bottom) Uto Hogerzeil; page 8 (top) Uto Hogerzeil; page 8 with kind permission of Christ Church Cathedral archives.

Other images: Section 1 pages 1, 2, 4, 7 (top left) from the Bayeux Tapestry; page 6 bottom from Grose's *Antiquities* Vol 1. Section 2 page2 from Grose's *Antiquities* Vol 1.

If any involuntary infringement of copyright has occurred, sincere apologies are offered and the owners of such copyright are requested to contact the publisher.

DEDICATION

To my Aoife

ACKNOWLEDGEMENTS

With thanks to Nathan Reynard and Katharine Simms

for their helpful feedback on earlier drafts of this book.

Contents

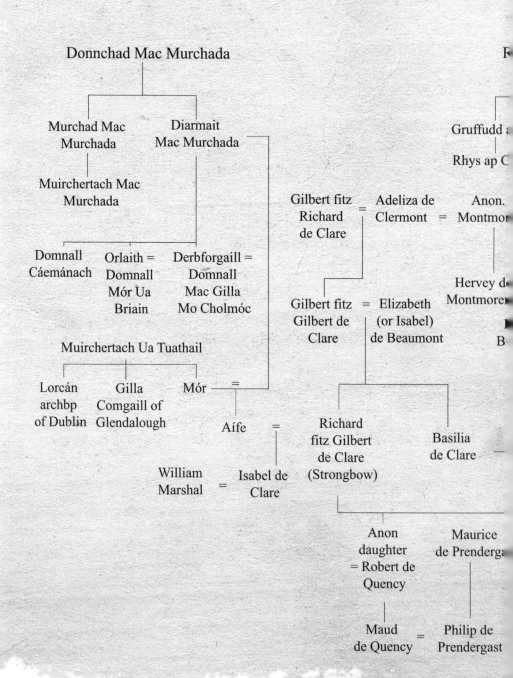

Donnchad Mac Murchada

Murchad Mac Murchada

Diarmait Mac Murchada

Muirchertach Mac Murchada

Gilbert fitz Richard de Clare = Adeliza de Clermont = Anon. Montmor

Gruffudd a

Rhys ap C

Domnall Cáemánach

Orlaith = Domnall Mór Ua Briain

Derbforgaill = Domnall Mac Gilla Mo Cholmóc

Gilbert fitz Gilbert de Clare = Elizabeth (or Isabel) de Beaumont

Hervey d Montmore

B

Muirchertach Ua Tuathail

Lorcán archbp of Dublin

Gilla Comgaill of Glendalough

Mór =

Richard fitz Gilbert de Clare (Strongbow)

Basilia de Clare

Aífe =

William Marshal = Isabel de Clare

Anon daughter = Robert de Quency

Maurice de Prenderga

Maud de Quency = Philip de Prendergast

ical Table

ewdwr

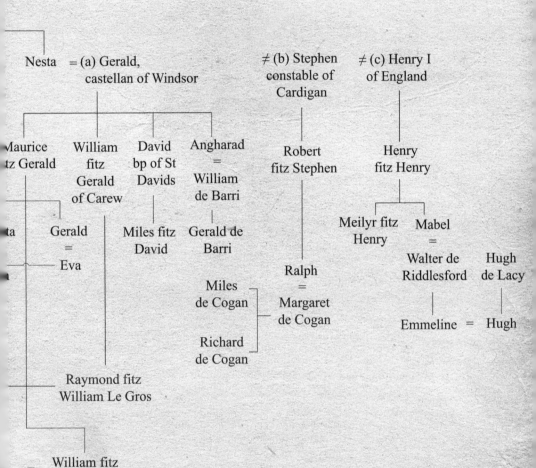

Nesta = (a) Gerald, castellan of Windsor ≠ (b) Stephen constable of Cardigan ≠ (c) Henry I of England

Maurice fitz Gerald | William fitz Gerald of Carew | David bp of St Davids | Angharad = William de Barri | | Robert fitz Stephen | | Henry fitz Henry

ta | Gerald = Eva | | Miles fitz David | Gerald de Barri | | | | Meilyr fitz Henry | Mabel =

Miles de Cogan | Ralph = Margaret de Cogan | Walter de Riddlesford | Hugh de Lacy

Richard de Cogan | Emmeline = Hugh

Raymond fitz William Le Gros

= William fitz Maurice

List of Historical Figures

Aífe Mac Murchada, Leinster princess

Asculv Mac Turcaill, ruler of Dublin

Basilia, sister of Strongbow

Derbforgaill, wife of Tigernán Ua Ruairc

Diarmait Mac Murchada, king of Leinster

Domnall Cáemánach Mac Murchada, Leinster prince

Domnall Mac Gilla Pátraic, king of Osraige

Gerald de Barri, cleric and historian

Henry II, king of England

Hervey de Montmorency, adventurer and Strongbow's uncle

Hugh de Lacy, Norman lord

John the Wode, Viking hero

Lorcán Ua Tuathail, archbishop of Dublin

Maurice de Prendergast, leader of Flemish troops

Maurice fitz Gerald, Norman knight

Meilyr fitz Henry, Norman knight

Miles de Cogan, Norman commander

Miles fitz David, Norman knight

Muirchertach Mac Lochlainn, high king of Ireland

Raymond Le Gros, Norman commander

Robert fitz Stephen, Norman commander

Ruaidrí Ua Conchobair, high king of Ireland

Strongbow, Richard fitz Gilbert de Clare

Tigernán Ua Ruairc, lord of Bréifne and Conmaicne

Chronology

1110   Birth of Diarmait Mac Murchada.

1115   Murder of Diarmait's father by the Hiberno-Norse of Dublin.

c.1122   Tigernán Ua Ruairc becomes lord of Bréifne and Conmaicne.

1126   Diarmait becomes ruler of the Uí Chennselaig and is proclaimed king of Leinster, but is overthrown by the high king.

1128   Tigernán Ua Ruairc plays a prominent part in a raid against the Uí Chennselaig, Diarmait is forced to give way.

1130   Birth of Richard fitz Gilbert de Clare, 'Strongbow'.

1132   Diarmait attacks Kildare Abbey.

1138   Diarmait and his allies thwart an incursion from the high king and Tigernán Ua Ruairc.

1141   Seventeen local rivals murdered or blinded by Diarmait.

1148   Strongbow inherits his father's lands and titles.

1151   The battle of Móin Mór, Diarmait survives on the winning side.

1152   Diarmait, allied with Muirchertach Mac Lochlainn, defeats Tigernán Ua Ruairc. Derbforgaill, Tigernán's wife, elopes with Diarmait.

1154   Strongbow faces ruin arising from the hostility of Henry II.

1155   King Henry II of England proposes an invasion of Ireland, but is dissuaded by his court.

1159   The battle of Ardee. Diarmait allies with Mac Lochlainn and, in another brutal conflict, defeats Tigernán and his allies, the warriors of Connacht.

1166   Muirchertach Mac Lochlainn is killed by Tigernán Ua Ruairc and his allies. Ruaidrí Ua Conchobair becomes high king and in the company of Tigernán inflicts a heavy defeat on Diarmait. Diarmait flees to Bristol. That autumn, Diarmait seeks out King Henry II of England and offers to become Henry's vassal in return for support.

1167   The fateful meeting of Diarmait and Strongbow. Diarmait returns to Ireland and rallies the Uí Chennselaig, but is immediately attacked by

Ruaidrí and Tigernán. Diarmait is forced to pay honour price to Tigernán for taking Derbforgaill fifteen years earlier.

1169, 1 MAY

The arrival in Ireland, at Bannow, of Robert fitz Stephen, Miles fitz David, Meilyr fitz Henry, Maurice de Prendergast and Strongbow's uncle, Hervey de Montmorency.

1169, SUMMER

Maurice de Prendergast attempts to leave Ireland and, when prevented from doing so by Diarmait, defects to the king of Osraige.

1169, AUTUMN

Ruaidrí Ua Conchobair confronts Diarmait and Robert fitz Stephen, leaving Leinster with hostages and the promise that the Norman troops will be sent back across the Irish Sea. Maurice de Prendergast and his troops escape ambush to report back to Strongbow.

1170, 1 MAY

Raymond Le Gros, acting for Strongbow, arrives at Dún Domnaill near Waterford and wins a battle against the Hiberno-Norse and their local Irish allies.

1170, 23 AUGUST

Strongbow sails for Ireland against King Henry II's commands. Two days later, Waterford is stormed and Strongbow marries Aífe Mac Murchada in the aftermath of the slaughter.

1170, 21 SEPTEMBER

The Hiberno-Norse of Dublin are taken by surprise, while negotiating with Strongbow and Diarmait, and the city is captured.

1171, *c*1 MAY

The death of Diarmait Mac Murchada.

1171, *c*16 MAY

The deposed ruler of Dublin, Asculv Mac Turcaill, along with John the Wode, bring a Viking army to regain the city, but are defeated by Miles de Cogan.

1171, SUMMER

Siege of Dublin by the high king and his allies, ended by a surprise attack on Ruaidrí's camp and the rout of the Irish army.

1171, LATE AUTUMN

Tigernán leads the third attack of this year on Dublin and once again Miles de Cogan defends the city, routing the Irish army.

1171, 17 OCTOBER

The arrival of King Henry II of England in Ireland (near Waterford). From 11 November, Henry spends the winter in Dublin.

1172, 17 APRIL

Henry II leaves Ireland, having taken oaths of submission from most Irish kings and also having created divisions among the Norman lords remaining in Ireland.

1172

Tigernán is betrayed and murdered while in negotiations with Hugh de Lacy, the new Norman lord of Meath. Tigernán's head is placed over the gates of Dublin Castle.

1173, AUGUST

Strongbow fights in Normandy for Henry II.

1173, AUTUMN

Mutiny against Strongbow by his soldiers in Ireland who want further conquests. Raymond Le Gros returns to Waterford to lead these troops and is promised the hand of Strongbow's sister, Basilia.

1174

At Cashel, Strongbow retreats from a punitive raid. A surge of Irish and Hiberno-Norse risings take place.

1175

The capture of Limerick by Raymond Le Gros.

1176, 20 APRIL

Strongbow dies of an infection spreading from his foot.

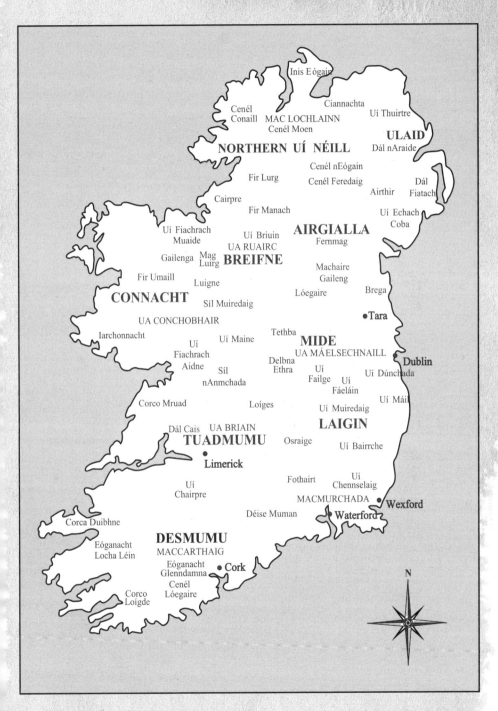

Ireland before the Normans.

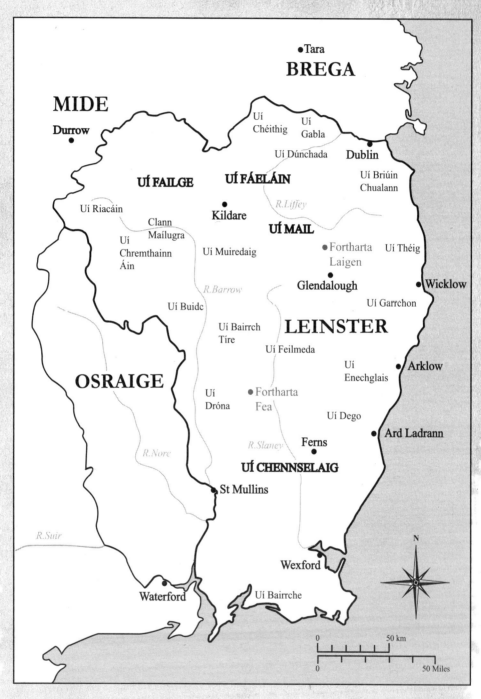

Leinster before the Normans (following FJ Byrne, *Irish Kings and High Kings*).

Ireland, Wales, England and Normandy.

Preface

ay 1169. Dispersed groups of armoured men are wielding long axes in a meadow on the southwest border of Leinster. They are sweating in the sunshine and would welcome the opportunity to rest in the shade of a nearby line of trees. It is not timber that these men are hacking but heads from the several hundred corpses that are lying in the tall grass. Blood has been sprayed over the yellow marigolds and buttercups and has collected in dark, scarlet pools. Longhaired, bearded or bald, the severed heads are picked up and brought to be counted and paid for at a distinct gathering of soldiers, whose banners are as colourful as the spring flowers. There, one man in particular dominates the scene.

Diarmait Mac Murchada, king of Leinster, cannot contain his feelings of satisfaction as the pile of heads before him grows. His teeth are clenched and a bitter, vindictive joy is evidently coursing through him. From time to time the king leaps into the air, clasping his arms above his head in glee. Despite the gore, Diarmait recognises the features of men whom he hated passionately and revels in the fact that they will never defy him again. Their threats have proven empty. Their cruelties towards Diarmait have been answered. In the vicious life-and-death struggle that has over the years favoured one side and then the other, Diarmait has ultimately emerged victorious. It is finished with now and forever.

Beside the king are three knights clad entirely in chainmail: from the coif over their heads − currently thrown back so they can feel refreshed after their exertions − to their feet. Their names are Robert fitz Stephen, Maurice de

Prendergast and Hervey de Montmorency and they are conscious of being foreigners in this land. If these knights think the behaviour of the king is unbecoming, they are wise enough not to display their disapproval. Instead they look on with apparent equanimity as the elderly man jumps around the grisly display, the satisfaction of vengeance fulfilled evidently providing him with boundless energy.

The king of Leinster is a tall man who at fifty-nine years of age still retains some of the muscular physique of his youth. But his bearded face also bears the lines of a man who has brooded in sorrow and anger for many years. And Diarmait's voice, once capable of giving a roar as loud as a charging bull, is husky now, worn out from the din of battle. Of his many sorrows, one of the greatest was the blinding of his eldest son, Énna Mac Murchada. It was the men of Osraige, the kingdom on Leinster's south-west border, who had made Énna their prisoner and, after holding their captive for two years, it was they who had put out his eyes and made him ineligible to ever inherit the king-ship. It is the same warriors of Osraige who carried out this mutilation whose bodies are lying still under the blue sky and whose sightless eyes roll as their heads are tossed onto the bloody heap.

As he turns over the ruined faces to examine them, one in particular excites Diarmait more than all the others. He grabs it by the hair and holds it up for all in the field to see. Everyone pauses to watch. With a husky laugh of tri-umph, Diarmait suddenly lunges at the head and bites the nose and cheeks of his defeated foe. This action will reassure his superstitious warriors that the ghosts of the slain will not return to haunt them.

The king of Leinster had a lot of enemies; at one time nearly the whole of Ireland was united against him. But the fact that his neighbours from Osraige had joined in the coalition to oust him had been a particularly heavy blow and Diarmait had hardly dared dream that the day would come when he could make the traitors pay. Now they were dead and their corpses were his to abuse. Let the word spread throughout the land: Diarmait Mac Murchada was back. If you had been one of those traitors who had turned against him and driven him to seek the assistance of foreigners, then you would shiver at the news of the king of Leinster savaging the features of his old enemies. It could be your head in his hands before long.

Out of sight of the Irish king, the three Norman lords exchange glances with each other and look back to the far end of the field where a handful of knights and a much larger number of archers are gathered after the battle. Before that morning's conflict began, Robert fitz Stephen had addressed the Norman army. The handsome, clean-shaven knight had emphasised the justice of Diarmait's campaign; the treacherous nature of the men of Osraige, who had committed a crime when they had taken over half of Diarmait's former lands; and the honourable nature of the king of Leinster. If that attempt to exalt their nominal overlord as a model of chivalry now appears rather false, there are nevertheless no shocked stares or insubordinate mutterings from among Robert's followers.

These soldiers from south Wales are hard men with a professional commitment to war and no illusions as to the character of the princes who lead them. And that morning there had been another point made by Robert in his rallying speech that had struck home and made them more loyal to Diarmait's cause than any of the king's own Irish followers. 'Perhaps,' Robert had said, 'the outcome of this present action will be that the five divisions of the island will be reduced to one, and sovereignty over the whole kingdom will devolve upon us in future. If victory is won and Mac Murchada is restored with the aid of our arms, if by our present assaults the kingdom of Ireland is forever preserved for us and for our descendants then what renown we shall win!'

Renown, yes, and a comfortable living as the recipients of the wealth that made its way up from those who worked the land and cattle to those who lived in halls and castles. There was opportunity, here in Ireland, to supplant the local nobles. That was the real appeal of Robert's speech. Let Diarmait behave as a pagan king of biblical times if he wished. It did not matter. What was important about this campaign was that after Diarmait was gone, it would be their turn to enjoy the fruits of victory.

CHAPTER 1

Normanitas

In the autumn of 911 the foundations of a duchy were laid, the warriors of which were to dominate Europe's military affairs for over two hundred years. Despite their very modest origins, from Palestine to Ireland Norman knights would conquer kingdoms and make empires tremble. At the small town of Saint Clair on the river Epte – a tributary of the Seine – Charles, king of the Franks, whose unaffected manners earned him the nickname 'the Simple', came to agreement with a Viking troop that they should desist from their depredations upon the French and, instead, settle the land. For more than a generation the descendants of the great emperor Charlemagne had been humbled by raids of swift-moving Viking armies. The Norsemen were difficult to contain and even when cornered and forced into battle they proved to be ferocious warriors, clad as they were in sturdy chainmail hauberks and wielding iron weapons of the highest craftsmanship.

The leader of the Vikings who met with Charles was a warrior called Hrólfr (Latinised by those who subsequently came to write about him as 'Rollo'). Hrólfr was a massive man, so bulky in fact that no horse could carry him far and thus he earned the nickname, 'the walker'. The band of Vikings that Hrólfr led were more than a short-lived raiding party; their comradeship was a way of life and they had stood together for more than twenty years: sailing, raiding, fighting on either side of the English Channel and living off the tribute that the nobles of France and England offered up to appease their violence. The initial impulse that led Hrólfr to raise his banner — whose design was the left wing of a red bird — and for hundreds of warriors to rally to it was a desire to live freely.

Back in Norway, a king had for the first time fought his way to such power that the whole country was obliged to serve him. Harald Finehair, it was said, had been spurned as a teenager by the high-spirited Gyda, who had replied to his advances that she would only become his wife if he could rule Norway with as little opposition as the kings of Denmark and Sweden faced in their realms. On hearing this, Harald vowed that he would win Gyda and that he would not cut or comb his hair until he did so. When at last his goal was fulfilled, it was the revelation that, after cleaning and unknotting, Harald's hair was actually a striking, bright blonde that earned the king his nickname.

Subduing one small Norse kingdom after another, Harald rallied a sizeable section of the defeated Viking élite to him by crushing the free farming class as he marched. The king imposed such taxes upon the *bonder* that those the king appointed *jarl* could live better under Harald than they had managed independently of him. But Vikings prided themselves as much on their freedom as on their consumption of food and drink, so the stronger Harald Finehair became, the more entire communities of warriors took ship, to settle the Faroe Islands and Iceland and to trouble northern Europe.

One summer Hrólfr returned from Russia and raided territory that had fallen under King Harald's sway. In consequence, Hrólfr was banished and no amount of pleading from his high-born mother could reverse the decision. As a result she made a prediction:

> *Evil it is by such a wolf,*
> *Noble prince, to be bitten;*
> *He will not spare the flock*
> *If he is driven to the woods.*

The wolf crossed the North Sea to the Hebrides, gathered more ships and, on 17 November 876, planted his giant frame firmly on the heavy soil of northern France. For the Christian church a nightmare had arrived; not only did the Viking army plunder directly from the churches and monasteries but the royal authorities drew on church wealth to buy off attacks on towns. The church had accumulated a great deal of wealth in the form of precious ornaments and delicate works of art, but this was now all taken from them. If there was one positive effect to derive from the pagan Vikings' lack of appreciation of such cultural artefacts, it was that the Norsemen released into circulation once more the church's gold and silver; melting it down to make ingots for trade. The commodity that the Vikings were most interested in was iron. The Vikings cared more for iron than any other metal, because iron made their ships sturdy, their armour strong, and their swords the finest weapons in Europe. Those settlements in the former Carolingian province of Neustria (the northern part of present-day France) that were now under Viking control began to prosper, with a lively trade and flourishing of craftsmanship.

Accepting that the Norsemen were here to stay, Charles the Simple decided to try to end the pattern of raids and tribute-giving for once and for all. A treaty made at Saint Clair gave all the land from the river Epte to the sea to the Norsemen and as a result this land became known as Normandy. In return for this grant, Hrólfr was to be baptised a Christian, take Charles's daughter Gisela as his wife and accept the French king as his overlord. A twelfth-century verse history of this moment, however, reports a striking incident that is said to have taken place when Hrólfr came to make his submission, an incident that testified to the continued determination of the Viking host to assert their freedom.

Surrounded by his nobles and the senior figures of the French church, Charles met Hrólfr to ratify their agreement. But for Charles the meeting got off on the wrong foot, literally. The French king attempted to impose his authority from the beginning by having his heralds explain that before discussions could begin, the Vikings should show due deference to the monarch by kissing his foot. After some murmuring on the Viking side, one of their warriors strode forward and bent down. Then, clasping Charles firmly by the ankle, he stood up again and raised the royal foot, causing the king to dangle in a most undignified manner. The Viking warrior then fulfilled his obligation of kissing the king's foot, before letting go of Charles who collapsed back towards the cries of consternation and outrage coming from the royal entourage. But scandalised as they were, the French nobility could not retaliate, not while they needed the good will of the leaders of the Viking army.

Despite their very different attitude towards authority, the Vikings and the French came to an agreement. The Vikings did not exactly turn their swords into ploughshares; they still needed to be able to mobilise an army to face their neighbours or the possibility of attack by rival Viking fleets, but they did take up farming in a land that was far more fertile than the rocky mountains of Norway. Whereas yields of grain crops were rarely more than three to one in Scandinavia at the time, the fields of Normandy returned up to fourteen times the grain sown. And the Vikings knew all about the use of a heavy iron-tipped plough to break through the thick clods of northern soil and get the most from the land.

Swords and Ploughshares

Elsewhere in France, a great deal of aristocratic disdain existed towards those who performed manual labour. But the early records from Normandy show a keen interest by owners in their tools; they made extensive lists of their iron-tipped mattocks, spades, hoes and other equipment. Hrólfr announced decrees to ensure that farmers need not fear the loss of their ploughs or tools from theft.

According to one medieval historian, a farmer's wife thought to take advantage of this ruling, and when her husband left ploughshare, coulter and tools behind in the field as he went to rest, she moved them all to a secret location and the farmer, naturally, thought that they had been stolen. Facing ruin, the farmer went to Hrólfr, who gave him the considerable sum of five *solidi*. But the duke did not leave the matter there and had the incident investigated further; suspicion fell upon the wife and she was forced to take the ordeal of hot iron to prove her innocence. When she failed that, she was whipped until she confessed her crime. The duke then asked the farmer, 'Did you know your wife was the thief?' and the farmer answered, 'Yes, I did.' At this Hrólfr said, 'You wicked man, your mouth condemns you,' and he ordered both to be hanged. The severity of punishment for theft in Normandy in Hrólfr's time was such that a story grew up claiming that when he left golden bracelets hanging from an oak tree after removing them for a meal, the gold remained safe and untouched for three years.

One of the most significant revolutions in the Norman way of life compared to that of their neighbours was the effective abolition of slavery. Slavery did exist in Normandy up until the mid-eleventh century, but in the form of a few slaves serving in the homes of the rich, rather than large numbers of slaves working in gangs on the fields, or, as in the Irish case, working with herds of cattle. Not that the Norman élite had a benign attitude to their workforce, it was just that they found the system of serfdom a more efficient one than that of slavery. When a gang of slaves goes out to work the land, they do not care whether tools get broken or not, or whether the field can be expanded through new drainage systems, or whether it is worth doing the backbreaking work of cutting bushes and shifting rocks to bring more land into use by the plough. A slave resents every task. A serf or a crop-paying farmer on the other hand, one whose land was granted to their children and grandchildren (albeit on making a payment to the lord), is motivated to improve the yields of their seed and livestock. Not quite slaves, the serf did at least have a stake in the crop, taking a share for themselves.

The life of a serf was better than that of a slave, but barely. To be a serf was to surrender yourself to the lord who owned the land and from the point that you ceremonially attended him with a rope around your neck you no longer had any freedom to leave the land or even marry without the lord's consent. And the lords were brutal in maintaining their grip on the lower classes. When the Norman peasantry tried to resist new exploitative burdens, such as taxes on the use of traditional paths and river ways, their overlords could be very severe. In 996, Rodolf, count of Ivry, and his nephew Duke Richard II of Normandy, caught peasant delegates in the act of assembling to discuss methods of rebellion against such new impositions. The lords had the hands and feet of the peasants cut off. The point of this particular form of harsh punishment was that these impudent serfs would live on, a burden to their communities and a warning to anyone who dared to resist the knightly class.

From Vikings to Normans

With generous revenues and a military force capable of seeing off those who might rob them, the former Vikings slowly, over the next four or five generations, inter-married and prospered and in the process they reinvented themselves. By the middle of the eleventh century the consistent development of their farms and their efficiency at squeezing the lower classes had provided the Norman knight with the wealth for developing the finest arms and armour west of Constantinople and for breeding the stoutest warhorses on the continent.

The Normans took a direct interest in the development of their farms and especially in the purchase and breeding of horses. The destrier, so-called because it was led by the right hand (*dextra*) of a squire, was a powerful beast, capable of carrying an armoured warrior into battle. Costing some thirty times more than a palfrey – a light horse suitable for couriers – muscular destriers in the fields and stables of the knights were one of the most visible forms of the growing wealth of Normandy. The Vikings had long known of the use of the stirrup and treated stirrups as precious items, to judge by the fact that their riding equipment, made from bronze or iron, often accompanied their owner in burial. It was on the grassy fields of Normandy, however, rather than the mountainsides of Norway that the art of fighting from horseback was perfected. Within a few generations, from Spain to Byzantium, the Normans were praised as masters of horsemanship, riding horses that had been trained to be surefooted in the tumult of battle and to turn at the touch of a hand.

Knights and Clergy

Culturally the Norman élite had changed over the years. They still remembered their Viking origins and Norse was used as a language among them for several generations. Viking zoomorphic art, the swirling-tailed animals that decorated metal goods and cloth, remained popular in Norman crafts. But by the eleventh century it was clear there had been great changes since Hrólfr's day.

Socially, the former warriors had copied developments among their continental neighbours and, where they could achieve it, the richer amongst them had become a distinct nobility, concentrating on improving their knightly skills by riding to the hunt almost every day that they were not actually riding to war. Not all the descendants of Hrólfr's Viking army had become lords of the labour of others, many were still free farmers of varying degrees of wealth, but, on the whole, the aristocracy of Normandy by the end of the first millennium could trace their origins back to Viking ancestors.

In their religion, there was an enormous contrast between the pagan values of the original invaders and their descendants. As part of his agreement with King Charles the Simple, Hrólfr had been baptised. As a result, the practice of beheading captured Christians in honour of the old gods came to an immediate halt. Indeed, at the end of his life Hrólfr distributed a hundred pounds of gold through the churches in honour of the Christian God. Was he genuinely converted? It would appear so, judging by these donations. Hrólfr's conversion in order to sign the key treaty was clearly a political decision, but the distribution of great wealth back to the church — albeit in the face of death — he once plundered shows a great deal of respect for the religion.

Understandably, though, it took the church some time to regain its confidence and function once more in Normandy. For much of the ninth and tenth centuries, bishops, such as those of Avranches, Bayeux, Lisieux and Sées, were not appointed or, if they were, lived in exile. But when the Christian religion was consolidated among the Norman nobility, the new lords began to compete with each other in their efforts to endow monasteries and churches. Evidence for just how skilled the masons and carpenters of Normandy were at this time remains in the landscape even today, especially in the form of the restored church buildings of the eleventh century. Huge stone buildings, employing the latest techniques in construction, sprang up over the duchy as each magnate established his own religious foundation.

These clerical and monastic communities fulfilled an important service for the new Norman nobility, in addition to that of spiritual welfare. A religious endowment provided a setting for the retirement and final resting place of a knight and his descendants. The clergy were also essential in estate management, being literate where the knight, typically, was not. In marked contrast to the Irish lay nobility, which included poets with extraordinary technical prowess, the Norman knight generally did not trouble to learn to read.

One knight who might have come to an early appreciation of the practical value of written records was William the Bastard, later 'Conqueror'. As a young lad of seven, William, along with several other boys, was summoned to a meeting at which his father, Duke Robert the Magnificent, had just reached agreement with Humphrey de Vieilles over the foundation of a monastery at Saint-Pierre at Préaux. Duke Robert smacked his son hard in the face. Humphrey did the same to young Richard of Lillebonne, who was carrying the Duke's greaves (leg armour). When Richard asked Humphrey why this strong blow had been struck, Humphrey answered, 'Because you are younger than me and perhaps you will live a long time and you will be a witness of this business whenever there is need.' For good measure, the adults then gave a solid crack to Hugh, son of Count Waleran of Meulan. Hitting youths was not a very efficient method of record keeping but perhaps William was to learn from this hard lesson: in later life he was to commission the greatest documentary survey of people and property of the medieval era: the Domesday Book.

Over time the dukes of Normandy found in the clergy useful and effective allies in the suppression of the near-constant warfare that threatened the stability of the political structures of the region. At large assemblies of knights, clergy and free farmers in the time of William the Conqueror, decrees were passed announcing general 'truce' and 'peace' legislation: the former outlawing warfare on all days but Tuesdays and Wednesdays, the later banning attacks on the unarmed and their property. The penalty for ignoring these decrees was excommunication and a heavy fine, payable to the church.

Castles

One striking symbol of the restless efforts by lords to promote themselves at the expense of their rivals was the rapid proliferation of castle-building. The Norman knights led the world in the development of the castle, largely because they had the resources to invest in the considerable labour and craftsmanship required. But Normandy, too, had social conditions that impelled the art of castle construction forward. Although tactically the castle is a defensive building, strategically, the castle is used offensively. By locating a castle in disputed land and on river crossing points, a lord fashions a base from which his knights can range far and wide into enemy territory and from which they can demand revenues from the local peasantry. In a word, a castle means domination. At least forty castles were erected in Normandy before 1066 and there would have been many more, but for William the Conqueror's intervention, halting castle construction except at his discretion. William decreed that:

'No one in Normandy might dig a fosse in the open country of more than one shovel's throw in depth nor set more than one line of palisade, and that without battlements or alures [wooden walkways]. And no one might make a fortification on rock or island and no one might raise a castle in Normandy and no one in Normandy might withhold the possession of his castle from the lord of Normandy if he wishes to take it into his hand.'

In Ireland, in the eleventh and early twelfth centuries, there did not exist the same drive to build castles. Clearly, those lords who founded such impressive constructions as the monasteries of Mellifont or Baltinglass had the resources and the access to skilled artisans necessary to build castles. But why would they, when the source of wealth in Ireland was mobile? Build a castle near enemy territory and the enemy would simply move their herds of cattle away from it. Nor were there administrative structures in Ireland which were centralised in the same way as, for example, the English financial centre at Winchester or governmental centre at London. When the Normans conquered England, they immediately built castles in both cities to ensure control of them. But the retinues and functionaries of Irish kings, like the kings themselves, were itinerant. They had favoured residences, of course, but like their wealth, they were constantly mobile.

In a mistaken belief that Irish society before the coming of the Normans was sufficiently like that of northern Europe to warrant an expectation that the Irish aristocracy used castles as their primary residences, some historians and archaeologists have looked for evidence of pre-Norman castles. They have searched in vain and they will continue to do so. The only possible exceptions were the various Uí Chonchobair fortresses described with the loan words *caistél* or *caislén*, located beside rivers, where control of such key crossing points might have repaid the investment of the king. But even if – as they certainly could have – the Uí Chonchobair rulers had hired experts in castle construction and built something similar to a Norman ringwork or motte, it would still have served a rather different function to the castle as it was developed in Normandy. There is no suggestion by the Irish sources of these forts being residences for lords or centres of administration. For a Norman knight, by contrast, establishing jurisdiction over a 'fief', allotted to him by his lord, meant creating a fortified residence to control the revenues of those ploughing the land and to threaten the revenues of those within riding distance. And if the fief were on conquered territory in England, Wales, Italy, Palestine, or Ireland, there was no question but that the residence would be a castle. The generation living at the time of the conquest of England would see over a hundred castles appear on the landscape, and by the time the Normans came to Ireland a century later, there were over a thousand castles in England.

The early Norman castle was a wood-and-earth affair. It came in two basic forms, either that of a ringwork, where the defensive system depended entirely on the ditch and palisade that surrounded the stables and residential buildings, or a motte-and-bailey, where the main defence was a high mound (the motte) on top of which perched a wooden tower for additional defensive height advantage. In the latter form of castle, the residences and other buildings were usually at the foot of the hill surrounded by a ditch and palisade (the bailey). By 1066, the Normans had become adept at throwing up a motte castle in a hurry. When they invaded England, for example, they built a castle at Hastings within fifteen days. Once their foothold on a territory was consolidated, the Normans then built more substantial structures.

The same pattern was even more evident in the partial conquest of Ireland a hundred years later, when about five hundred earth-and-timber castles were constructed within the space of a decade or two, covering the eastern half of the country. Having secured their presence in Ireland in this way, the Anglo-Normans then built more permanent and much more impressive stone castles, such as that at Trim, which was constructed on top of the early timber ringwork castle.

Conquests

If there was a golden rule of European high politics in the period from AD1000 to 1200, it was not to let the Normans become involved in your realm. For not only were they the finest warriors in Europe, but they were also intensely ambitious, restless, and devoted to the goal of achieving fame. Wherever a Norman force encountered weakness among an existing ruling élite, whether friend or foe, they ended up supplanting the old aristocracy and taking their land.

Despite intense rivalry between them, the Normans also knew when to band together to take advantage of an opportunity. They had no fear of the sea, having inherited from their Viking forbears the techniques of building seaworthy craft capable of transporting their cavalry, as well as a knowledge of weather, tide and coastal landscape. As a result, the Normans made some extraordinary conquests, including the amphibious invasions of England, Sicily and Ireland.

William the Conqueror

The most famous Norman leader both in his day and in modern times was William, who in later life was known as 'the Conqueror', but who from child-hood was termed 'the Bastard'. For William was born from a liaison between Duke Robert the Magnificent of Normandy and Herleva, the daughter of a lowly leather worker. The duke took responsibility for Herleva and later married her. This did not prevent William's enemies from mocking him in regard to his grandfather's profession. When, around the year 1050, he was besieging the town and castle of Alençon, a group of knights and footsoldiers cried down from a stockade at William's troops, banging on the protective leather hides:

> *The skin, the skin of the tanner*
> *That belongs to William's trade!*

Such taunting was rather reckless, since as soon as the town's outer defences were overcome, William picked out those involved and had their hands and feet cut off. The feet were then catapulted into the castle to demoralise the defenders.

Partly because of his lowly origins on his mother's side, but more due to the desire of all Norman lords to throw off any authority above them, William faced enormous challenges in becoming an effective ruler of the duchy. Duke Robert left on a pilgrimage to Jerusalem in 1035, when William was just eight years old. William's father never came back, dying on the return journey at Nicaea. And although the Norman lords had all sworn loyalty to the boy in front of the archbishop of Rouen at Fécamp, they immediately set about fighting one another and building castles to protect their independence. At one point, in 1042, when William was fourteen or fifteen, a conspiracy to murder the young duke nearly caught him unawares. One evening after hunting in Valognes, he was woken by a jester called Goles beating on the walls of his room.

'Open up,' Goles cried, 'open up! You will all be killed, get up, get up! Where are you lying, William? Why are you sleeping? If you are attacked here, you will soon be killed. Your enemies are arming themselves. If they can find you here, you will never get out of the Cotentin and not live till the morning.'

With just breeches and shirt and a cloak around his shoulders, William grabbed a horse and set off. In great fear and distress, the teenager could not risk going to any major town until he knew who remained loyal to him. With the pursuit close behind, William came to the castle at Reys, where he was relieved to find that Hubert of Reys was willing to aid him. Sending William on with his three sons as escort, Hubert met the rebel party and while pretending to share their goals, escorted them down the wrong path, allowing William the time he needed to reach safety.

The turning point for William's extraordinarily successful rise to power was a battle, that of Val-ès-Dunes, near Caen, in 1047. There, on a wide, sloping battlefield William, aided by King Henry I of France, met his enemies. Before the battle began, a significant incident took place. Ralph Taisson had once been a part of the rebel army and had sworn to strike William if he got the chance. Now, however, along with hundred and forty knights, he wanted to reconcile himself to the duke. Riding up to William, Ralph took off his gauntlet and slapped the young man with it, saying:

'I am acquitting myself of what I swore. I swore I would strike you as soon as I found you. I have struck you in order to acquit myself of my oath, because I do not wish to perjure myself.'

'My thanks to you for this blow,' replied William. And the two fought together thereafter.

The press of this battle was particularly fierce, with knights in tight formation clashing against one another. Lances sought openings in armour; maces and swords clattered against shields. No one wanted to earn the ignominy of fleeing and so on both sides they persevered despite the blood and horror. William and Henry were in the thick of the press and at one point the French king was unseated by a blow from a lance. Only the strength of the hauberk that he was wearing saved Henry from death and the proud peasants of Cotentin remembered the fall of the king hundreds of years later, with the couplet: 'from the Cotentin came the lance, which struck down the king of France.' Despite being trampled in the mud, Henry was raised back up to his saddle and rallied his knights, riding around to make sure they could see him and thus quell the rumour that he was dead.

It was rare for the most senior lords of a realm to be killed in eleventh- and twelfth-century European battles. Normally, their opponents would prefer to capture them alive. But whether because of the near-death of the king of France or the bitterness engendered by the rebels' previous attempt to assassinate William, the duke and his allies showed no mercy once they got the upper hand. As men fleeing the battle were killed while trying to cross rivers, their bodies floated off downstream in such numbers that all the local watermills became choked for miles around.

After Val-ès-Dunes, William was never seriously challenged again and his authority was such that he could undertake the adventure for which he became famous, the conquest of England.

1066

England was a country with vastly greater wealth and resources than Normandy; it had also gone much further in the eleventh century in the formation of a central administration than had its neighbours. Under the impact

seem as though Harold Godwinson had won. But then the Norse reinforcements arrived to prolong the struggle. Due to the heat of the day and their lack of water, these men who had run from the ships were exhausted and they too fell to the English axes.

Stamford Bridge was a great victory for Harold Godwinson and one that would have given him the platform to become a powerful and successful ruler of England. The chance to savour his achievement, however, was short-lived. Three days after the battle, the Normans set sail.

William's invasion was a triumph of Norman logistical ability. Some seven thousand knights, along with their horses, thousands of archers, tens of thousands of arrows, all their armour and weapons, and hundreds of craftsmen and all their tools were safely brought across the Channel to Pevensey in Sussex. Then the army was moved to Hastings and it was there, on 14 October 1066, a battle took place, the consequences of which would completely overshadow the battle of Stamford Bridge.

Having marched swiftly from London, Harold hoped to catch William unawares, as he had the Vikings at Stamford Bridge three weeks earlier. The Normans, however, had put on their armour every day since arriving in England and were not to be caught by surprise. At around nine in the morning the two armies eyed one another from opposing hillsides. From William's perspective, the arrival of the English king was welcome news. Clearly, a confrontation had to happen and the sooner the better. The longer it was delayed, the more chance Harold could gather in troops from right across England.

In terms of the quality of the two armies, the Normans had two great advantages. They had powerful warhorses and knights trained to ride in formation and they also had a great superiority in the numbers of archers and the technology of their bows. It was probably this latter aspect of the Norman army that won the day for them at Hastings. For the English army, with its core of iron-clad housecarls, was well able to defend itself against cavalry charges. Sending their own horses to the rear, the English formed up on a hill a 'shield wall' that bristled with axes and spears, proving impenetrable to repeated charges by the Norman cavalry. What the threat of the Norman knights did create, however, was a great immobility in the English ranks. Fear of allowing the cavalry a breakthrough meant that the shield wall had to be held tight, even while the Norman archers were creeping close to the English lines. Slowly but surely, over a long day, the clouds of arrows made a slaughter of the poorly armoured and also found their mark in numbers of housecarls. Despite strong iron helms, the English warriors were vulnerable at their eyes, mouths and the neck above the top of their chain hauberks.

Not that the Normans were always in control of the battle. When the Norman knights' efforts to break down the shield wall came to nothing, their formations were disrupted and, after being repulsed, they began to turn tail, especially when the rumour began to spread that William had been killed. When sections of English warriors broke from the shield wall to scatter the Normans, it seemed that they were on the verge of victory. But as the less experienced 'thegns' in Harold's army were drawn far from the hill and away from the more heavily armoured and experienced housecarls, the joy of the English troops at their apparent success turned to horror as the Norman cavalry rallied as one, turned and cut down their former pursuers. This pattern of Norman cavalry appearing to flee, but regrouping to turn on their attackers, repeated itself several times over the day, and bled the English army dry.

At one point during the day-long battle, Gryth, Harold's brother, had come face to face with the Duke of Normandy and, having successfully thrown a spear at William's great stallion, had forced the Norman ruler to dismount. But the other riders with William overran Gryth's position before the Duke was in any great danger, killing the English prince. William then demanded the horse of a nearby knight of Le Mans, who reluctantly yielded the mount. Not that it fared any better than William's favoured steed. For a second time, William's horse fell beneath him, this time due to 'the son of Hellox', a lightly armoured Englishman, who followed up his attack by going hand to hand with the Norman duke. With the second disappearance of William into the fray, rumours began to spread that he had been killed and the Normans, along with their Breton and French allies, were losing heart in face of the bloody resolution of the English shield wall. Even so, William had overcome his assailant and riding to his aid came Eustace of Boulogne, who willingly dismounted and helped the duke back in to the saddle. William then rode around his troops, helm tipped back so that all could see he still lived.

By evening the outcome was still in the balance, although in terms of attrition, English losses throughout the day had been higher than their Norman attackers. King Harold and his bodyguard were in a tight knot at the top of the hill, still suffering from the constant rain of arrows, when William demanded yet another effort from his knights and led the decisive charge. At last, the English shield wall disintegrated and the mounted knights could utilise the advantage of height and power to the full. Riding through the last stand of the housecarls, the Normans toppled the English dragon banner and trampled over piles of bodies, among which lay that of Harold Godwinson. After months of preparation and one day of ferociously violent fighting, William had won himself a crown. As a result of victory in this battle, the path was opened to a thoroughgoing conquest of England and the replacement of the aristocracy of the country with new Norman rulers.

Robert Guiscard

While William was proving the superiority of Norman horsemanship and fighting technique in the north of Europe, the same lesson was evident in the south. In some ways, the achievements of Robert of Hauteville, nicknamed 'Guiscard' – the cunning – and his brothers in Italy and Sicily were more impressive than those of William, for William had begun life in a high position, whereas Robert had almost nothing, just his sword and a genius for the art of war.

When he arrived in Italy in 1047 or 1048, with five knights and thirty foot-soldiers, Robert Guiscard came to join a force of Normans led by his older half-brother Drogo. Fraternal loyalty did not mean easy gains for Robert and he was put to the test by being sent, with his small number of troops, against Byzantine-controlled towns and villages. As with the English and the Irish at the time, the southern Italians were not accustomed to the use of castles. They built forts at the major towns, but did not control the surrounding land through the construction of castles. Robert, however, was a master of the strategic use of the castle and he built a small but effective motte-and-bailey at Scribla (today 'Il Torrione' in the commune of Spezzano Albanese) and soon afterwards another at San Marco Argentano. With these castles as his base, Robert was able to raid far along the valley of the river Follone and divert farm rents away from the Byzantines, while at the same time he could retreat and defend himself when his opponents mustered strong forces to try to deal with him.

As Robert strove to master the upper valley of the river Follone, the call came to rally all Normans and French warriors in southern Italy, for Pope Leo IX himself was leading an army from Rome to oust them before they become too strong. It was unprecedented for a pope to act as general for an army, but Leo IX was not afraid of innovation. Having striven to emancipate the papacy and the senior Roman clergy from the control of the local aristocratic families, in 1053 Leo IX felt the time had come to rid Italy of the disruptive Normans. With contingents sent by the Byzantines and some Swabian cavalry sent by the western emperor, along with troops from the Italian lords, whose power was disintegrating from the manoeuvres of the Normans, the pope led his army to Civitate. There, on 17 June 1053, the pope was humiliated.

The far more accomplished Norman cavalry cut the papal allies to pieces, with only the Swabians showing any discipline. While all other troops scattered, the Germans held steady with the pope until the last, but this bravery earned them only death and a later papal pronunciation that they had earned a place in heaven. Of the Norman leaders, it was Robert Guiscard who attracted the most praise for his conduct in the battle, showing both a strong grasp of cavalry tactics and individual bravery when called upon to do so.

Having captured Leo IX, the Normans were careful to treat the pope with the greatest respect. There was no need to look for vengeance; instead this was an opportunity. Back in Normandy the descendants of pagan Vikings had learned that the church was an invaluable ally in the governances of the duchy. Now the former mercenaries had a chance to create the same kind of relationship with the Italian church. Cleverly, the Normans pledged themselves to be servants of the pope and offered to make annual payments to the church. As a result, Leo IX had considerable incentive to accept that they were a legitimate part of the political landscape and allow monasteries such as the vibrant community at Monte Cassino to provide the Normans with church services and competent administrators.

Success followed success and, as Robert's elder brothers died or retired, he became the leader of a now significant Norman presence in Southern Italy. When his younger brother Roger arrived in the early 1060s with fresh forces from Normandy, the two brothers came to an agreement to share all that they conquered. Their military actions began by securing Calabria, but their ambition was extraordinary. Their next goal was to take the island of Sicily from its Arab and Berber rulers and, after that – since they had defeated the Byzantines in Italy – to challenge the Byzantines in Greece.

In 1059 a papal synod was held in Melfi, the strongpoint of Norman Apulia, where a new understanding was reached between the Normans and the recently elected Pope Nicholas II. There the Normans swore to assist the papacy with their troops and regular financial tribute. The pope in turn recognised Richard of Aversa, son of the first Norman to have risen to prominence in the region, Rainulf, count of Aversa from 1029, as the legitimate prince of Capua, while Robert was invested 'Duke of Apulia and Calabria, as well as Sicily yet to be conquered'.

A 'duke', with equal status to that of William back in Normandy, recognised as such by the pope, and Robert Guiscard was still only forty-four. There was plenty of vigour in his frame and ambition in his heart. So in the year following the new agreement with the papacy, Robert and Roger set about building ships and testing the defences of Sicily. Although nominally vassals of the Zirid

sultan of Mehdia in north Africa, the Muslim rulers of the island were effectively autonomous. They were, however, bitterly divided: the west of the island
was ruled by an emir called Abd-Allah ibn Manqut; the south and centre by
Ibn al-Hawwas; and the east by Ibn Maklati. None of the three rivals was able
to dominate the whole island and soon their rivalry produced an opening for
the Normans.

Ibn Maklati was deposed by an upstart emir, Ibn Timnah, and killed in his
capital city of Catania. To consolidate his new position, Ibn Timnah married
the widow of Ibn Maklati but, understandably, his new wife did not appreciate
the changed circumstances and the murder of her husband. Matters came to
a head in a drunken night of attempted vengeance, after which Ibn Maklati's
widow fled to the protection of her brother, the ruler of the south of the island,
Ibn al-Hawwas, whom she encouraged to war upon Ibn Timnah. A series of
events that had already carried a curious foreshadowing of those which took
place in Ireland a hundred years later, then became an even more explicit prediction of the future, when the success of Ibn al-Hawwas forced Ibn Timnah
to flee westwards across the sea to Calabria. There the exiled emir offered the
Normans lordship of Sicily if they would help him back into power.

Before Roger and Robert fully committed their forces to such a risky ven-
ture, they sent reconnaissance parties over to the island. From the skirmishes
that ensued, one fact became clear: small numbers of Norman soldiers could
defeat considerably larger Muslim forces. The Muslim knight could easily out-
perform their Norman opponent with the bow, but when it came to hand-
to-hand fighting, their heavier armour, their horses trained for close combat,
and their ability to charge with the lance saw the Normans triumph. In May
1061, the Norman invasion began in earnest. While Robert manoeuvred with
the larger part of their fleet off the coast of Calabria, to draw away the Muslim
war galleys, Roger crossed to Sicily at night with three hundred knights. These
proved enough to capture Messina, with its vital harbour, and, as a result, the
Muslim admirals became demoralised. It was no longer realistic to hope to intercept the Normans, who now simply had to wait for the Muslim fleet to leave

the Straits of Messina, which they had to do to take on water or to seek shelter from rough weather. Then the Normans could sail across the short distance to the secure harbour.

Once Robert had arrived with the full army, the two brothers consolidated the defences of Messina and set out with about a thousand knights and the same number of footsoldiers, guided by Ibn Timnah and his followers. Their target was the strongest of the Muslim emirs, Ibn al-Hawwas, whom they encountered in the summer of 1061 on the banks of the River Dittaino, east of Castrogiovanni. There, despite being considerably outnumbered, the Normans battled hard and eventually scattered the Muslim army. This was a remarkable success and their advance had been rapid up to this point, but the full conquest of the island took another thirty years. The main reason for this was that Roger, and more especially Robert, were needed back in Italy, where the struggle to oust the Byzantines from the country was ongoing. With Messina as a bridgehead the Normans could return to Sicily and keep the pressure on the other emirs, until such time as a decisive campaign became feasible.

The eventual domination of Sicily by the Normans was mostly the work of Roger; Robert Guiscard came to the island only twice more, for he had raised his eyes even higher and was looking towards the east and the possibility of becoming an emperor.

Under pressure from Seljuk Turks to their south, the Byzantine Empire began to disintegrate and already one adventurous Norman had sought to take advantage. Having once fought alongside the Hautevilles in southern Italy, Roussel of Bailleul had moved east to serve on behalf of the Byzantines in Asia Minor as a mercenary leader of a band of warriors, at whose core was a body of Norman knights. Turning on his former employers, Roussel plundered the eastern states of the empire and defeated the Byzantine generals sent against him, creating a principality for himself based on Ankara. Roussel was undone, however, by the Turks, who in return for recognition of their conquests, agreed to a peace treaty with the Byzantine emperor at the heart of which was an agreement to destroy the Norman usurper. Despite a period in prison in Constantinople, Roussel was released in 1077 because the Byzantine emperor, Michael VII Dukas, desperately needed Norman military support to deal with a rebellion. Roussel, however, once more turned against his employers, joining the rebellion, and was again defeated by a Byzantine treaty with the Turks. This time there was to be no comeback; Roussel was executed, having been brought back to Constantinople.

What Roussel's wild career had proven to Robert Guiscard was that the Byzantines were no longer the mighty power they once had been. Moreover, the Byzantine élite made the mistake of asking for military aid and offering a marriage alliance. They intended to flatter a man they saw as barbaric but useful. Instead, Robert interpreted the offer as a sign of weakness. Michael VII offered his younger brother as husband for one of Robert's seven daughters in return for the services of the Norman general and his knights. In order to test the Byzantines, Robert delayed an answer, looking to see what else they might offer him. In March 1074, the Byzantine offer was indeed improved. The marriage alliance would be between Michael VII's own son, then a baby, Constantine, and one of Robert's daughters. In addition, Robert Guiscard, the once lowly knight of Hauteville, was offered the highest position available to someone not born to the purple, that of the court rank of *nobilissimus*. Robert agreed and his daughter, re-christened Helena by the Greeks, arrived in Constantinople in 1076.

In March 1078, Michael VII's career ended, as did that of so many Byzantine emperors in this period, through a military coup directed against him. Unlike many of his predecessors and successors, Michael avoided execution or blinding and retired to be a monk of St John Studios in Constantinople. The new emperor, Nikephoros III Botaniates had a more hostile approach to the Normans of southern Italy and broke off all dealings with Robert. They were done with him, but Robert was not done with the Byzantines.

Backing an impostor claiming to be Michael VII, Robert began to mobilise his army and prepare to invade Greece, with the object of putting his puppet on the throne and rescuing his daughter. Sending his eldest son, Bohemond, across the Adriatic in March 1081 to establish a beachhead on the island of Corfu, Robert followed two months later with a force of around 1,300 knights and many more footsoldiers. The conquest of the island was completed by 21 May 1081. The Norman fleet then conducted the army to Albania but here, in a rare occurrence for a Norman amphibious operation, they misjudged the weather and were caught by a summer storm. Despite losing part of his army, Robert landed sufficient troops in Albania that he could march on Durazzo, a port town that had the potential to unlock the empire as Messina had Sicily.

By this time, Robert's opponent had changed, due to yet another coup. Alexios I Comnenus was now on the imperial throne and in Alexios, Robert met a skilled adversary. Moreover, many of Robert's military cadres, the veterans of his campaigns in Italy, thought this too risky an enterprise and had not crossed the Adriatic with him, sending younger relations in their stead.

Of the hundreds of problems facing the empire, Alexios treated the Norman invasion as the most urgent. Raising funds by the risky act of melting down gold and silver owned by the church, the new emperor brought an army to the relief of Durazzo. He also negotiated a treaty with Venice and the city's fleet proved crucial in cutting off the Normans from their home territories. The situation looked to be a dangerous one for Robert, but his first encounter with Alexios proved favourable to the Normans. By utilising their cavalry skills to the full, the Normans lured the Varangian guard, the mercenary shock troops of the Greek army, into a premature charge. Many of the Varangians were Anglo-Saxons who had fled William's conquests in England, only to find the same enemy in Greece. Isolated, they were cut down and the Greek army thrown back, allowing Robert to enter Durazzo after an eight-month siege.

News from Italy meant that Robert could not press the attack on Greece in person. He was needed to put down rebellions in Apulia and guard against the German king, Henry IV, who had crossed the Alps. Leaving Bohemond in charge of the campaign, Robert found he was kept fully stretched for the next three years and could not reinforce Bohemond as he wished. His son, however, proved very competent in keeping control of Durazzo and twice obliged

Alexios to withdraw from attempts to take the city.

Only after three year's campaigning in Italy could Robert cross the Adriatic and resume battle with Alexios. Here the intervention of Venetian fleets cost him dear, cutting his supplies in the winter of 1084 and contributing to a terrible outbreak of disease that claimed the lives of some five hundred knights. Bohemond was struck down and returned to Salerno, where he recovered. But Robert himself became victim of sickness in the summer of 1085 and died of fever on the island of Cephalonia.

Although Robert Guiscard fell just short of becoming the effective ruler of the Byzantine empire, his career was an incredible one all the same. That a poor knight could set out on his travels from Normandy as a teenager and become a ruler of huge swathes of territory in Italy, that the papacy would honour him as a duke, and that he could challenge for the rule of the Byzantine empire is testimony to the extraordinary economic and military advantages the Normans had over their neighbours.

Bohemond

It was intended that the first-born child of Robert Guiscard was to be called Mark at his baptism, but the stocky size of the infant boy was so impressive that he was given the nickname Bohemond, 'the giant', and the child grew into a man of a stature that deserved such a name. San Marco Argentano, the second castle constructed by Robert Guiscard, was the birthplace of Bohemond and as eldest son, he might have expected to inherit all of his father's lands. But although Bohemond was entrusted with the leadership of Robert's troops and fleets, he had a rival for the role of leader of the Italian Normans. For Robert married a second time, to the daughter of the ruler of Salerno (before Robert went on to capture the city) and by Sichelgaita, he had a son, Roger Borsa, who stood to gain all of the inheritance.

In 1096, Bohemond was in alliance with his uncle, Roger I of Sicily, against his rival half-brother, besieging the city of Amalfi. Suddenly, the possibility of an extraordinary new adventure opened to Bohemond. Warriors began travelling through Italy on their way to Constantinople to join up with a mighty crusade – the first of its kind – to liberate Jerusalem and place the Holy City in Christian hands. Seizing on the excitement generated by the crusade, Bohemond offered to lead those Italian Normans who wished to take part. Demonstratively, he cut up his most valuable cloak to make crosses. Hundreds of knights who had been vassals of his uncle rallied to his banner. Lamenting the loss of his army, Roger was forced to abandon the siege of Amalfi and return to Sicily.

The First Crusade was a chaotic enterprise, with perhaps as many as a hundred thousand participants, many of whom were non-combatants: farmers, their wives, children, the elderly, monks and nuns. Because of its disparate nature, there was no overall command structure, although the papal legate, Adhemar of Le Puy, was held in great regard. Of all the warriors on the crusade, it was Bohemond and his Norman followers who came to dominate military decisions. Whenever the crusade faced a military threat, it was Bohemond who was chosen to direct the army.

The son of Robert Guiscard earned this respect for his ability to match the tactics of the Turkish opponents of the crusading army. At the core of the Turkish fighting forces were light cavalry, whose riding ability equalled that of the Normans, albeit in a different style. For a Turkish warrior was trained to fire a powerful horn-and-sinew composite bow over his shoulder while riding away from the enemy. Again and again, these riders had destroyed enemy armies by luring them into false charges by feigned retreat, only to turn and encircle their enemies when the momentum of the charge was lost. Qilij Arslān I, sultan of Rūm, met the crusading army near Dorylaeum in central Anatolia on 1 July 1097 and in a storm of dust, his ten thousand riders attempted to draw the Christian army out of position.

In Bohemond, however, the crusaders had a leader thoroughly aware of the tactic of the feigned retreat. Norman cavalry had practised it often enough and Bohemond himself had used it to destroy the Byzantine Varangian guard in 1081. Mounted rows of Norman knights formed the centre of the Christian defences, weathering the storms of arrows, assisted by women bringing water up from the rear for thirsty men and horses. The moment Bohemond was waiting for was the arrival of the crusade rearguard, several hours away, and although impetuous troops were drawn into rash charges, the discipline of the Christian army held. Late in the afternoon, the Turks were shocked to find that their opponents, immobile for so long, were now moving into action, reinforced by the fresh arrivals. Worse, they were outflanked. Adhemar of Le Puy had come around the far side of a mountain to intercept the Turkish riders as they withdrew from battle. From a feigned retreat, Qilij Arslān's army was suddenly in genuine rout and many of his troops fell to the Christian lances. The path towards Jerusalem was open.

It was during the siege of Antioch, however, that Bohemond showed that not only was he a master of the cavalry charge, but also he had craftiness worthy of his father. Antioch was a rich city, a slave trading entrepôt on the river Orentes, secure behind walls that rose up the sides of a mountain. Although past its most glorious days, Antioch was still a major trading centre and a near autonomous Seljuk garrison was based there under the command of Yaghī Siyān. The Christian forces had arrived at Antioch on 21 October 1097 and they were not to capture the city until 3 June 1098.

During this long siege, a number of battles were fought against relieving Muslim armies, perhaps the most crucial being that of 9 February 1098 against the forces of Ridwan ruler of Aleppo. The night before, an emergency council of the princes of the crusade had taken place. All agreed that the crisis called for one person to command the entire crusading forces and that person should be Bohemond. The Norman lord did not hesitate and, despite the risk, ordered all the available knights to mount up that night and ride out in darkness in order to set up an ambush. The total Christian force was less than a thousand riders.

As dawn came, so did a light rain, ideal weather for Bohemond's plan; for rain reduced the effectiveness of the Muslim bow. While Ridwan's army approached, confident the Christians were still some twelve miles away, the crusader cavalry rode over the crest of a large hill and surprised the Muslim army with a thunderous charge. To create the impression that the crusaders were there in great numbers, all the banners had been brought from the camp. This ruse, and the ferocity of the charge, was a complete success. The vanguard of Ridwan's army recoiled back upon the main force, adding confusion to fear. Not that victory was assured for the Christians. Outnumbered some twelve to one, the momentum of the first charge was not enough to win the battle and the fighting grew fierce. Sensing the critical moment had come, Bohemond now committed his Norman reserves, leading them into the thick of battle. The sight of the red banner flying high, moving deep among the Muslim force, rallied the whole Christian army and the Muslim enemy riders scattered. Bohemond had secured an extraordinary victory, with very few losses to the remaining knights of the crusade.

Antioch fell on 3 June 1097 in a manner that echoed Robert Guiscard's capture of Durrazo after a long siege. A traitor from within the city, named Firouz, had approached Bohemond with an offer to allow the Norman lord into the city in return for rewards and protection. Bohemond played his hand very cleverly, hiding the knowledge of this offer from the rest of the Christian army. An enormous Turkish army under Kerbogha, atabeg of Mosul, was on the march and only when the Christian scouts had confirmed its proximity did Bohemond ask for a meeting of all the princes of the crusade. Before revealing his plan, Bohemond asked all the others to swear an oath that whoever could deliver the city should become ruler of it. Nearly all of the princes agreed: after all, the situation was so desperate that if Bohemond could get them into Antioch, he would be saving the crusade and would deserve to become lord of the city.

Once the Christians had secured the city and seen off Kerbogha's army, they recuperated for several months, before moving off towards Jerusalem. Bohemond, however, and most of his Norman followers, remained in Antioch, the capital of a new principality. There he ruled, part Norman prince, part oriental emir. The fame of Bohemond's deeds spread throughout Europe, to the great pride of the Normans and, indeed, all of France. In 1105, Bohemond went to France in search of a bride and enjoyed a triumphal reception throughout the land, culminating in his marriage to Constance, daughter of King Philip I. Success in battle had made Bohemond a prince and now even the descendants of Charlemagne honoured him by giving him a princess as a bride.

Norman Military Dominance

For several generations, the Normans were the most powerful warriors in Europe and beyond. Their great destriers, heavy protective chainmail surcoats, skilled horsemanship, their improvements to the bow, and above all, their use of castles, allowed them to wrestle their way to power wherever the opportunity presented itself. Not only did they have these technical advantages in warfare, but they also had a pugnacious spirit to match. Norman knights valued bravery, ambition, feats of arms, guile and, above all, success. They were not chivalrous, in the later sense of the term, they were pragmatic. Whether by ruse, intimidation, marriage, or ferocity in battle, what mattered was the result. Each of them held a belief that they could end their lives in a far better position than that to which they had been born. And in the cases of William the Bastard, Robert Guiscard and Bohemond they had clear examples of just how dramatic an advance was possible.

The last of the Norman adventurers in this tradition was a lord called Strongbow and his opportunity to sieze a realm came as a result of a political crisis in Ireland.

CHAPTER 2

Humiliation

Twelfth-century Ireland had undergone enormous changes from the days of the Celts, but it was still a country for heroes. For it was possible that any warrior born into one of Ireland's numerous royal families could emerge from comparative obscurity to become a king; possible, providing he was skilled in building alliances and capable of impressing his peers. Such a warrior would also have to be sufficiently brave and able enough in warfare to win the obedience of his neighbours and the surrender of their hostages and, above all, he would have to be ruthless.

Firstly, a rising warrior would win the leadership of his own kin group to become lord of a *túath*, a family dynasty of a fairly localised region, about a fifth the size of a modern county. Secondly, if his fortune held, his lordship might be recognised across a number of such regions. The major figures of twelfth-century Irish political life were those kings who ruled one of the five provinces of Ireland and could command the obedience of several local dynasties. For our warrior to win that position in the twelfth century was nearly impossible unless he was born a close relative of a previous provincial king. If he achieved such a high status and if he managed his affairs well enough, it could be that the whole island would acknowledge him high king, *ard rí*. Ever since the Uí Néill monopoly on that title had ended in 1002 there had been a constant striving by the regional kings of Ireland to win that accolade, but only a handful of men could boast of ever having done so.

Early medieval Ireland was a country great at boasting. No other country at the time gave such high status to the professional poet and in no other country did the poet carry such influence. No lord or lady shone quite so brightly in their actual lives as they did in the praise work of the poet. A swan could not rival the lady for grace in motion; the prowess of Hector could not match the feats of the lord as he returned triumphant from battle. And if the prize of war was merely a herd of cattle, what of it? Had not the whole of Ireland once shivered with the marching of armies to decide the ownership of just two bulls? More powerful still than the poet's ability to praise, was his ability to shame. Woe betide the noble who earned the anger of a poet, for scornful verses – of masterful craft – would soon humiliate him across the island.

The story of the invasion of Ireland by the Normans begins with humiliation.

In 1152, only two of the five provinces of Ireland had the strength to challenge for position of high king: the northern region of Tír Eógain (modern Tyrone) and the westerly province of Connacht. In the south, the once powerful Uí Briain of Munster – descendants of renowned Brian Bóruma – were in disarray, with rival branches of the family fighting over the inheritance and with their strongest leader having suffered a decisive defeat to an alliance led by the king of Connacht at the cruel battle of Móin Mór in 1151. The province of Meath was weaker still, its western regions in the hands of the traditional ruling dynasty and the eastern half divided between two bitter rivals, the battle-scarred Tigernán Ua Ruairc of Bréifne, and the king of Ireland's fifth province, Leinster, Diarmait Mac Murchada. It is with these two protagonists that we come to the irreconcilible feud that would eventually bring the Normans to Ireland.

Diarmait Mac Murchada

Diarmait Mac Murchada was born in 1110, a noble of one of the most power-ful dynasties in Leinster, the Uí Chennselaig, whose core territories were those of modern-day County Wexford and south County Carlow, east of the river Barrow. The urban settlement of Ferns was the setting for the most important Uí Chennselaig residence, for it was there they had constructed a fortified palace. Not that the boy Diarmait spent much of his youth at Ferns, for like most members of the nobility, as an infant Diarmait was placed in fosterage.

Fosterage

Placing your child with a foster family was an important way of creating close ties of mutual alliance between dynasties. The point of the system was that the foster family was not of the same lineage as the child and its members were therefore unlikely to become rivals for the lordships and the kingships to which the child was heir. As a result, foster brothers and boyhood friends were generally more dependable allies and more helpful for the youth's prospects in later life than his actual blood relatives. When the Normans came to Ireland they were shocked by the level of rivalry between family members and equally impressed by the strength of the ties created by fosterage. Our main Anglo-Norman source for these events, Gerald de Barri, or Gerald of Wales as he is commonly called, was a raconteur who soon after the Normans came to Ireland wrote two books about the country. In Gerald's eyes it seemed that if the Irish people had any love or loyalty, it was kept only for foster children and foster brothers.

In Diarmait's case, his foster-kin were the Uí Cáellaide, an up-and-coming aristocratic family to the west of the Uí Chennselaig. The Uí Cáellaide had recently become rulers of Uí Buide in Laigis (modern-day County Laois) and had become lords of Uí Berrchon, a region between modern-day Arigna and the Barrow, along the valley of the Nore from Rosbercon to Inistioge. There, they were in the territory of Osraige, and, indeed, were potential candidates for the kingship of that realm, despite the fact they were considered lowly upstarts by their enemies.

Given that the kings of Osraige had, back in 1037, managed to obtain the kingship of Leinster, it was important to the Uí Chennselaig dynasts to keep an eye on developments in Osraige. To prevent any possible repeat of that success, and to obtain support for their own goals, some Uí Chennselaig families sought allies in the region.

An event took place in 1103 which cleared the way for the rise of the Mac Murchadas. A Uí Cháellaide prince blinded Donnchad mac Énna Bacaig of Uí Chennselaig. The blinding of a nobleman was a common event at the time, and an Irish annalist could rarely complete a page of his work without having to record the blinding of one lord by another. The practice arose as a way of eliminating a competitor without committing the greater sin of killing him, and it makes grim reading to find that brother often blinded brother and fathers their own sons. So, for example, the annalists for 1136 record that Aed, son of the king of Connacht, was blinded by the king himself.

It was Diarmait Mac Murchada's family who gained most from the blinding of Donnchad mac Énna Bacaig, as this act removed their main rival for the lordship of the Uí Chennselaig. Less than a decade after the mutilation, in an act expressing his approval, the father of Dairmait Mac Murchada, Donnchad, placed his infant boy Diarmait with the Uí Cháellaide and it was there the young man was brought up in relative safety, despite a turn against the fortunes of his family. For, despite having gained leadership of the Uí Chennselaig and having brought them to a dominant position in Leinster, Diarmait's father was killed by the people of Dublin in 1115.

Twelfth-century Dublin

The medieval city of Dublin was populated by the descendants of Vikings and retained a different culture from the rest of the Irish population, so that contemporaries viewed them as a distinct grouping, labelling them with terms such as *Ostman*, 'Easterner'. These Hiberno-Norse people had turned Dublin into a huge entrepôt, one of the largest in Europe ('the rival of our London in commerce and importation', said William of Newburgh, writing around 1200), with its most valuable commodity being human slaves. Ireland, more than any other Christian realm at the time – with the possible exception of Iceland – needed slaves. The main source of food and wealth in the country was that derived from cattle. Milking cows, churning butter and making cheese was arduous, backbreaking work and it was performed by the people from the lowest level of Irish society, the female slave. So fundamental was the slave to the Irish economy that the same term for a female slave, *cumal* was also used as a basic unit to reckon value, applicable to land as well as moveable goods.

Irish Viking ships roamed far and wide in search of slaves, especially after 1102 when the kingdom of England outlawed the trade. The Welsh, however, around the same time drew up legislation to confirm the rights of victors in battle to sell the conquered. An entry for the Welsh *Book of Llandaff* in 1125 explained that the Norse wanted slaves for Scandinavia and also for the great market of Ireland. When dealing with these Dublin merchants, even in the relative safety of a port, you would be unwise to turn your back on them. Many an unwary person was kidnapped from the docks and shipped back to Ireland. Their fate would be either to serve Irish farmers or, perhaps even less enviable, be exported to Iceland, where the demand for slaves was equally high.

Tuarastal

The Dubliners used their fleet for war as well as commerce. No ruler of Leinster, nor any aspirant ruler of Ireland, could do without their services and the Dubliners were happy to sell their obedience to the strongest Irish king in return for a kind of payment – *tuarastal* – of cattle. In the twelfth century the bestowing of *tuarastal* meant more than a simple payment in return for military service. It also defined a form of vassalage, where the defeated in battle, for example, might accept *tuarastal* from the victor, symbolising that they were now in his service. To have the army, fleet and crafts-persons of Dublin as vassals, though, was expensive. When Ruaidrí Ua Conchobair came to the city in 1166, he brought with him a huge herd of four thousand cattle to win over the city after its surrender to him.

From the perspective of the Hiberno-Norse Dubliners, it was far better to owe service to a distant king, from say the Uí Chonchobair of Connacht or the Meic Lochlainn of Tír Eógain, than to the local rulers of Leinster and Meath. The more distant the king, the less likely he was to mobilise Dublin's fighting forces, to extract hostages, to demand rent, or to interfere with judicial affairs. So when Diarmait's father, Donnchad, had become so powerful that he felt he could dictate to the Dubliners in their own council chamber, they mutinied and slew Donnchad in order to transfer their allegiance to the Uí Briain of Munster. To make it clear how proud they were of their tradition of self-government and how contemptuous they were of the king of Leinster, the Hiberno-Norse warriors buried Donnchad's body along with that of a dog in the large building they had erected for their assemblies. Every time they met and stood over the bones, they refreshed the insult.

From the age of five, then, Diarmait had reason to hate the population of Dublin and reason to nurse a desire for vengeance upon them.

Ambition

Following the death of his father, the child Diarmait became a pawn in the struggle for the kingship of Leinster and, as a result, the high-stakes rivalry for the high kingship of Ireland. The Uí Chennselaig had many rivals for the control of Leinster, especially from dynasties in the north of the county, but eventually Diarmait's older brother Énna secured the inheritance, only to die in 1126.

Tall and well-built, with long red hair, Diarmait may have been a fresh-faced sixteen-year-old at the time of his brother's death, but he was ambitious. By lineage as well as in his determined manner, he was the best candidate to retain

Uí Chennselaig dominance over their province. His followers quickly had Diarmait proclaimed king of Leinster. Their most immediate rival in this move was another family member, Máel Sechlainn Mac Murchada, and for many years Diarmait was vulnerable to opposition from within the Uí Chennselaig focused on Máel Sechlainn. Moreover, the question of who ruled Leinster also had national implications and on Énna's death, the high king of Ireland, Tairdelbach Ua Conchobair, set out from Connacht to try and take advantage of the situation.

Late in 1126, Tairdelbach arrived in Leinster with an irresistible army, irresistible at least to a young noble who had few vassals and fewer allies. Helpless, Diarmait, Máel Sechlainn, and all the rival Murchada dynasts bent the knee to Tairdelbach, surrendering many hostages from their family to the high king. In defiance of all pre-existing tradition, but quite in keeping with the race to national power that was the spirit of the age, Tairdelbach then made his own son Conchobar ruler of Leinster and Dublin. This imposition, however, was too ambitious and Conchobar was unable to govern even those who were nominally supporters of Tairdelbach. All of Leinster promptly rebelled and, as a result, for the first time but not for the last, Diarmait forfeited the lives of the hostages he had given earlier in the year.

Hostages

The practice of taking hostages in medieval Ireland was not just a symbolic matter. In theory, the hostages were persons of such status or such close relatives to the hostage-giver that no one would risk undertaking acts of disobedience for fear of their hostages being killed. In practice, too, many an ambitious dynasty was held in check by the vulnerability of its hostages, whether kept in chains or as honoured guests. But Diarmait was not to be numbered amongst the lords who feared the death of their family members: both as a young man and later as a father, whose grown son was being held hostage, Diarmait proved willing to risk the lives of his family and foster-family members for the sake of his crown.

From Tairdelbach's point of view, to show humanity to the Leinster hostages he had taken once the rebellion had begun, to spare those he had wined and dined, would be to collapse the value of all his other hostages. Reluctantly, Tairdelbach sent for the axeman and the rebels of Leinster received back the heads of their family members. The hostage system was not one conducive to stable alliances. Rather, it was a system that bred feuds and murderous hatreds.

Faced with rebellion in Leinster, as well as a simultaneous challenge from Munster, in a year described by the annalists as 'a storm of war', and one which required Cellach, the archbishop of Armagh, to travel continuously in order to pacify the warriors of Ireland, Tairdelbach retreated. Accepting Conchobar could not rule the province, Tairdelbach instead tried to divide the Leinster dynasties by decreeing that Domnall Mac Fáeláin would be the new king. Domnall was from a north Leinster dynasty, the Uí Fáeláin, who before the dominance of the Uí Chennselaig could boast of holding the title king of Leinster. Naturally, Diarmait resisted this attempt to deprive him of his father's kingdom and, equally naturally, Domnall set out to enforce his rule over the teenager. Marching with Domnall, at the head of the most vigorous and harsh fighting troops at his command, was another ambitious young prince, Tigernán Ua Ruairc of Bréifne.

Tigernán Ua Ruairc

In or around 1122, Tigernán Ua Ruairc became lord of Bréifne and Conmaicne, modern-day counties Leitrim, Longford and Cavan. There is an old Irish saying, 'the three rough places of Ireland are Bréifne, Bairenn and Bérre (Breifne, the Burren and the Beare peninsula)' and this was not just a statement of geography.

Bréifne, especially to the north and west, was a wilderness of lakes, marshes and abrupt heights. 'A grim and wooded territory', as far as the Normans were concerned. Its position in Ireland was of strategic importance. An aspirant high king from Connacht who had the allegiance of the fiercely autonomous people of Bréifne could rely on them to check incursions from the north and could bring his own armies safely through the more difficult terrain to the plains that led to Dublin.

Although one of the last regions of Ireland to adopt Christianity, by the twelfth century the people of Bréifne were far removed from their pre-Christian practices. No longer did they believe, for example, that the health of the land was reflected in the health of their ruler. For it was acceptable that Tigernán was lord of Bréifne, despite his loss of an eye. In an earlier era, such a wound would have caused an Irish king to forfeit his position.

Tigernán's father had hardly been a devout figure, however, as he raided Kells in 1117, killing the abbot of the church along with a sizeable number of clergy. The historical record suggests that Tigernán later tried to make amends for this deed by donating lands to the church of Int Ednén, although the piety of this act was undermined by the fact the land in question was in disputed territory on the borders of Meath, a province upon which Tigernán had set his eyes.

An alliance between the Uí Chonchobair of Connacht and the Uí Ruairc of Bréifne made sense to both parties to such an extent that – rather unusually for the period – it lasted, with occasional lapses, over sixty years. Tigernán gave backing to Tairdelbach Ua Conchobair until Tairdelbach's death in 1156 and subsequently to Tairdelbach's son and successor, Ruaidrí. Tigernán was well rewarded for his services, gaining a substantial proportion of east Meath and, indeed, he was considered effective ruler of all Meath by the Normans at the time of his death in 1172.

The alliance of Bréifne with Connacht meant confrontation with the Uí Chennselaig, who in the person of Diarmait refused to give up their claim to the kingship of Leinster and denied Tairdelbach Ua Conchobair's right to give the position to Domnall Mac Fáeláin. And so in 1128, Tairdelbach along with Domnall, the new king of Leinster, invaded Uí Chennselaig territory as far as Wexford, before successfully making an entire circuit around south Leinster, leaving a trail of slaughtered cattle. And it was Tigernán Ua Ruairc and his troops who came away from the expedition with the greatest reputation for savagery. For the first time, the two men whose bitter enmity was to bring the Normans to Ireland had faced each other across the field of battle, and it was Diarmait who had given way. For all the shame of allowing such a brazen foray by his enemies and the discontent of his own people, Diarmait was still leader of a powerful dynasty and, lacking any other options, he learned to bide his time, waiting for the opportunity to strike back.

From Tigernán Ua Ruairc's point of view, this hosting was a great success and he followed it with an act of enormous notoriety as far as the Irish church was concerned. For in the same year, 1128, Tigernán violated the tradition of allowing the clergy to travel unmolested, by plundering the cavalcade of Cellach, the archbishop of Armagh, killing several of the clergy. This was an unprecedented attack and it had the consequence of making all the clergy of Ireland terrified of travelling, when − except while marching to war against rival churches − they had previously felt secure. But if Tigernán was to earn a dark reputation for ill deeds towards the clergy, so too was Diarmait.

Kildare Abbey

The abbey at Kildare was one of the great ecclesiastical centres of Ireland, with the reigning abbess a successor to its founder Brigid, the early sixth-century patron saint of Ireland. As head of affiliated monasteries across the country, Kildare was sufficiently important that the obituaries of its abbesses were recorded over the centuries in the major annals. Until the synod of Kells in 1152, the abbess of Kildare was given precedence over bishops. The position of abbess of Kildare was not just that of a spiritual leader, however, as the same annalistic entries show the abbess playing an important political role in Irish affairs, both national and local. As such, the position was coveted by the lords of Leinster and whenever possible the Uí Chennselaig strove against their north Leinster rivals the Uí Fáeláin and the Uí Failge to place a noblewoman from their royal family as head of the abbey.

In 1112, after the death of the abbess Gormlaith, a member of the Mac Murchada family, the Uí Fáeláin gained control of the abbey. In turn, however, they lost out to the Uí Failge after a short but bloody battle in 1127. The victorious Uí Failge appointed one of their own, Mór, as abbess. In 1132, taking advantage of this conflict between his Leinster rivals, Diarmait made the first move of a campaign to regain the kingship of Leinster and attacked Kildare.

The raid led to bitter fighting around the abbey and although Diarmait gained the upper hand, the defenders fought on bravely, preventing the entry of the Uí Chennselaig warriors. Diarmait had to set fire to the church before he could drive Mór and her supporters out of the building. The damage to the church was considerable, as was the loss of life. Diarmait's next action, the equivalent to blinding a potential rival to disbar them from office, was to put Mór 'into a man's bed'. Having been raped, Mór was no longer a virgin and no longer fit to be a successor to Brigid. The position of abbess was now vacant and the new appointee, Sadb, was a Mac Murchada and a close family member of Diarmait's.

Both Diarmait and Tigernán were proving themselves ambitious and ruthless lords and both were finding their power growing, albeit with opposition. Within the Mac Murchada family, Diarmait's main rival was Máel Sechlainn, but in 1133 — the year following his mastery of Kildare Abbey — Diarmait heard the welcome news that Máel Sechlainn had been killed in battle by north Leinster dynasts led by Augaire Ua Tuathail. This deed earned Augaire a special place in Diarmait's esteem and the two lords joined forces to go to war. The campaign of 1134 was short-lived. Unfortunately for Diarmait, his new ally was killed early on in the conflict, which was between the Uí Chennselaig and the men of Osraige along with their Hiberno-Norse allies from Waterford. The slaughter Diarmait subsequently conducted on his enemies, it was said, went some way to revenge the loss of Augaire.

If the year 1133 was a major one in Diarmait's career, in that his rule over the Uí Chennselaig was henceforth without major opposition, for the people of Ireland it was remembered as a time of massive catastrophe; a plague broke out among the herds of cattle in the country, the worst, said the annals, in nearly five hundred years, leaving behind just a small remnant of the island's cattle population. While the nobles continued to play out their political ambitions in raids and warfare, the farmers and slaves of Ireland starved.

The Rivalry Deepens

By the late 1130s Diarmait and Tigernán were figures of national importance and had to consider their attitude towards those just above them in terms of power and wealth: the aspirant high kings. Given that Tigernán and the Uí Ruairc were aligned with Tairdelbach Ua Conchobair and the Connacht host, then inevitably Diarmait was willing to ally with Tairdelbach's opponents, the Uí Briain of Munster and the Mac Lochlainn of Ulster. The nearer of these, Conchobar Ua Briain of Munster, was looking for assistance in subduing the important Hiberno-Norse port of Waterford, while Diarmait, along with the Hiberno-Norse populations of Wexford and Dublin, also had an interest in defeating one of their major trading rivals.

A lucrative exchange with Poitou meant that, despite a lack of vineyards, there was no shortage of wine in Ireland. The merchants of Waterford traded animal hides and bird skins in return for wine and were growing ever richer. For many years now the citizens there had thrown off nominal vassalage to the Uí Briain, instead looking to the Mac Carthaig kingdom of Desmond, centred on Cork in the southwest of Ireland. It was time to check Waterford's progress towards independence and, in 1137, with Conchobar as leader, Diarmait with the Uí Chennselaig army and two hundred ships from the Dublin and Wexford Hiberno-Norse fleets besieged the city. The campaign was successful, obliging Waterford to surrender hostages to Conchobar. He, in turn, before returning to Thomond, visited Diarmait in Ferns and bestowed the hostages to Diarmait in recognition of both Diarmait's assistance in the siege of Waterford and to encourage the Uí Chennselaig to assist in the future against Conchobar's southern neighbours.

Not wishing to see this potentially dangerous southern alliance progress any further, Tairdelbach Ua Conchobair brought the Connacht army south the following year, 1138, picking up his ally Tigernán Ua Ruairc and also the south Ulster army of Donnchad Ua Cerbaill and the Airgialla.

Their first target was Murchad Ua Máel Sechlainn, king of Meath, who had recently agreed a treaty of mutual defence with Diarmait. The wording of the treaty allowed for Diarmait to avoid having to face this very dangerous invasion. In return for control over certain territories in north Leinster, Diarmait was to assist Murchad, providing they were facing a similar sized army to their own. The combined army of Leinster and Meath was considerably less than that led by Tairdelbach Ua Conchobair, and Diarmait could have used that excuse as a reason not to fight the aspirant high king. What made the confrontation more of an equitable one and brought Diarmait into the field was the decision of the Dubliners to march out and help bring the invasion to a halt. The Dubliners may have come to their decision to assist Diarmait and Murchad while standing on the bones of Diarmait's father, but Donnchad Mac Murchada was a long-defeated enemy, while the ruler of Connacht and his allies appeared to be a much more immediate threat to the city's autonomy.

The two armies met at Largy in Meath and camped either side of a wood; they were so near to each other that they could view each other's movements through a pass between the trees. Once again Diarmait and Tigernán were in sight of each other. Ten years earlier Diarmait was young and alone; this time he had the Dubliners serving with him, temporarily at least, and he also, rather more sincerely, had the king of Meath as an ally. The terrain favoured the defenders and Diarmait was determined not to give way. A day passed. Then another. Tairdelbach Ua Conchobair did not want to risk his army in an engagement here. After a week, the king of Connacht gave up. To the horror of Donnchad Ua Cerbaill and Tigernán Ua Ruairc, Tairdelbach returned to Connacht, allowing the Leinster and Meath allies free rein to punish those who had thought to prosper by Tairdelbach's intervention. So thoroughly did

Murchad's army burn and destroy the crops of the Airgialla that in the following year in the southern parts of the kingdom there was an appalling famine.

The Leinster-Meath allies then attacked the notable Uí Cherbaill monastery of Inis-Mocht. The lake island of Mochta on the border of Meath and
Louth was a wealthy prize, but only in years of extreme cold – such as had
occurred in 939 and 1036 when the lake froze solid – was it vulnerable to
attack. In 1138, the attackers set out across the water in rafts with the stronger
swimmers in the lake all around them. But the Uí Cherbaill were well prepared and countered by launching sturdy boats full of warriors, who were
easily able to spear their vulnerable assailants. Although a party of attackers –
including some prominent nobles – made it across the lake to firm land, it was
only to meet their deaths. In modern times, with the lake long since drained,
the land beside the monastery has yielded a great number of human bones:
testimony to the large numbers of attackers who sank beneath the cold water
during that ambitious but ultimately reckless attempt to take the monastery.
After this setback, there was no enthusiasm among Diarmait's troops for the
pursuit of Tigernán Ua Ruairc, who had retreated to the safety of Bréifne.

Cruelty

The tradition of writing *specula principum*, moral works to advise rulers on how
they ought to behave, was in full swing in the twelfth century. One exponent
of the genre and author of a notable book on the subject was the Welsh cleric
Gerald de Barri, our main Norman source for the invasion of Ireland. When
Gerald came to write about Diarmait, it was natural for him to assess the Irish
king on a scale that ran from a prince who ruled through the affection of his
people to one who ruled through terror. Gerald's opinion was that Diarmait
was a ruler who preferred that all should fear him rather than esteem him. An
oppressor of nobles, Diarmait raised up the inferior. Hostile even to his own
people, he had nothing but hatred for foreigners. The hand of all was against
him and his hand was against all.

Gerald's last observation was a formulation taken directly from Genesis (16.12) and it was a rather clever one. For it derives from a description of Ishmael, who despite being ostracised and isolated to the point of death in the desert, miraculously survived to found twelve tribes through his sons. The image of Diarmait as returning to power despite once having all hands against him was, as we shall see, very apt, but so too was Gerald's implicit invocation of an observation made by Saint Paul about the story of Ishmael and his half-brother Isaac. For Paul made the point that the brothers were symbols for Judaism and Christianity: Ishmael the older, but rejected brother, being overtaken in God's plan by Isaac. Gerald's allusion was intended to place Diarmait's actions in a similar light: the Irish king had an important place in history, but ultimately, just as with the medieval Christian view of the role of the Jewish people, Diarmait's significance was that he paved the way for the true authority.

That Gerald had some factual basis for his comment about Diarmait's severity is evident from the Irish annals, which make it clear that both Diarmait Mac Murchada and Tigernán Ua Ruairc adopted an approach to governance that was merciless. In 1139, Tigernán assassinated Fergal, a son of the ruler of a rival Bréifne dynasty, even though Tigernán's own men and the clergy of Bréifne had sworn on shrines and on relics that Fergal was safe. Even more dramatically, Diarmait, in 1141, launched a ruthless and bloody coup to eliminate all his Leinster rivals. Despite truce agreements and the *de facto* recognition of Diarmait as king of Leinster, his assassins set out as one to find their given targets: seventeen important local nobles. Within a few weeks, all were either murdered or blind. Included among those ambushed and struck down was Diarmait's main rival to the title of king of Leinster, Domnall Mac Fáeláin. It had taken Diarmait thirteen years, but he had revenged himself upon the man who had claimed the title and who – in the company of Tigernán – had once marched through Uí Chennselaig territory, destroying all their cattle.

Gerald de Barri, accustomed to the presence of a strong royal authority capable of intervening in factional struggles and administering justice, saw in these violations of solemn oaths nothing but outrage. Moreover, ever since the Norman conquest of England in 1066 a more chivalric culture had been established among the nobles, one where the breaking of oaths and mutilation of opponents was frowned upon. Reflecting the more delicate approach to feuding that he was familiar with, Gerald devoted a long passage to condemning acts such as those undertaken by Diarmait and Tigernán against their enemies.

'Above all other peoples,' he wrote, 'the Irish practise treachery. When they give their word to anyone, they do not keep it ... When you have employed every safeguard and used every precaution for your own safety and security, both by means of oaths and hostages, and friendships firmly cemented, and all kinds of benefits conferred, then you must be especially on your guard, because then especially their malice seeks a chance ...

'Among many other tricks devised in their guile, there is this one which serves as a particularly good proof of their treachery.

'Under the guise of religion and peace they assemble at some holy place with him whom they wish to kill. First they make a treaty on the basis of their common fathers. Then in turn they go around the church three times. They enter the church and, swearing a great variety of oaths before the relics of saints placed on the altar, at last with the celebration of Mass and the prayers of the priests they make an indissoluble treaty as if it were a kind of betrothal. For the greater confirmation of their friendship and completion of their settlement, each in conclusion drinks the blood of the other which has willingly been drawn especially for the purpose.

'O! How often in the very hour of this alliance has blood been so treacherously and shamefully shed.'

Disgusted with the kinds of oath-breaking and violence he witnessed and heard about, Gerald continued by stating that 'one seems here to be allowed to carry out whatever one desires; people are so concerned not with what is honourable, but all of them only with what is expedient.' In his own – pejorative – manner and with an outsider's lack of appreciation of the fact that the Irish nobility had, in fact, their own very strong notions of heroism (more to do with extraordinary physical deeds, with besting a powerful enemy, and with the composition of thrilling phrases, than adhering to vows made in church), Gerald nonetheless grasped the underlying cause of the frequency of ambushes and blindings in Ireland when he spoke of expediency. Given the constantly shifting alliances of the other lords, a medieval Irish prince could not afford to let down his guard for an instant. An abrupt loss of the use of his eyes would be the only reward for the man who followed the advice of monks.

The curious parallels between the careers of Diarmait and Tigernán continued in the 1140s with both of them receiving a sharp setback in their otherwise impressive march to becoming dominant figures in Irish life. Whether because of his assassination of Fergal or whether it was because Tigernán temporarily abandoned the traditional alliance between Bréifne and Connacht in order to destroy a wicker bridge that Tairdelbach Ua Conchobair had constructed across the river Suck at Ath-liag, his own warriors rose up against him and in 1140 Tigernán was temporarily ousted from power.

Diarmait did not fall so far, but, in 1141, he suffered a major military defeat. Having launched a raid into Laigis that began well, Diarmait was encumbered with a great herd of cattle and his enemies caught up with him and turned all his gains into severe losses. The destruction of significant numbers, both of his core troops and those of his allies, made Diarmait vulnerable and, for the first time in over a decade, the Uí Chennselaig were on the receiving end of a raid, when Tairdelbach Ua Briain of Munster took the opportunity to swipe thousands of cattle from them.

Both Diarmait and Tigernán, however, returned to full strength through a series of opportunistic alliances and wars, mostly revolving around the power vacuum that existed in Meath. Both of these princes were careful not to antagonise Ireland's strongest ruler, Tairdelbach Ua Conchobair. In order to fulfil his obligations to Tairdelbach and to avenge the Ua Briain cattle raid of 1141, Diarmait participated in the mightiest battle of his generation. In 1151, Tairdelbach Ua Conchobair led an army into Munster to face his Uí Briain namesake. The two armies met at Móin Mór where the men of Munster suffered horrific losses.

Open-field battles in medieval Ireland tended to result in the scattering of the defeated armies, but not in their annihilation. Given that political fortunes could rise and fall rapidly, it was rare for a prince to feel the necessity to fight to the last drop of blood. Better to flee and regroup than make an all-or-nothing stand. The battle of Móin Mór was a grim exception, with the Uí Briain army resolved to make this the moment that they restored their fortunes. Instead, they met with such catastrophic losses they were never to recover. *The Annals of Tigernach* state that 'until sand of sea and stars of heaven are numbered, no one will reckon all the sons of kings and chiefs and great lords of the men of Munster that were killed there, so that of three battalions of Munster that had come hither, none escaped save only one that was shattered.'

1152: The Crucial Year

Medieval politics in Ireland was a fickle and unsentimental business and the decline of the once-powerful province of Meath provided pickings that drew even the great national rivals together to share the spoils. In 1152, Muirchertach Mac Lochlainn journeyed from Ulster and Tairdelbach Ua Conchobair from Connacht to dismember Meath. Diarmait, along with his old ally from the days of holding the forest pass, Murchad Ua Máel Sechlainn, were invited to the feast. Meath was divided in two, with the part west of Clonard Abbey on the Boyne given to Murchad and the eastern part to his son Máel Sechlainn Ua Máel Sechlainn.

One of those who lost out greatly from this new arrangement was Tigernán Ua Ruairc, whose ambition to rule Meath now collapsed along with his control over parts of West Meath. Despite being isolated, Tigernán brought his army to battle with some courage, but had no hope against such a strong alliance. Not only did he lose all the territory in Meath that he had gained with such persistence over the previous thirty years, but the core Bréifne lands of

Conmaicne were taken from him too. A fort at Bun-cuilinn (modern-day Dangan, County Roscommon) was burned and the son, a dynastic rival, was raised up to the lordship of Conmaicne.

From Diarmait's perspective, these events were positive enough, in that he was driving his old enemy eastwards and away from influence over north Leinster and Meath. But even more exciting was an opportunity that came Diarmait's way to heap further indignity upon the ruler of Bréifne.

Tigernán was married to Derbforgaill, daughter of Murchad Ua Máel Sechlainn, the new king of West Meath. Aged forty-three, Derbforgaill was a woman of independent wealth – represented by her herd of cattle and many donations to the church – and high aristocratic lineage (Derbforgaill was a direct descendent of Brian Bóruma). Derbforgaill's marriage to Tigernán had been arranged during one of the short-lived periods of truce between Bréifne and Meath, but for most of their years together Tigernán had been at war with her father and now he was being deprived of East Meath by her brother Máel Sechlainn.

With Tigernán in retreat, even from his core territories, Derbforgaill saw the opportunity to escape her husband. Although she had been placed on an island in the heart of Bréifne, Derbforgaill was able to send a messenger to Diarmait. Who better to be the means of her revenge than this longstanding enemy of Tigernán's? Moreover, from time to time, as opportunity allowed, Diarmait had paid his compliments to Derbforgaill by letter and through messengers, expressing sympathy for her plight. He had long made it clear that if Derbforgaill wanted to escape Tigernán, Diarmait would take her in, perhaps even as his third wife.

Once informed as to Derbforgaill's location, Diarmait did not hesitate for a moment. Quickly, for Tigernán was defeated but not destroyed, the Uí Chennselaig troops rounded up all the queen's cattle and bundled up her furnishings. Riding off to Ferns, Diarmait rejoiced in having delivered an unprecedented insult to Tigernán.

To lose in battle was not necessarily shameful; it could be a sign of bravery if, although defeated, all your wounds were on the front of your body. To have your wife elope with a rival prince, however, that was humiliating indeed. The news of the shaming of Tigernán Ua Ruairc quickly travelled the length and breadth of the island. Contemporary historians could think of no Irish examples with which to compare the event and, especially given the consequences of this incident, they turned instead to the tale of the fall of Troy. The capture of Derbforgaill by Diarmait was seen as the equivalent to the seizure of Helen by Paris: daring, passionate, but ultimately ruinous. For Gerald de Barri, there was a misogynistic conclusion to be drawn from the parallel between Derbforgaill, Helen and, indeed, the fall of Mark Anthony: he observed that nearly all the great evils of the world were brought about by women. Despite his endorsement of the medieval Christian Church's prejudice against the female gender, Gerald's conclusion did, at least, show some understanding of the perspective of the Irish nobility: from their point of view the elopement of Derbforgaill would indeed have appalling consequences.

In 1152 then, Tigernán Ua Ruairc was hurt by two blows: the loss of his territories and the loss of his wife. It was the latter that pained him the most. Although it was to take him nearly fourteen years, he was set upon obtaining vengeance upon Diarmait no matter what the cost. A rage was upon him that could no more be quenched than that of the mythical Cú Chulain, whose temper as a youth was such that were he thrust into a vat of cold water while angry, the water would steam and the cauldron burst. Seeking assistance for his new goal, Tigernán Ua Ruairc set out for Connacht and Tairdelbach Ua Conchobair with one thought in mind. If Tairdelbach would march on Leinster to destroy Diarmait, Tigernán would lay Bréifne at his feet.

Tairdelbach was more than willing to capitalise on his ally's desire for vengeance and came south the following year. Facing these significantly superior forces, Diarmait retreated, surrendering Derbforgaill back to Tairdelbach. It cost him little to do so. Diarmait's interest in Derbforgaill had never been for any other reason than the harm he could do to Tigernán, and her year in Leinster had been one of relative isolation.

For a few months Derbforgaill resided with her father, Murchad Ua Máel Sechlainn in Meath. Relations between Tigernán and Derbforgaill were quickly stabilised and, later that year, she returned to Bréifne and her husband. In public, at least, such as at the sumptuous consecration ceremony in 1157 for the Cistercian Abbey at Mellifont, near Drogheda, the couple kept up a harmonious appearance. Nor did Tigernán lay hands on Derbforgaill's cattle and belongings. She was able to live out her life as a patron of the church until her retirement to Mellifont in 1186, where she died seven years later, in her eighty-fifth year.

The invasion of Leinster in 1153 caused Diarmait to worry that he would lose more than Derbforgaill and, in particular, that Tairdelbach and Tigernán might capture the prisons that held the hostages which Diarmait relied on to keep his main enemies in check. Rather than let these hostages be released, Diarmait set free Niall Ua Mórda lord of Laigis of his own accord, but not before blinding him and ensuring that henceforth he was a broken man. Niall was a major rival of Diarmait's foster kin, the Uí Cháellaide, and Niall's troops had bested Diarmait in the king of Leinster's failed raid a decade earlier. Although Niall's safety as a hostage had been sworn to by Diarmait before the laity and the clergy, such oaths were of little consequence to a man who understood that the competition between lords in Ireland brooked no scruple. Success brought its own vindication and failure brought mutilation or death. It was the same for all and in a land famous for its saints, there were none to be found among those who were eligible for a crown.

Tigernán pursued his vendetta against Diarmait, even without the presence of the Connacht army, and, in 1154, conducted a raid of Diarmait's territories in south Kildare, successfully returning to Bréifne with his spoils, although without meeting his rival in battle. For at the same time as Tigernán was attacking from the north, Diarmait had been attempting to stave off an invasion of Uí Chennselaig territory by the army of Osraige in the southwest and had suffered considerable losses in doing so. And if the lands of Leinster were troubled enough by cattle raids, the misery of the general population was increased this year by a cattle murrain.

In 1156, the strongest lord in Ireland, Tairdelbach Ua Conchobair, died. Of his sons, Ruaidrí moved quickly to secure the kingship of Connacht; in recent years Ruaidrí had fought his way back into favour with Tairdelbach, having once been in danger of exile or blinding. Straight away, Tigernán gave hostages to the new king and re-established the Bréifne-Connacht alliance that he hoped would bring about the fall of Diarmait. The king of Leinster, however, had an equally powerful ally in Muirchertach Mac Lochlainn and, snubbing the accession of Ruaidrí, instead gave hostages to the northern prince.

Once more the weakness of Meath drew down the contending armies of the aspirant high kings. Murchad Ua Máel Sechlainn, Diarmait's off-and-on ally, king of West Meath and father of Derbforgaill, had died in 1153, just as he had concluded an alliance with Mac Lochlainn which had secured him in West Meath and given him hopes of rule over East Meath and even the northern parts of Leinster. Murchad's son, Máel Sechlainn, stood to inherit his father's lands, having earlier blinded one potential rival, his nephew, but before Máel Sechlainn could consolidate his position, he was poisoned, in 1155, while feasting on St Brigid's Day. Poison was a rare instrument of assassination in medieval Ireland, so rare in fact that Gerald de Barri thought that, along with poisonous snakes and reptiles, the land and air of the country acted as a preventative that blunted the toxicity of imported poisons. Poison was, however, effective here and, at the age of thirty, Máel Sechlainn was dead.

The king of West Meath had many enemies who may have organised the poisoning, among them Tigernán Ua Ruairc. Tigernán had also recently been conspiring to overthrow Donnchad Ua Máel Sechlainn, the king of East Meath, and, despite having been checked by Diarmait in alliance with the Hiberno-Norse army of Dublin, Tigernán eventually met with success. Donnchad Ua Máel Sechlainn had killed a captive for whom both Tigernán and Diarmait had given surety and, as such, both were deeply shamed by the insult to their reputation. For a moment, in 1158, Tigernán and Diarmait found themselves in uncomfortable alliance, insofar as both participated in the synod that deposed Donnchad in favour of his brother.

Given this massive instability in Meath — partitioned and with the rulers of the respective east and west sides of the division now ousted or slain — it was inevitable that the two great princes of Ireland would march to the region, each to try to stamp their own mark on the question of who should rule the fragmented province. Matters came to a head with another bloody battle in 1159, on the banks of the river Dee, near Ardee, County Louth. This was more than a battle to determine the future of Meath, it was the moment that would decide whether Ua Conchobair or Mac Lochlainn would be high king of Ireland. Fortunately for Diarmait, he picked the winning side by fighting with Mac Lochlainn, while Tigernán's army fled along with the warriors of Connacht.

The battle was a ferocious one, and it is notable that Diarmait Mac Murchada was the only commander in Ireland to have emerged victorious from the two most hard-fought battles of his generation: Móin Mór and Ardee. Clearly, he did not shirk when the fighting grew fierce and his veterans were capable and grim. Diarmait was well rewarded for his decision to back Mac Lochlainn. Not only was he now absolutely secure as king of Leinster, but from 1161 Mac Lochlainn awarded him rule over East Meath and, in 1162, the ever-pragmatic Hiberno-Norse rulers of Dublin acknowledged Diarmait as their overlord. Obedient to Diarmait's orders, the Dubliners sent their war fleet as he directed, and an annalist noted that Diarmait's influence over the city was such that had not been seen for a very long time. While superficially the Dubliners were acquiescent in fulfilling their obligations to Diarmait, the Hiberno-Norse people hated the fact that they were caught in a vice between Leinster and Ulster and that their men were dying in causes that did little to further the wealth and success of their city.

The considerable political control that Diarmait exerted over his core territories and beyond was reinforced by his patronage of the church from local to the highest levels. Again, it was the alliance with Mac Lochlainn that allowed Diarmait to have an effective relationship with the church. Mac Lochlainn's rule as high king of Ireland had the full support of Gilla Meic Liac, archbishop of Armagh, and this support transferred to Diarmait. In 1162, the king of Leinster presided over a national synod held at Clane, County Kildare, at which a papal legate and twenty-six bishops were present. It was as though the attack on Kildare Abbey had never happened. Soon after the synod, Lorcán Ua Tuathail, brother to Diarmait's wife Mór and a former hostage of the Uí Chennselaig, was consecrated as archbishop of Dublin by Gilla Meic Liac.

Lorcán Ua Tuathail as archbishop was an ardent reformer and would later obtain the powers of a papal legate from Alexander III. The main abuses that he was anxious to eliminate from the Irish church were those of clerical marriage – which had led to family dynasties emerging in a great number of churches and monasteries – and the related problem that Ireland's secular nobility thought it their right to place family members into high church position rather than allow the clergy to elect their leaders free from external pressure. At first sight, it seems to be a startling contradiction that a man who owed his position to a powerful prince should pursue such an agenda, a prince, moreover, who had deposed the former abbess of Kildare in a brutal fashion in order to replace her with his own kinswoman. But Lorcán had never been the kind of churchman who pandered to the needs of secular princes, and he had won the respect of the clergy in his own right, through his ascetic practices and deeds as abbot of Glendalough. Despite Lorcán's independent spirit, Diarmait was willing to see him elected archbishop of Dublin, for Diarmait had good reason to champion church reform.

In order to consolidate his position as king of Leinster, Diarmait had been systematically undermining venerable local and neighbouring dynasties by replacing them with families who were new to the highest levels of lordly power, or with nobles fleeing defeat and exile from elsewhere in Ireland. As part of this process, wresting churches and monasteries out of the hands of his rivals and making them answerable only to the papacy was an effective tactic. Nor was there any harm in the fact that by promoting church reform in this way, Diarmait won approval from the leading voices of the international clergy.

Bernard of Clairvaux, the leader of the Cistercian order and the most influential churchman of the twelfth century, wrote enthusiastically to Diarmait around 1148, the year that the king of Leinster founded the Cistercian abbey of Baltinglass, County Wicklow. The monastery had as its first abbot a Norman monk from Lincolnshire, Gilbert, and became a daughter house of Mellifont Abbey. Its establishment, one of many monastic foundations by Diarmait, provides a good example of Diarmait's thinking. Baltinglass at the time was in Ua Tuathail hands and while – after some conflict early in his career – this minor Leinster dynasty were nominally supporters of the king, it was important to Diarmait not to let them become too strong. The foundation of Baltinglass took place shortly after the Uí Thuathail had gained territory in the Wicklow mountains to the northeast of their demesne lands. The new monastery cut them off from the mountains and, as the Cistercians were to do all over Europe, transformed the intervening region into an economic powerhouse. Within a generation, the monks of Baltinglass were arranging three-year trading agreements with Italian city states for the wool of their rapidly expanding flock of sheep. Similarly, when Diarmait and Lorcán confirmed the establishment of a Cistercian monastery at Kilkenny, they were ensuring that a wealthy establishment under the control of no rival secular ruler would control the strategic route from Dublin to the south coast.

Abandonment

No Irish ruler of the twelfth century ever drew sufficiently ahead of their rivals that they could feel secure in power. Make a mistake and there was a host of restless lords willing and able to bring you down. In 1166, Muirchertach Mac Lochlainn made a mistake, one that soon after caused his own death and, as a consequence, caused Diarmait's unstable pyramid of supporters to come crashing down. Despite having defeated a northern rival, Eochaid Mac Duinnsléibe, and given away his lands, Mac Lochlainn thought it necessary to follow this up by blinding Eochaid, in violation of oaths taken before the archbishop of Armagh.

This action, usually an effective one, was a risk, as it was no longer clear that Mac Lochlainn had the forces to deal with all contenders. The high king had seen some of his support in the north waver, following the defeat of his main ally in Scotland. The violation of his oaths gave the opportunity for Mac Lochlainn's enemies to test the mood of the country and see if the high king was still as strong as when, in 1161, he had forced Ruaidrí Ua Conchobair into submission and the surrender of hostages. Nevertheless, it would be a courageous prince who first raised the standard of rebellion, as in the event of failure Mac Lochlainn's response would not be merciful.

With great daring and hope that the pendulum of fortune was once more swinging his way, it was Tigernán Ua Ruairc who bravely mustered his troops and marched north. Donnchad Ua Cerbaill of the Airgialla joined him, despite the fact that Tigernán had once betrayed Donnchad (a half-brother of Tigernán's on his mother's side) by incarcerating him for ransom on an island on Loch Sileann for six weeks until Donnchad managed to escape. The main reason for Donnchad's alliance with Tigernán was that Donnchad had stood surety for Eochaid and so Eochaid's blinding at the hands of Mac Lochlainn was a personal insult. These two lords now dared to march on Tir Eógain, Mac Lochlainn's home territory. They should have been slaughtered. But the former allies of Mac Lochlainn in Ulster stood aside and let him face the invasion with only his core troops. These were not enough, and one of the few Irish rulers ever to deserve the title of high king fell, sword in hand, in a small battle in south County Armagh. The contrast between the wide scope of Muirchertach Mac Lochlainn's rule and the small numbers involved in the fighting that killed him was not lost on the contemporary annalists, who wrote that 'the Augustus of North-west Europe for valour and championship was killed in a slight skirmish' and 'a great marvel and wonderful deed was then done: to wit, the king of Ireland to fall without battle, without contest'.

Donnchad did not live long to enjoy his fame as one of the two princes who had dared face the might of Mac Lochlainn and triumphed. Just two years later, he was enjoying a drunken feast when a serving attendant from among his own people – for unstated reasons – cut him apart with an axe. Tigernán, however, made the most of the fruits of such a surprising victory. For him the time had come to inflict a decisive reckoning on his oldest and bitterest enemy.

Joining with Ruaidrí Ua Conchobair, Tigernán and the Connacht army enjoyed a triumphant march to Dublin, where the citizens too rejoiced at the collapse of Mac Lochlainn's power. In Dublin, Ruaidrí was 'inaugurated as honourably as any king of the Irish was ever inaugurated'. The three allies, Connacht, Bréifne and Dublin, now turned towards a reckoning with Diarmait. As the mighty army drew near, Diarmait was abandoned by all his former supporters, great and small. Of course the rulers of the neighbouring counties were delighted with the turn of events. Donnchad Mac Gilla Pátraic, king of Osraige, was more than happy to recognise Ruaidrí as high king and agree to the fall of Diarmait. Similarly, there could be no question of Diarmait retaining control of East Meath, and the leading candidates for kingship there swiftly turned to Ruaidrí. From the point of view of the Normans, these were terrible acts of treachery, but in Irish terms, it was perfectly well understood that vassalage to a neighbouring king was something that would be broken as soon as the dominant king could no longer threaten reprisals at the head of a punitive army.

In Diarmait's own eyes a more disgraceful example of treachery was that arising from the behaviour of the other leading Leinster dynasts. Of course the Uí Fáeláin and the Uí Failge of north Leinster refused to come to Diarmait's aid; they had every reason to hate Diarmait for the havoc he'd wreaked upon their nobles through blindings and assassinations. But there were several dynasties that Diarmait had promoted during the course of his rise to power in Leinster; they also failed to come to the muster called by their king. As Gerald de Barri imagined it, they 'recalled to mind injustices which they had long concealed and stored deep in their hearts. They made common cause with his enemies and the men of rank among this people deserted Mac Murchada along with his good fortune. He saw that his forces were melting away on all sides.'

One such family to desert the cause of Diarmait Mac Murchada was that of Murchad Ua Brain and his son Dalbach. The Uí Brain (not to be confused with the great Uí Briain of Munster) had been driven out of north Leinster by the Uí Fáeláin and sought assistance from Diarmait. He had set them up as lords of a region north of Enniscorthy, between the river Slaney and Black-stairs mountains; there they guarded the strategically important pass of Fid Dorcha, 'the dark wood', which allowed passage from the mountains to the core Uí Chennselaig territories. In 1166, as Ruaidrí Ua Conchobair, Tigernán Ua Ruairc and Asculv Mac Turcaill (ruler of the Hiberno-Norse of Dublin) marched southwards towards him, Diarmait sent messenger after messenger to Murchad and Dalbach. Their silence was ominous.

Taking matters into his own hands, with just a few bodyguards, Diarmait galloped from Ferns to obtain counsel from the Uí Brain lords. He antici-pated that they might judge defence of the pass impossible, but what shocked Diarmait was that Murchad and Dalbach would not even meet him to discuss a common strategy to face the crisis together. Rather than breaking their treaties with Diarmait outright and risk the death of their hostages, Murchad and Dalbach hid themselves and pretended that they did not know of Diarmait's visit. But Diarmait was wise to this ruse and implemented one of his own. Having returned to Ferns, Diarmait went to the abbey of St Mary the Queen, an abbey he had founded six years earlier for Augustinian Canons who followed the rule of Arrouaise. There he borrowed a religious habit and returned to the Ua Brain strongholds disguised from head to toe. The warrior king of Leinster seems to have made a convincing pilgrim. When at last Diarmait came within sight of Murchad, his worst fears were confirmed. On recognis-ing his overlord, Murchad shouted out, 'Wicked king, what are you looking for? Go away, I order you! And if you do not go at once, I will make you swing in the wind.'

With only his Uí Chennselaig troops to fight at his side, the position was nearly hopeless, but Diarmait made the best defence of his realm that he could, bringing his small army to Fid Dorcha. What Gerald de Barri failed to appreciate about the Irish lords is that the same ambition that led them to break oaths also drove them to acts of great courage and defiance, such as trying to hold a pass against a much larger army. This time, courage was not enough. Diarmait's men were driven from the forest with enormous loss. Irreplaceable Uí Chennselaig veterans of Móin Mór and Ardee lay slaughtered among the bracken, which was prematurely coloured rust by their blood. In this fighting it was the Uí Failge who acted as the vanguard for the united army, avenging – amongst other slights and insults – the rape of Mór, the former abbess of Kildare.

Before following up their victory, the allies cleared a path through the wood wide enough to allow future armies an easier path for the invasion of Uí Chennselaig territory. Then they pressed on to confront the defeated king of Leinster. Determined not to give his enemies any material reward for their attack, Diarmait himself set fire to Ferns before sending messengers asking for terms from Ruaidrí Ua Conchobair. This action, the burning of his own residence, was a stark signal about Diarmait's character. The message of the smoking ruin was this: you may force my back to the wall but I will not surrender, not even to save my own people. If I must fall, then all must fall with me. It was a message that Tigernán, in his moment of triumph, did not read.

For Ruaidrí Ua Conchobair, it was not necessary to seek the complete destruction of Diarmait's power. When Diarmait submitted to the new high king, gave four hostages, and abandoned claims to the kingship of Leinster, Ua Conchobair was perfectly willing to leave Diarmait as lord of the Uí Chennselaig. Ruaidrí was taking into consideration the balance of power across the length and breadth of Ireland and for him the priority was to use the tide that was flowing in his favour to gain more submissions, with Osraige his next goal. Ruaidrí did not need to make irrevocable enemies of the Uí Chennselaig, just weaken them and use their vassalage to his own ends. Ultimately, Ruaidrí intended to circle through the entire south and oblige the lords of the region to bring their troops in massive strength to Ulster, which is where he faced the only real threat to his status as high king.

By contrast, Tigernán Ua Ruairc looked at the situation through the perspective of a publicly humiliated man. Here was Diarmait on his knees: his alliances broken, his residence burned. So long as Diarmait remained at liberty, however, there was a chance the pendulum of fortune would swing back and one day it would be Tigernán whose world was in ruins. After all, as a young man Tigernán had savaged all these lands, only to see Diarmait recover his fortune. There could never be a stable compromise between them. One or the other would end their lives triumphant in the feud and Tigernán was intent on making this moment the decisive one.

No sooner had the high king returned to Connacht than Tigernán assembled an alliance of those with the greatest interest in completing the destruction of Diarmait. From Dublin came Asculv Mac Turcaill and a Hiberno-Norse army relishing the opportunity of adding Diarmait's bones to those of his father. The Uí Fáeláin and the Uí Failge marched once more, as did Diarmait Ua Máel Sechlainn, determined to break the recent pattern of kings of Leinster also becoming rulers over East Meath. These allies met with no resistance, for Diarmait was utterly without support. Even among the Uí Chennselaig it was thought his time was over and there was talk of a coup, to put Diarmait in chains and send him to Ruaidrí Ua Conchobair; a captivity he could not expect to survive, certainly not with his sight intact.

In triumph, Tigernán trampled on the stones of Diarmait's residence at Ferns, now toppled to the ground. Even so, these were not Diarmait's bones and so long as he lived, Ferns could be rebuilt. The game of thrones was not yet over. In a purely Irish context, Diarmait had no more options, but Leinster, and the Mac Murchadas in particular, had strong ties with England, which now offered a line of retreat to the defeated king.

England

Diarmait was a direct descendant of the great Leinster king Diarmait mac Máel na mBó, who was killed in battle in 1072. This ancestor of Diarmait Mac Murchada had given shelter to Harold Godwinson, the future king of England, and his brother Leofwine, in 1051 when the Godwins had scattered to avoid capture, having fallen out of favour with the king of England, Edward the Confessor. Again, in 1066, after the battle of Hastings and the death of Harold at the hands of the invading Normans, the king of Leinster played host to two of Harold's sons, Godwin and Edmund. Two years later, having been assisted by the Hiberno-Norse warriors of Dublin, these two tried to reinvade England with a fleet of fifty-two ships. William the Conqueror's grip on his new land, however, proved unshakeable.

Leinster's political intrigues with these English royal dynasts was a result of a strong economic connection between Ireland and England. For centuries the ports of Chester and Bristol had been busy with the trade of merchants sailing back and forth across the Irish Sea. Chester in the eleventh and twelfth centuries was a major urban centre whose patron, St Werburgh, is buried in the cathedral. An indication that significant numbers of people originating from Chester resided in Dublin is the fact that one of the pre-Norman parishes in the city was dedicated to St Werburgh. Until the ban of 1102, Chester exported slaves to Dublin in return for marten skins.

The other major English port dealing with Irish commerce was Bristol, and from the early eleventh century, when Bristol began minting coins, the townspeople seem to have modelled their coins on those of the Dublin mint, presumably to facilitate exchanges between the two cities. The scale of English exports to Ireland were such as to cause one twelfth-century historian, William of Malmesbury, to observe that without them, Ireland would be worthless. 'For what value would Ireland be, if goods were not brought to her by trade from England?'

Bristol was also a favoured city in the eyes of the current English king,

Henry II. Not only had the port supported Henry's mother, the empress Matilda, in a protracted civil war with King Stephen of England (from 1139 to 1154), but Henry had spent four years as a youth being tutored in Bristol. In 1166, the main representative of royal authority in the city was Robert Harding, lord of Berkeley, reeve of Bristol. An eighty-year-old man, Harding had been at the heart of Bristol's adherence to the king's mother during the years of strife with Stephen. Harding was also someone from whom Diarmait could hope to receive a sympathetic response to his plight. The two lords had not only overseen the regulation of trade between England and Ireland, but they shared a common patronage of the Augustinians.

With his power in Ireland crumbling and with his former supporters turning against him, Diarmait fled, escaping both the danger posed by opportunistic traitors within his immediate family and the invading armies. Meeting no resistance, Tigernán, with the approval of Ruaidrí Ua Conchobair, was able divide up the Uí Chennselaig territory between Murchad, Diarmait's brother, and Donnchad Mac Gilla Pátraic of Osraige; the latter also obtained as a prize Diarmait's son and heir designate Énna, who had not managed to escape with his father. It was a massive defeat for the once-mighty dynasty, one that suggested their future might be to fragment and disappear as a force capable of ruling Leinster. But even as he was savouring his victory, did Tigernán have any presentiment that with Diarmait still alive and free, his own future could not be assured?

Despite his many enemies, Diarmait had slipped away with his wife, Mór; daughter, Aífe; a navigator from the Hiberno-Norse community of south Wexford, Amlaib Ua Cinaeda; and some sixty men. Fearing that every hand was against them, this body of refugees took ship at a small fishing village, St Keran, where the river Corock flows into the Skar estuary at Bannow Bay. The skies were clear and the wind south-westerly. Leaving catastrophe behind, on 1 August 1166, Diarmait sailed for Bristol and Robert Harding. But he was not looking for refuge. His goal was revenge. Revenge against Ruaidrí Ua Conchobair, the Uí Fáeláin and the Uí Failge; revenge against his brother; against Donnchad Mac Gilla Pátraic of Osraige; against Asculv Mac Turcaill and the Dubliners; against the people of Wexford; against Diarmait Ua Máel Sechlainn and the people of Meath; against Murchad and Dalbach Ua Brain. Above all, revenge against Tigernán Ua Ruairc. And if the easing of Diarmait's brooding heart meant the fall of Ireland to Normans, so be it.

CHAPTER 3

Alliance

When Diarmait Mac Murchada arrived in Bristol he was supported by the elderly reeve of the town, Robert Harding, who housed the exiled Irish king and his family near the Augustinian monastery. From there, Diarmait kept up a regular correspondence with Leinster, seeking news from every ship that docked at the busy port. He also sent back word to Ireland to encourage more of his followers to cross the Irish Sea and join him. From Diarmait's conversations with Robert, it seemed that his best course of action was to seek assistance from the king of England himself, Henry II. Indeed, Robert suggested that the king might be interested in bringing an army to Ireland, as in his youth he had once planned to do so. So gathering up his small entourage, Diarmait set out for the royal court, then residing in France.

Having travelled back and forth in Normandy and sent messages in every direction, Diarmait eventually found Henry II directing affairs from Saumur castle in the Loire valley, and the exile was given a royal audience. Once before the court, Diarmait conducted himself well and made a favourable impression with his manners and his words:

May God who dwell on high

save and protect you, King Henry,

and grant you also

the courage and the desire and the will

to avenge my shame and my sorrow

which my own people have brought on me!

Hear, noble King Henry,

where I was born and in what country:

I was born a lord of Ireland,

in Ireland I was acknowledged king,

but my own people have wrongfully cast me out

from the kingdom.

I come to appeal to you, fair sire,

before the barons of your empire.

I will become your liege man

for as long as I live,

provided that you will help me,

so that I do not lose everything.

I will call you lord

in the presence of your barons and earls.

Vassalage

The promise to become Henry's 'liege man' was a significant one. It often arose in Normandy and France and, after 1066, in England, that a knight held lands as fiefs from a number of different lords. If those lords should ever come into conflict, that knight then faced the difficulty of owing military service to both of the rivals. To resolve this issue, the practice had evolved of swearing loyalty to a 'liege lord': one and only one prince whom the knight was obliged to serve above all others and regardless of any other oaths. Diarmait was offering to place himself in exactly this subordinate relationship to the king of England

and leader of the Normans. If his goals were achieved, Diarmait would be restored to power, but as a vassal of Henry and of Henry's descendants. Such a situation could potentially create major difficulties. A king of Leinster in such a relationship would no doubt have to provide troops for Henry's many military campaigns, not to mention pay regular and heavy tribute. But clearly Diarmait would prefer such vassalage to exile and in any case, in Irish terms, vassalage was something that could be shrugged off as soon as one's lord was sufficiently distant or weak (assuming you were prepared for the execution of your hostages).

From Henry's perspective, Diarmait's was, naturally, an attractive offer. After all, back in 1155, shortly after coming to power, Henry had contemplated an expedition to conquer his western neighbour. A few preliminary steps had been taken. At a meeting of the king and his most senior nobles in Winchester, 29 September 1155, the idea of attacking Ireland was discussed, but rejected on the advice of the young king's experienced and powerful mother, the empress Matilda. This was a disappointment to Henry at the time, as he had sufficient forces available for the enterprise and matters had gone so far as to set up the expectation that William, Henry's younger brother, would be made king of Ireland in due course. Moreover, Pope Hadrian IV had been solicited to endorse Henry's proposed action.

The intermediary between the English royal court and the papacy at this time was one of the great intellectuals of the twelfth century, John of Salisbury. Visiting the pope at Benevento from November 1155 to July 1156, John wrote that: 'at my entreaties, Pope Hadrian IV conceded and gave Ireland to the illustrious king of England, Henry II, to be possessed by an hereditary right, as his letters at this day witness. For of ancient right all islands are said to belong to the Roman Church by virtue of the Donation of Constantine, who founded and endowed her. He sent also by me a golden ring, decorated with a very fine emerald, with which ring the investiture of law in conveying Ireland should be made and the ring is as yet ordered to be preserved in the public archives of the court.'

John of Salisbury is a very reliable witness and the specific reference to a ring that would have been known to the readers of John's books reinforces the idea that Hadrian IV was willing to sanction some kind of English intervention in Irish affairs; but there is considerable doubt as to the terms of such an intervention. The only record of Hadrian's thinking is a supposed papal bull, recorded in the history of Gerald de Barri, known by its opening word, *Laudabiliter* (laudably). Very many historians even today take this document at face value, but the balance of modern scholarship suggests that Gerald rewrote it to strengthen the idea that the papacy supported an invasion of Ireland by Henry II. After all, Gerald was quite capable of putting words in the mouths of popes if it suited his goal of justifying the invasion of Ireland by his relatives. His history contains a letter from Alexander III which is recognised as an out-and-out forgery.

If *Laudabiliter* had been written in 1155 in the form that Gerald de Barri has it, and if it had returned to England with John of Salisbury, a copy would have been kept in the English exchequer archives, which is where the kings of England kept all their charters. The bull does not exist there, nor does it appear in the 'Black Book' of the exchequer that was drawn up around 1207 for King John and is an assembly of precedents for the English crown. In that collection are three letters from Pope Alexander III concerning Ireland, written after the fact of the invasion, and none of these refer to a previous grant of the country to Henry II. Had such an important papal grant as *Laudabiliter* existed, it would have been referred to in all subsequent papal letters on the subject.

Thanks to the fact that medieval papal bulls were very formulaic, it is possible to discern the fault lines of Gerald's tampering. Restoring the paragraphs of the bull to an appropriate order for a document issued by the papacy at the time gives it a very different sense. Yes, the pope was willing to have Henry II assist the Irish church, but not without consultation with 'the princes, churches and people of the region', a formulation Hadrian IV definitely did use in a known letter in regard to the proposal of the kings of France and England to crusade in Spain. This lukewarm phrase was hardly the ringing endorsement

Henry II was seeking in 1155: the pope had not given an unequivocal grant of Ireland to the English crown, and it is no wonder there was no copy kept of the 1155 letter in exchequer records.

By 1166, Henry had a much better foundation for intervention in Ireland than a papal letter urging him to consult with the Irish. With the quite unexpected arrival of Diarmait Mac Murchada, Henry gained a direct invitation from the king of Leinster to become liege lord of that province. Of course the king of England promptly accepted Diarmait as his vassal. Unlike in 1155, however, Henry had no troops to spare from his wars in France and the king was also embroiled in a bitter dispute with Thomas Becket, archbishop of Canterbury. This was no time to set about creating a fleet and an army to assist Diarmait. Henry did not, however, entirely disappoint Diarmait. After dismissing the Irish king and suggesting he return to Bristol, Henry sent a messenger to Robert Harding to urge his old friend to give everything necessary for Diarmait to reside in Bristol with his family and followers and that Robert should unreservedly respect Diarmait's commands.

For several weeks, therefore, Diarmait lived in Bristol with an abundance of the pleasant things in life, following developments in Ireland as closely as he could. As it became clear that Henry was unlikely to mount a military campaign in Ireland, Diarmait decided he could no longer tolerate a life of idle luxury, not while his desire for revenge burned so strongly. After travelling around the Bristol region and into south Wales, Diarmait succeeded in spreading word of his mission to receptive ears; for his plight and his promises came to the attention of Richard fitz Gilbert de Clare, lord of Strigoil (Chepstow), a Norman knight more commonly known as 'Strongbow'.

Strongbow's Inheritance

Strongbow had one of the most illustrious pedigrees of any descendant of the Norman conquerors of England. One of Duke William's close supporters in his invasion of England was Richard de Bienfaite, a grandson of Richard I, Duke of Normandy. As a result of the victory at Hastings and William's ascendancy to the throne of England, Richard de Bienfaite was rewarded with enormous swathes of English land, over a hundred and seventy lordships, the most important being Clare Manor in Suffolk, where he promptly built a castle. Due to the importance of this estate, Richard's descendants were named after the manor. Richard was the eighth wealthiest in the list of lords who benefited from the conquest. By the time of Richard's death in 1091, one son, Roger, inherited the Norman patrimony centred on Orbec and Bienfaite, while another, Gilbert fitz Richard, became lord of Clare, and the sixth wealthiest magnate in England.

Gilbert faced a crisis on the death of William Rufus, the new king of England, who had been killed by an arrow while hunting with Gilbert in the New Forest late in the afternoon on 2 August 1100. This accident meant that the king's younger brother could hastily be crowned Henry I, just before the older brother, Robert Curthose, duke of Normandy, completed his journey home from crusade and claimed the title. Several senior magnates, including Gilbert, would have preferred Robert as king and for a few months the Clares hinted that they might favour the Duke of Normandy by dragging their feet in response to Henry's efforts to mobilise his fighting forces. But in 1101 Gilbert shifted decisively over to the younger claimant and in backing Henry he chose wisely.

Once Duke Robert's efforts to conquer England that year petered out, the tide began to turn as Henry slowly but surely consolidated his position in England. In 1105, Henry felt confident enough to launch a major invasion of Normandy. By September 1106 the English king had destroyed Robert's following and captured the duke himself as a result of a major battle at Tinchebray in southwest Normandy. Among Gilbert's rewards for loyalty to the king was an 1110 grant of the lordship of Ceredigion in Wales. This brought the family close to Ireland, although there was a great deal of conflict with the Welsh before their rule over the region was secured.

On Gilbert's death, his son Richard took over the Welsh inheritance of the family fortune and managed it well, at least, up until a major rebellion by the Welsh in 1136. Then Richard was killed at Crickhowell in an ambush and nearly the entirety of Ceredigion was lost to Owain and Cadwaladr, sons of King Gruffudd ap Cynan of Gywnedd. Only the de Clare castle at Cardigan held out against the rebellion. Thanks to the efforts of royal intervention — King Stephen I sent Miles of Gloucester into Wales with a small rescue force — Richard's widow, Alice, along with important Clare vassals who had survived the uprising were brought to safety.

Naturally, this branch of the Clare family were well disposed towards Stephen, all the more so when Walter de Clare died and Stephen awarded the estates of Strigoil, Caerleon and Usk to Gilbert fitz Gilbert, Richard's younger brother and the new master of the Clare interests in Wales. In 1138, Stephen made Gilbert an earl, and Gilbert took the title 'Earl of Pembroke'. It was this Gilbert who was first referred to as 'Strongbow', earning the proud sobriquet for his prowess with the weapon. 'Strongbow' became the name of Gilbert's eldest son, Richard, more as an inheritance — along with the potentially enormous de Clare holdings in south Wales — than because Richard too had great strength and talent in using the bow.

It was natural then that when, in 1139, civil war broke out between King Stephen and his rival, Matilda, western empress and daughter of Henry I, the Welsh branch of the Clares gave their support to Stephen. Not that this support was a resolute and uncompromising one. Far from it, like many of the senior magnates in England at this time, Gilbert swapped sides more than once in an effort to take advantage of the weakness of royal authority. When Gilbert died, 6 January 1148, however, and the eighteen-year-old Strongbow became leader of the Welsh de Clares — inheriting not only the extensive family lands in south Wales but also the lordships of Orbec and Bienfaite in Normandy — he made the mistake of supporting Stephen wholeheartedly.

Putting all that he had at the disposal of Stephen, while loyal and honourable, was a disaster for the young Strongbow's fortunes as he was ultimately to find himself on the losing side. Matilda's son, Henry II, came to the throne in 1154. Although Strongbow had been styled 'Earl of Pembroke' in Stephen's proclamation of the 1153 Treaty of Wallingford (the treaty which acknowledged Henry as Stephen's heir and effectively meant the surrender of Stephen to his opponents), subsequently Strongbow appears in the sources as simply 'lord of Strigoil'. It was clear that the new king was not going to be easily reconciled to his former opponents, and a sign that the de Clares were now out of favour was that no one dared refer to Strongbow's title of 'earl' when it was treated with such contempt by Henry.

Agreement

By the time that Diarmait Mac Murchada appeared in south Wales seeking military aid, Strongbow was in a miserable position. He was thirty-seven years old and his fortunes had been declining for the latter half of his life. In part, this was because Henry II had taken most of Strongbow's lands in Ceredigion and granted them to one of Strongbow's cousins. In part, also, it was because the dynamism of the Welsh princes of the region had eroded the Norman presence there and most of the castles and towns once owned by Strongbow's great-uncle Walter were in the hands of Rhys ap Gruffudd, prince of Deheubarth (south west Wales). If Strongbow were to see a rise in his fortunes, he would either have to contract a successful marriage with an heiress – an action that would almost certainly be denied him by the king – or make military conquests. The problem with the latter perspective was that to subdue the Welsh would take a strategy of castle-building and a unified approach to a campaign agreed between all the local Norman lords. Again, Henry would not allow this. All major campaigns against the Welsh were to be conducted by the king himself, lest any of his magnates become too successful, and Henry carefully fuelled rivalries between his lords. From 1154 to 1166, Strongbow was kept in check and in a state of bachelorhood.

As Gerald de Barri put it, Strongbow was a man 'whose past was brighter than his prospects, whose blood was better than his brains, and whose claims of succession were larger than his lands in possession'. Gerald also gave a physical and psychological description of the Marcher lord. Strongbow had reddish hair and freckles, grey eyes, a feminine face, and while tall, his neck was short. Unlike his uncle Baldwin, who had been given the task of addressing King Stephen's troops at the battle of Lincoln (1141), Strongbow's voice was weak. An easy-going and generous man, Strongbow could be persuasive in negotiations and used this skill to make up for military setbacks. In battle, he was all that you could want in a leader. When he took up his position in the thick of the fighting, he stood firm as an immovable standard, around which his men could rally and take refuge. On campaign he was steadfast and reliable, regardless of whether fortune was favouring him or not. No feelings of despair overwhelmed him at times of adversity, nor did lack of self restraint ever cause him to run away with himself when successful. During peace times, however, Strongbow preferred to listen and accept council than take the initiative. In that sense he had more of the air of a rank-and-file soldier than the charisma of a leader.

Gerald was writing with the benefit of hindsight, and early in 1167, when Diarmait met Strongbow, the qualities of the lord of Strigoil, and especially his prowess in battle, would have been largely unknown. In fact, Strongbow would have compared very unfavourably with the enterprising Norman leaders of the previous century. But this was due to changed circumstances, rather than any personal failings. By the mid-twelfth century, Normandy's neighbours had adopted the successful economic and military practices that had once given the Normans such a dramatic advantage over their rivals. In particular, a traveller through France, Flanders, Lotharingia, Burgundy and England would have seen the same kind of social landscape, with the small manorial centre at the heart of farming practice, dominated by a castle and adjacent to this fortress, evidence of a small but growing town. Now that there was a more level playing field, the prospects for a dramatic rise in power of a Norman lord were much diminished and the most restless and ambitious knights of these regions were casting their eyes further afield: to Spain, Palestine, the Slavic lands and the Baltic region.

Moreover, while in the eleventh century the pioneering Duke William of Normandy, Robert Guiscard and Bohemond had been answerable to no one, the French and English states had been growing stronger over the century and more able to crush independent activity by an ambitious magnate. The process towards centralised royal power had gone the furthest in England, where not only had William the Conqueror inherited a sophisticated tax-collecting bureaucracy, but also he could impose a tight discipline on his knights through the threat that if they fell out with one another, the resentful English population would rise up and drive all the Normans out of the country. Although the senior nobles of the land had taken advantage of the fighting between Stephen and Matilda to improve their own autonomy, and in particular to get their hands on strong castles, with the coming to power of Henry II in 1154, England had a king with enormous resources, easily enough to bring utter ruin to any individual family that defied him. Strongbow's difficulties in the 1160s, then, were not due to timidity or a passive nature. He simply could not advance his dynasty until such time as Henry ran into major difficulties elsewhere. It is, in fact, testimony to Strongbow's suppressed sense of daring that when he met Diarmait, Strongbow committed himself to an enterprise that risked Henry's wrath, but which promised him a kingdom.

At last, hearing of someone who offered him more than just good wishes, Diarmait and his companions travelled to the river Wye. There, dramatically situated on cliffs overlooking the river, was the *caput* of the lordship of Strigoil, Chepstow Castle. Welcomed by Strongbow, the exiled king of Ireland set out his plight: a tale of woes, banishment and injustice. Diarmait outlined the opportunity that now dawned for Strongbow. The conquest of Leinster, argued Diarmait, was possible, with the deposed king's support. On their own, the arrival of Norman troops would achieve very little, other than to unite the Irish princes to drive them out. With Diarmait rallying the Uí Chennselaig and advising Strongbow, however, the two of them could secure the province. After that, Diarmait would seek to establish Strongbow as his successor.

A marriage alliance between Strongbow and Aífe – 'the person most dearest to him in the world' – would do a great deal to integrate Strongbow with the Uí Chennselaig. Aífe was Diarmait's eldest daughter from his current marriage to Mór. This would also bring Strongbow the support of her uncle, Lorcán Ua Tuathail, archbishop of Dublin.

Then there were Diarmait's sons, the eldest Énna, Conchobar and Domnall Cáemánach – named from his fosterage, at Cill Cáemánach – all born to Diarmait's previous wife. Of these sons, Énna was in the hands of Donnchad Mac Gilla Pátraic of Osraige, but Conchobar and Domnall were still free and Domnall, in particular, was in a position to assist his father with his own strong following. Diarmait could assure Strongbow of the full commitment of all of his sons to the plan of designating Leinster to a Norman lord. Énna had very little hope of surviving at all, certainly not with his sight intact, and what little hope he did have depended on Diarmait regaining power and being in a position to bargain for his release. Conchobar and Domnall also fully understood that, without assistance, their branch of the Meic Murchada was doomed to decline in power. Nor were they giving away an assured inheritance: under the Irish system anyone from an extensive family group could challenge for the mantle of a deceased king and, given how weak their current position was, Diarmait's sons were not sacrificing a great deal by the offer.

The Norman lord was interested in Diarmait's proposal. So too were the knights of his household. Having listened carefully to the Irish king and consulted with those whose lives were about to be staked upon the enterprise, Strongbow assembled his full court. There Strongbow and Diarmait clasped hands for all to see and made their oaths, the feudal 'oath of equals'. With the important caveat, that he would have to find a way of getting the expedition off the ground without incurring the wrath of Henry II, Strongbow swore faithfully that once he felt the political conditions allowed, he would bring his army to aid Diarmait in Ireland. In return, Diarmait replied for all to hear that Aífe would be given to Strongbow in marriage as soon as the lord of Strigoil arrived in Ireland with his vassals.

LIVM: CON·TRA·HAROL

Above: Norman warriors revolutionised European warfare, not least due to their skill in fighting from horseback while wearing heavy armour.

Right: This early twelfth-century Bible image, created at Citeaux, shows Goliath in Norman armour.

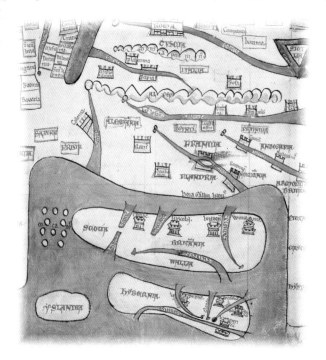

Left: A late twelfth-century map of Ireland.
Below: Inheriting the shipbuilding technique of their Viking ancestors, the Normans had no fear of organising amphibious invasions of neighbouring territority.

Above: Norman castles, initially earth and timber constructions, transformed the landscape of the lands they conquered.

Above: Intense fighting between Norman cavalry and Anglo-Saxon infantry at the Battle of Hastings, 1066.

Left: Diarmait Mac Murchada.
Right: Robert fitz Stephen.
Below: A Victorian war memorial, built as a round tower, marks the spot of Robert fitz Stephen's first castle at Wexford. Clearly, the site was chosen to dominate the River Slaney.

Above: Baginbun, the landing site for Raymond Le Gros with the first substantial forces sent to Ireland by Strongbow. The traces of Norman and older earthworks can still be seen.

Below: Strategically located on the banks of the Barrow, St Mullin's Church was the rendevous point for Maurice de Prendergast and Domnall Mac Gilla Pátraic of Osraige.

Above left: The Norman warriors took their hunting birds with them to war and in so doing introduced to Ireland the practice of using sparrowhawks in their hunts.

Above right: Norman propaganda in a manuscript illumination: Gerald de Barri claimed Irish nobles were untrustworthy and were always ready to strike with the axes they carried in hand.

Below: Strongbow's castle at Chepstow, dominating the River Wye.

Above: The Black Castle, Wicklow. The original medieval castle
at Wicklow, dramatically located on the coast, was constructed by
Maurice fitz Gerald, after the surrounding lands were granted to him by
Strongbow. Today ruins of a later stone castle are all that remain.

What did they see in each other, these two men who had been born to lead warriors and rule great territories but whose fortunes were battered and shaken? As they clasped hands and looked into each other's eyes, they must have recognised in each other a grim determination and an absolutely heart-felt commitment. For, in this pivotal moment for the history of Ireland, a comradeship was created that was to withstand the pressures of life-and-death decisions and the wild vicissitudes of ever-unreliable war. History offers many examples of people forming profound alliances from their very first meeting, the foundation of such alliances usually being a positive one, such as a shared passion for a new perspective on politics or the arts. Here, the cement of the relationship was much more negative but just as effective. It was a shared fury against the people who had ground them down and discarded them. Despite their seeming emasculation, these were still dangerous men and they desired nothing more than the opportunity to prove themselves to the world. For Diarmait, the aristocratic inhibition against giving outsiders a foothold in Irish affairs was now of negligible weight against the balance of his perceived injustices. For Strongbow, the disdain of his class for what they saw as the barbaric culture of the Irish was as nothing to the fact that mighty deeds in that land would give him a name that Henry II would otherwise take from him.

They clasped hands, looked at each other, and in this moment at least, they meant every word they uttered.

Robert fitz Stephen

Revitalised by his meeting with Strongbow, Diarmait immediately made his way to the port of St Davids, in the westernmost part of south Wales, from where Ireland was just visible, merging with the clouds on the horizon. The former king of Leinster was allowed to move freely through the territory of the Welsh prince Rhys ap Gruffudd. A bitter opponent of Norman advances upon Wales — in 1164 Rhys had driven the de Clares out of Ceredigion — Rhys could see the potential in this adventure for deflecting his Norman enemies away from campaigning in south Wales.

In 1166, Rhys had captured the strategically important castle of Cardigan, which he would soon rebuild in stone and make his main fortress. A little further up the river Teifi was the castle of Cilgerran, where a valiant Norman knight had been in charge of the defences and had been imprisoned in chains as a result of its capture. This knight was Robert fitz Stephen.

A well-built and sturdy man of above average height, Robert was a good-looking man. Although Gerald de Barri had great admiration for Robert, the medieval historian could not help but condemn Robert for the fact that when free, the Norman knight was over-fond of wine and women. At the time Diarmait came to south Wales, however, Robert was languishing in a dungeon owned by Rhys ap Gruffudd. In the course of making plans for Strongbow to come and assist Diarmait in Ireland, the Norman lord had made the point that Diarmait should meet Rhys and plead for the release of Robert fitz Stephen and his men. When the matter was raised with the Welsh prince, he was happy to oblige. Rhys had, in fact, for some time sought a way to release fitz Stephen, as Robert was a first cousin, albeit a dangerous one: Robert's mother, the Welsh princess Nesta, was Rhys's aunt. So long as Robert refused to swear an oath that he would fight Henry II on his release, Rhys kept his truculent relative in chains; after all, Robert's father was the former constable of Cardigan castle and Robert would no doubt try to regain his inheritance as soon as he was free. But Diarmait's plans gave Rhys a new way of diverting his cousin from resuming battle in Wales.

Having accepted certain guarantees from Robert's relatives, Rhys freed the Norman warrior from captivity to facilitate a meeting with Diarmait. Also present at the discussion were two half-brothers of Robert's, both sons of Nesta by an earlier relationship: David, bishop of St Davids and Maurice fitz Gerald. Again, this meeting was the seed of enormous changes for Ireland. Diarmait once more recounted his woes and injustices. But this time his tale ended with the news that Strongbow, as soon as he could safely escape the attention of Henry II, was coming to Ireland. If they so desired, Robert and

Maurice could share in the spoils. For while Leinster had been promised to Strongbow, the Hiberno-Norse ports of the province were not yet spoken for. In particular, if, with the agreement of Strongbow, Robert and Maurice came to help Diarmait take the town of Wexford, Diarmait would confer the town upon them, along with two large manors – known as cantreds – beside Wexford, corresponding to the Hiberno-Norse agricultural hinterland.

For Robert, this was a far more attractive proposition than returning to his chains and hoping that royal intervention would free him: not that any assistance was likely to be forthcoming. Henry II preferred peace with Rhys than to honour a debt incurred in 1157. That year, in a battle at Colsehill Woods, near Rhuddlan in north Wales, Henry had found himself in perilous difficulty, to the extent that his army thought him dead and the royal standard fallen. Among those alongside Henry as he struggled to escape the forest was Robert fitz Stephen, who was badly wounded, and Robert's half brother, Henry fitz Henry, who was killed in the fighting. The king of England felt obligated to one of the few lords to have stayed with him during that crisis, but not so obligated as to risk his strategy of balancing the Welsh prince Rhys against the potentially powerful Norman lords of south Wales. No request had come for the release of Robert in almost two years, and no doubt the constable of Cardigan Castle had spent some of this time brooding on the ingratitude of kings.

Diarmait and Robert were the same age and Robert found the determination of his contemporary to return to power inspiring and convincing. Even though he had few followers – he could raise perhaps thirty knights from his family and dependents – Robert decided it was worth giving up his claim to Cardigan Castle, and agreed that at the first sighting of a swallow the following spring, 1168, he would sail to meet with Diarmait and lead the effort to establish lordships for the fitz Stephens and fitz Geralds in Ireland. More unassuming than Robert in physique and manner, Maurice also swore to assist the proposed expedition. Maurice was 'a man of few words', wrote his nephew, Gerald de Barri. But he was also 'sober, disciplined and chaste, steadfast, loyal and faithful'. In other words, he was a good man to have at your right-hand side. Another stout warrior pledged to the enterprise at this time was the youthful Miles, son of the bishop of St Davids. David had listened avidly to Diarmait's tale of opportunity and promised that Miles would also be there in the spring to assist Robert.

Free from his dungeon, under the fresh blue skies of St Davids, in the company of senior family members willing to help get him back on his feet, Robert must have felt his fortunes were on the rise at last.

Return

Impatient, now that he had the solemn agreement of these Normans that they would bring their troops to Ireland, Diarmait could not resist crossing the Irish Sea once more to determine how matters stood in Leinster. The risk of capture, ambush, or betrayal was high, but his scouts reported that Ruaidrí, the high king, and his ally Tigernán, were busy fighting elsewhere.

Earlier in the year, Ruaidrí had reinforced his authority over the whole of Ireland by hosting an impressive synod, at which all his major vassals and allies as well as the senior figures from the clergy had assembled and agreed to honour royal authority. Ruaidrí had become the most powerful king in Ireland's history, and respect for his rule meant that 'a woman could traverse the island alone'. Of course, there were always those who would challenge a high king and, in particular, the families of Tír Eógain had not forgotten the recent claim to the title by Muirchertach Mac Lochlainn. After the success of his synod, Ruaidrí mobilised for a summer campaign in the north, one which saw the high king successfully partition Tír Eógain and cripple his opponents.

It was on learning of Ruaidrí's endeavours in the north that Diarmait decided to commit his small following to a return to Leinster. His only foreign assistance at this time came from a minor lord called Richard fitz Godibert, with a handful of knights, archers and footsoldiers. Richard was a Fleming from Rhos Castle, near Haverford, south Wales, and if questions were asked about him by Henry II, Strongbow could deny any connection. But Richard was acting with the full knowledge of Strongbow, and Richard's family would later be well rewarded, founding the Roche dynasties of Wexford and Cork. On board ship, too, was a young son of the great Welsh prince Rhys (unnamed by the sources). Although careful not to violate his treaties with Henry II, Rhys nevertheless gave permission for his son to join the adventure, to keep the prince of South Wales informed as to developments on the other side of the Irish sea.

Scant though his forces were, Diarmait made a safe landing at Glascarrig, a small creek about twelve miles south of Arklow head. From there the band hurried along the short route to Ferns, to find the Uí Chennselaig in disarray. In Diarmait's absence, his brother Murchad had ruled over that part of their territories which had not been handed over to Donnchad Mac Gilla Pátraic of Osraige. But Murchad had no prospects of restoring Uí Chennselaig fortunes and therefore no base to resist even the small forces that — much to his astonishment — arrived in Ferns in August 1167. When Diarmait rallied the Uí Chennselaig with promises of Norman aid, of which Richard's presence was just a foretaste, and when Diarmait's son Domnall expressed his commitment to this strategy, then the Uí Chennselaig élite were won over and Diarmait resumed his royal seat.

No sooner had the news of the return of the former king of Leinster spread across Ireland than the old alliance that had unseated Diarmait in 1166 reformed. For Ruaidrí Ua Conchobair, well aware of the danger posed by the introduction of Norman troops into Irish politics, the main purpose of the hosting was to stamp hard on the first sparks of Norman intervention and put them out. For Tigernán Ua Ruairc, there was one matter above all that still burned and still drove him to battle with Diarmait: honour. Fifteen years on from his humiliation, the conflict was still about his wife. For the Dubliners and Diarmait Ua Máel Sechlainn of East Meath, the swift mobilisation was to ensure Diarmait never recovered his former position of dominance over them.

In 1166, when Ruaidrí had previously marched on Ferns, he had cleared a route through the 'dark wood', Fid Dorcha, that obstructed the pass down from the Wicklow mountains. This now served him in good stead because the Uí Chennselaig, with Diarmait at their head, once more sought to mount their defence at this point in the forest. The two armies, large and small, halted within sight of each other at Cill Osnadh (modern Kellistown, County Carlow). Negotiations began, with Diarmait urged to surrender in the face of such overwhelming odds. Richard fitz Godibert, the son of Rhys, and the other 'foreign' troops stood guard while their fate was being discussed.

Among the footsoldiers and cavalry of Connacht were those who thought the talks protracted and, indeed, unnecessary. It would be simpler to destroy the Uí Chennselaig army along with the foreigners. These Connachtmen attempted a surprise attack, but, to their dismay, the much smaller Leinster force was alert and stood fast. When the cavalry of Uí Chennselaig counterattacked, the Connachtmen turned in a panicked retreat. Six of the Connacht riders were killed, together with Domnall, son of Tadc son of Máelruanaid. Domnall was a distant relative of the high king's and a member of the royal dynasty of Mag Luirg, in north-east Connacht.

Although Diarmait's men had not been responsible for the skirmish, the death of Domnall was the trigger for Tigernán Ua Ruairc to let loose his own fierce troops in reprisal. This time the battle was no contest; twenty-five of the Uí Chennselaig were dead, as was the adventurous young Welsh prince, before Diarmait Mac Murchada surrendered to all the demands of his opponents. Coming before the assembly of victors, Diarmait bent the knee to Ruaidrí and presented the high king with seven hostages, in return for which the Uí Chennselaig were allowed to retain just ten cantreds of their traditional territory with Diarmait as their lord, provided all the foreigners departed. Then Diarmait turned to Tigernán.

Once equals, the contrast between the two figures was now marked. Through his alliance with Ruaidrí, Tigernán had gone from strength to strength and was famed throughout the land. Bréifne was expanding, triumphant and wealthy. In contrast, Diarmait looked like a beaten dog and the Uí Chennselaig an impoverished, truncated, and politically irrelevant third-rate power. The terms of Diarmait's surrender were that he pay one hundred ounces of gold to Tigernán Ua Ruairc for his honour. According to the Brehon Law tract, *Cáin Lánamna*, if a chief's wife were raped or stolen, the full honour price of her husband was owed. It was harsh to place the full responsibility on Diarmait for the abduction of Derbforgaill and even harsher to have him acknowledge that Tigernán's honour price was so extraordinarily high: something like five times that of Diarmait Mac Murchada himself. But then, Diarmait was a lord of what seemed now only to be a minor dynasty. Diarmait was forced to pay. He had to stay alive and at liberty long enough for his Norman allies to make the pain of this surrender a fleeting one. For Tigernán it was a moment of great satisfaction, and news of Diarmait's payment spread across Ireland, enhancing Tigernán's reputation as a famous and powerful king. But as he looked into the eyes of his old enemy, did Tigernán sense that the feud was not over?

For Richard fitz Godibert the adventure was over and he was lucky to still be free to leave the country, which he promptly did, bringing grim news for the prince of south Wales, but a slightly more positive report to Strongbow. Diarmait Mac Murchada had a long way to go before he could once more become a significant force in Irish politics. On the other hand, Richard had seen the high king's troops close up and had fought with them. The Irish lacked heavy armour and their archers had nothing more sophisticated than the hunting bow. A relatively small number of Norman knights would have every chance of besting the Connacht army.

For Diarmait, the next twelve months proved difficult in the extreme. Impoverished and, indeed, massively indebted from the payment to Tigernán Ua Ruairc, he was dependent on the assistance of the Augustinian monks of his own foundation in Ferns for his shelter and sustenance. The modest diet of a monk was hardly the regal fare he and his family were used to. Moreover, while the Uí Chennselaig still retained memories of Diarmait's former glories and their victorious role in the two defining battles of the era, Diarmait had lost most of his veterans in the defeat of 1166. He was exposed to assault from any of his innumerable enemies, great and small, and was saved from having to flee again mainly by the fact that Ruaidrí and Tigernán were occupied in taking advantage of two major crises in order to make their position unassailable. One province experiencing great political instability was Munster, where King Muirchertach Ua Briain was slain by a rival. The other was Meath, where Diarmait Ua Máel Sechlainn, the king who had so recently sided with Ruaidrí and Tigernán to punish the return of Diarmait Mac Murchada, had made the mistake of killing a hostage for whom Ruaidrí had stood surety. Forced by Ruaidrí to pay eight hundred cows compensation, the people of East Meath rose up against their king and ousted him.

1168 was a year to celebrate if you were a supporter of Ruaidrí or Tigernán. Their authority across the whole of the island could no longer be challenged by anyone, with Meath, Munster, Leinster and Ulster all partitioned and fought over by kings of only minor standing. But for Diarmait Mac Murchada it was a year of great misery, compounded by the fact that his son Énna was blinded by Donnchad Mac Gilla Pátraic of Osraige. Such a deed was Mac Gilla Pátraic's contribution to the collective effort of Diarmait's enemies to prevent the Meic Murchada from making a return to political prominence. And for all that blindings were commonplace among such rivals, it was another bitter blow. Diarmait, however, endured in hope, for he had felt the earnestness of Strongbow's grip.

The barn swallow is a conservative bird, in that it returns thousands of miles to the same nest at the end of its migratory journey; it begins to arrive in Ireland in late March, with the main influx in April. Whether March, April, or May in 1168, with the swallows that year came no sign of Robert fitz Stephen, Maurice fitz Gerald and Miles fitz David. In fact the whole year passed with Diarmait in a precarious position, more or less hiding in his monastery.

1169

Again, in 1169, the swallows returned, but there was still no news from Wales. The waiting must have been unendurable and Diarmait could not remain passive indefinitely. Sooner or later either a major army would raid through Uí Chennselaig territory or Diarmait's whereabouts would become known to a more local enemy and an ambush would be planned against him. The Normans had to come this year. So Diarmait sent his own interpreter, Maurice Regan, to St Davids with a letter and a speech memorised. Not only was Maurice to galvanize those who had previously offered to support the fallen king of Leinster, but Maurice should spread the word more widely:

> If anyone wishes to have land or money,
> horses, equipment or chargers,
> gold or silver, I will give him
> very generous payments;
> if anyone wants land or pasture,
> I will enfeoff him generously:
> I will also give him plenty
> of livestock and a rich fief.

From Robert fitz Stephen's perspective, the arrival of Maurice and the widespread dissemination of Diarmait's offer was the spur to action. He had indeed delayed, deterred by the report from Richard fitz Godibert and his own difficulties raising troops. Still, he had some thirty knights from among his nearest relatives and dependents.

In addition, a Flemish lord from Rhos, south Wales, Maurice de Prendergast, had responded to the message of Diarmait and was in St Davids with his men to hire a ship. This was reassuring to Robert – in an enterprise like this, the more knights the better – but also a challenge. Putting all his resources into the effort, Robert, together with Strongbow's assistance, could fill three ships with sixty mail-clad footsoldiers and three hundred archers. The latter would have to be protected by those in armour, being only lightly defended, but they were élite troops whose daily practice with their bows meant they could wreak destruction on an enemy force before it could close to hand-to-hand range.

On the last day of April, 1169, Robert fitz Stephen sailed for Ireland. With him were his family members – descendants of Nesta – Miles fitz David and Meilyr fitz Henry, and also with Robert was Hervey de Montmorency. Ten years older than Strongbow, entering his fiftieth decade, Hervey was Strongbow's uncle (Strongbow's grandmother Adeliz of Clermont had remarried after the death of Strongbow's grandfather Gilbert in 1117 and gave birth to Hervey, half-brother to Strongbow's other uncles and aunts). Hervey's presence on Robert's ships was in part due to the fact that Hervey had no better options in life. Gerald de Barri wrote that he was a 'fugitive from Fortune, unarmed and destitute'. But in part too, Hervey was also aboard in order to keep Strongbow informed as to the events taking place in Ireland. Although Gerald de Barri hated Hervey, for acting as an informant and constraining the later advances of fitz Stephen and fitz Gerald family members, the Norman historian wrote a favourable description of Hervey's physique: Hervey was tall and handsome, with prominent grey eyes. Nature had endowed him with many gifts and his overall bearing was all that a warrior could want.

Landing safely on what was then the island of Bannow (although shifting sands have meant that today Bannow is connected to the mainland), about sixteen miles from the hostile Hiberno-Norse town of Wexford, Robert waited anxiously while Maurice Regan hurried to contact Diarmait to tell his lord that at last the Normans had come. The next day a ship arrived with Maurice de Prendergast and seven other Flemish knights, along with some two hundred footsoldiers and archers. Their force was warmly welcomed, for Bannow island felt very exposed.

In the meantime, Diarmait had set out with the Uí Chennselaig cavalry, a force of about five hundred riders. News of the arrival of the Normans had travelled faster still and, as Diarmait rode towards Bannow island, he was met by messengers from two of the smaller Wexford dynasties, the Uí Lorcáin and the Uí Duibginn, promising loyalty and support. It was not for Diarmait to accuse these families of treachery and hypocrisy, to point out that they had previously deserted him, for such was the nature of Irish politics. There were certain families for whom there would be no forgiveness, but here, the first forces to rally to him were welcomed and would share in the rewards of his future success.

Before approaching the Normans in person, Diarmait sent ahead his son Domnall. The fact was, for all the planning and negotiations in Wales, Diarmait found his new allies something of an unknown quantity. Only after all their agreements were renewed and solemn oaths taken publicly many times over did the former king of Leinster and his Uí Chennselaig troops meet up with the Norman arrivals. There, Diarmait demonstratively kissed all the Norman leaders; the kiss of peace was a tradition of continental rulers, symbolising to all that the knight concerned was in favour and not to be harmed. Without further delay, the united army then drew up in battle order and marched on Wexford.

Wexford

The Hiberno-Norse warriors of Wexford had been gathering their numbers and sharpening their axes from the moment news arrived about the Norman landing. They rode out to meet Diarmait's new army, but as the Normans deployed their lines of archers and knights, ready to initiate combat, the Wexford men were dismayed. Normally, they would dismount to fight on foot with their fierce axes, and against Irish cavalry they had nothing to fear. They did not, however, like the look of so many archers and the heavy armour of the Norman knights glittered ominously in the sunshine. Rather than give battle, the Wexford men fell back to the walls of their town, setting fire to the suburbs around it so as to destroy materials and cover that might assist Diarmait's attack.

Diarmait and his Norman knights attempted to take the town by a *coup de main*, hoping to find a weakness in the defences. The allied troops charged headlong into the ditch and strove to climb up to the walls, all the while being covered by their archers. It was not a successful attack. The battle was harsh, but the citizens of Wexford kept up a barrage of heavy stones and wood against the attackers. One of the Normans in the thick of things was Robert, a brother of the historian Gerald de Barri. Gerald reports that, having climbed the ditch, Robert was under the walls of the town when he was struck by a heavy stone, which was deflected by Robert's helmet. Stunned, but alive, Robert fell back into the ditch, from where he was dragged away by his fellow soldiers. Curiously, sixteen years later, the impact of this blow was manifested by Robert's molar teeth falling out, with new ones having grown up beneath them. No other knight fared much better than Robert and it was clear that, without proper preparations of ladders and defensive wooden structures, the attack was only going to waste lives. Already, eighteen Norman soldiers were dead, with only three dead on the side of the defenders of the city.

Withdrawing from this attempt to breach the walls, Diarmait's army then went down to the estuary of the river Slaney to attack the boats in the harbour. While some ships in the harbour were successfully burned, a great prize, a ship full of wheat and wine, escaped the assault. In chasing this vessel, several warriors in their small skiffs, relying on their strength with the oar, were nearly swept out to sea, leaving them with an exhausting battle with the north wind to get back.

That night, Diarmait and his Norman allies were not discouraged, but the sound of timber being cut and made into ladders was ominous for those within walls that no longer felt so tall. When the sun was well up in the sky, the allied army heard Mass together, then proceeded to the town, carefully advancing behind their new protective hoardings and massing their archers so as to dominate a section of the walls. No longer confident in their ability to resist, the citizens of Wexford were relieved when Diarmait's messengers called upon them to surrender. They had been subject to Diarmait before, while still retaining a great deal of autonomy, they could bow to him once again. The negotiations were quickly concluded. The men of Wexford would accept Robert fitz Stephen and (when he arrived from Wales) Maurice fitz Gerald as their lords. Having surrendered four prominent men as hostages, the

Hiberno-Norse citizens vowed to assist Diarmait. In keeping with Diarmait's promise to Strongbow, that he would have control over Leinster, Strongbow's man, Hervey de Montmorency, gained Wexford's hinterland as his prize: two cantreds of land (about two hundred thousand acres) between Wexford and Waterford. Later, Strongbow would be happy to confirm the grant to Hervey.

Osraige

Returning to Ferns, Diarmait was delighted not to have to skulk any longer for fear of would-be assassins. His attention now turned to Osraige. Back in 1166, when Diarmait had been expelled from Ireland, Donnchad Mac Gilla Pátraic had been allotted half of the Uí Chennselaig territory. In the previous year, on hearing that Diarmait had returned to Ferns, Donnchad had blinded Diarmait's intended heir, Énna. Now was the time to regain those lands and obtain revenge upon the ruler of Osraige for the blinding of his son, although Diarmait's revenge would have to be upon Domnall, the successor to Donnchad Mac Gilla Pátraic, as Donnchad had recently died.

After three week's rest, which allowed some of the wounded Normans to return to the ranks, Diarmait summoned the Wexford axemen and, late in May, 1169, set out westwards, towards the ancient east-west route *Belach Gabráin*, the gap of Gowran, through the southern end of the Slieve Bloom mountains. As they travelled, the Uí Chennselaig, commanded by Diarmait's son Domnall Cáemánach formed the vanguard, the Normans and Flemish troops formed the centre of the army and acted as Diarmait's bodyguard, while the men from Wexford brought up the rear. The Hiberno-Norse warriors did not entirely trust Diarmait and at night made their camp a short distance from that of the rest of the army, mounting guards against ambush.

These disparate allies made their way along what was a heavily wooded six-mile valley between Slieve Margy to the north and Freagh Hill to the south. Domnall Mac Gilla Pátraic was alert to the danger from Leinster and had mobilised his full fighting force, some five thousand men. The army of Osraige moved to intercept Diarmait and on higher ground, in thick forest, their forces drew up behind three deep and wide trenches each topped with a palisade.

The battle to cross these defences was long and hard, lasting the entire day. As the shadows of the forest deepened, the Normans forced the last of the trenches and, with the army of Osraige fleeing the scene, the route was open for Diarmait's lightly armed cavalry to gallop through the enemy kingdom, raiding and looting. Success in the gap of Gowran was another step forward in Diarmait's march back to power, but it was a costly victory. Many of the Norman warriors had fallen, too many. At this rate, attrition would make his small force of foreigners ineffective.

Having gathered up booty from across the region, Diarmait ordered a return to Ferns, this time by a different route, hoping to shake off Domnall Mac Gilla Pátraic, who was still in the field with the army of Osraige, albeit reduced to some seventeen hundred troops. The route to the north of Slieve Margy, back to the valley of the Barrow river, was through much more difficult terrain and, worse, was laden with ill omen. Not only were the more remote parts of the region reputed to be inhabited by werewolves, but the path through the wilderness, the *fásach*, was thought to be *geis* (cursed) to the Uí Chennselaig, who had fought and lost three battles there. It was said that ghostly armies from other realms still marched this route and, as a result, when Diarmait made camp on the hillside his own cavalry were in a mutinous and terrified state of mind.

With morning came the unpleasant fact that only forty-three Irish riders, lead by Domnall Cáemánach, remained to assist the slower-moving Normans. The rest had fled during the night. Suddenly, the situation looked extremely precarious for the three hundred or so troops under Robert fitz Stephen and Maurice de Prendergast; nor was there any way of avoiding battle with the faster-moving Osraige troops who had been trailing Diarmait's army. The first pitched battle between Norman and Irish soldiers was inevitable.

It was Maurice de Prendergast who took charge during the crisis. Ordering a footsoldier, Robert Smith, to lie in hiding with fifty archers, Maurice then had the rest of the cavalry and footsoldiers rush towards higher ground, to get above the forest line. This was to be a feigned retreat, as, once well clear of the trees, the Norman troops were to turn and both cavalry and footsoldiers charge back down onto the two thousand strong Osraige army. It was to be that classic Norman ruse which served William, Robert and Bohemond so well: the feigned retreat. 'Flight,' shouted Maurice to the other knights, 'is out of the question: we either live or die here.'

Eager for battle, the lightly armoured Irish troops came after the retreating Normans with ferocity. They passed Robert Smith and his hidden archers, without noticing the enemy troops, and pushed on beyond the tree line. There, they were shocked to see the Normans turning, led by Maurice on his powerful pale destrier, *Blanchard*. Calling on St David to aid him and his Flemings, Maurice charged back down the hill, supported by Robert fitz Stephen, Miles fitz David, Meilyr fitz Henry and Hervey de Montmorency. All the footsoldiers, knights and squires of the Norman army charged and although few in number they smashed through the vanguard of the Osraige army. Of all the knights in battle that afternoon, it was Meilyr whose daring feats stood out.

Seeing the men from Osraige toppled from their horses and that those fleeing through the woods were running straight into an ambush, Diarmait's Irish followers regained their confidence. Emerging from their hiding places, they joined the scenes of carnage. Their priority was the decapitation of the injured and dead Osraige warriors, to make a pile of heads in front of Diarmait, in order to claim reward for them. Two hundred and twenty heads were taken, among them heads from several senior figures from the Mac Gilla Pátraic dynasty. It was the sight of these that had Diarmait dancing for pleasure and even using his own teeth to tear away the lips and nose of the most prominent of his fallen enemies. The behaviour was shocking to the Normans, but it was explained to them that this was one way to ensure the ghost of the enemy general did not rise again to lead a spirit army of all of the slain.

Following the victory, Robert fitz Stephen proposed that the united army remain for the night in possession of the battlefield and on the following morning re-enter Osraige in the hope of following up the victory and capturing Domnall Mac Gilla Pátraic. To be able to camp on the field of battle was, in Norman terms, the definition of victory. But Diarmait felt no need for the gesture; let Domnall Mac Gilla Pátraic return to obtain the headless bodies and claim what he liked, the brutal fact was that the Uí Chennselaig foray had inflicted great damage on the Osraige army and was returning laden with spoils. Moreover, Diarmait's own superstitious troops did not want to spend another night in the cursed wilderness. Instead, the allied army gathered up their wounded and pushed on to Leighlinbridge and the safety of its bridge over the Barrow. There they camped for the night and held a joyous feast to celebrate the success of their raid.

The following day, the elated army returned to Ferns and while the wounded and the Normans stayed in the town, Diarmait's Irish troops dispersed and the Hiberno-Norse axemen returned to Wexford. While the physicians were busy with their patients, packing spear and axe wounds with moss to promote clotting, Diarmait drew up his list of enemies and planned his next move. His star was beginning to rise again.

The Return of the King

The Uí Chennselaig victory over Domnall Mac Gilla Pátraic was news indeed and troubled many a Leinster dynast. If Osraige could not stand against the once-fallen king, then only a major power, such as the high king, or his right-hand man, Tigernán Ua Ruairc, could hope to oppose Diarmait. It was likely that Ruaidrí Ua Conchobair would soon take an interest in affairs in Leinster, but would his intervention come in time to prevent Diarmait obtaining vengeance against those who had deserted him? The more politically astute Leinster families sent their sons with tribute and praise for Diarmait, called him *rí ruirech*, provincial king, and offered to serve in his army. For Murchad and Dalbach Ua Brain (who in 1166 had abandoned the strategic pass of Fid

Dorcha and had refused to even meet with Diarmait and offer their counsel), however, there was nothing to be gained from such a submission. Nor too did the Uí Fáeláin and the Uí Failge of north Leinster have anything to offer but war. For the Uí Failge, in particular, there was the unforgivable rape of their princess, Mór, abbess of Kildare, who had died the previous year, to set against any suggestion they should seek to conciliate Diarmait. And of course Asculv Mac Turcaill and the Dubliners wanted only to put Diarmait's bones beneath their feet, along with those of his father.

Contemplating this list of enemies, Diarmait felt that his next move should be northwards, to modern-day Naas and the Uí Fáeláin. Calling on Robert, Henry and Maurice, the leaders of the Norman and Flemish troops, Diarmait ensured that each of them was willing to support the enterprise and that, while the Uí Chennselaig cavalry raided far and wide, the heavy troops of his allies would provide a personal bodyguard for Diarmait. To this the allied commanders answered respectfully, 'Sire, as you command'. The raid was entirely successful and when Fáeláin Mac Fáeláin attempted to stand against the Uí Chennselaig, he was driven from Kildare and the cattle of his people stolen. This time, away from cursed mountainside forests, the Uí Chennselaig did not shirk from the fighting and it was Domnall Cáemánach who led them in the vanguard of the allied army.

Returning to Ferns for eight days, Diarmait did not let the Norman troops retire to Wexford but instead proposed another swift raid upon an enemy. This time the target was the Uí Thuathail, who had not deigned to send a representative to come and parley with Diarmait, despite the fact that Diarmait's wife, Mór, was the sister of the dynast Gilla Comgaill Ua Tuathail and her brother was Lorcán Ua Tuathail, former abbot of Glendalough and archbishop of Dublin. In the now familiar battle order – Uí Chennselaig, Normans, Wexford – Diarmait marched to Glendalough to the cries of 'vengeance'. The raid was so swift and overwhelming that the Uí Thuathail mounted no resistance, allowing Diarmait once more to return to Ferns in triumph and with his fortune enhanced.

From the Uí Chennselaig perspective, the year so far had been a tremendous success. The poverty to which they had been reduced by Diarmait's payment to Tigernán was forgotten and the shame of their defeats partially avenged. For Robert fitz Stephen and Hervey de Montmorency it had been a good year too. The town of Wexford and the enormous grant of land promised them and their heirs a great fortune, albeit that they had yet to set up castles and manors to secure the land. The Flemish troops, led by Maurice de Prendergast, however, had fought hard but had yet to see any reward beyond their upkeep.

Again, after a few days feasting, Diarmait mobilised his army, to take advantage of the continued good summer weather and to test the loyalties of those who had offered to join him. Rich and poor, the Uí Chennselaig gathered in force alongside the axemen of Wexford. Those who needed weapons were provided with them and a war council was held. Representing the Normans and the Flemish troops were Robert, Maurice, Hervey and Meilyr. To cheers and universal approval Diarmait announced that he intended to invade Osraige once more, to confront Domnall Mac Gilla Pátraic, 'who was so treacherous to me in the past' and take revenge upon him.

Setting out with Domnall Cáemánach in the van, Diarmait had over five thousand troops and, surrounded by the heavily armoured Normans, must have felt like a king once more. There were still very powerful enemies at large, not least Tigernán and Ruaidrí, and no doubt the future held a bloody reckoning with them, one way or another. But already Diarmait was regaining his local authority and with Strongbow's army to come, there was every prospect of even greater power coming Diarmait's way.

This time Diarmait took the easiest route, through Fothair Fea (modern-day Forth, County Carlow) and his army spread out on the banks of the river Burren. The disadvantage of this path was that it required a crossing of the Burren and later the Nore, but Diarmait had such a strong army he did not fear opposition from Domnall Mac Gilla Pátraic at these points.

That night, as the army encamped near an old ringfort, the young knights Robert de Barri and Meilyr fitz Henry were sleeping side by side, as was their usual custom when on campaign, when suddenly it seemed as though they were under attack. Countless ghostly troops making a terrible din were striking all around with their axes. At these sounds, Diarmait's Uí Chennselaig cavalry scattered in terror. Fearing either treachery from the men of Wexford who were camped not far to the rear, or the presence of an otherwordly army, the horsemen galloped away to the nearby woods and bogs. Robert and Meilyr, however, armed themselves and having gone to Robert fitz Stephen's tent, helped organise the Norman troops, who on the whole held steady until the sinister figures and sounds had passed.

One unfortunate during this alarm was a knight called Randolf fitz Ralph, who was on duty guarding Diarmait. So amazed and alarmed was Randolf by the ghost army that shouting 'St David! Barons! Knights!' he drew his sword and convinced an enemy was present, smote one of his own companions a blow to the head that dropped the poor knight to his knees.

For Robert de Barri, on the other hand, the most important concern arising from this mysterious encounter was for his sparrow-hawk. Most hawking in Ireland was done with the lordly falcon and gyrfalcon, but Robert was the first person to introduce to Ireland the practice of hawking with a tamed domestic sparrow-hawk and he was much envied for it.

Despite the confusion and dismay, and a widespread belief among both Irish and Norman troops that a ghost army had ridden through the camp during the night, Diarmait reorganised his army the following morning and pressed on into Osraige. His prediction that he would be able to cross the Barrow and the Nore was well founded, for rather than defend the river crossings Domnall Mac Gilla Pátraic decided to make his stand on higher ground. At the pass of Achad Úr (Freshford, County Kilkenny), on the river Nuenna, about three miles above where it joins with the Nore, the army of Osraige had dug a deep trench, behind which they had erected a palisade of stakes and hurdles. It took Diarmait another day and night to reach his enemy, and when he did so, he ordered the Hiberno-Norse troops of Wexford to lead the way. The subsequent fighting was desultory, with the Wexford axemen having no desire to sacrifice themselves for Diarmait's ambitions, and for two days there was a standoff. On the third day, however, the Normans and Flemish troops took matters in hand. Relying on the strength of their iron hauberks to cope with the missiles that bombarded them, and with their own archers providing lethal volleys of covering fire, the knights fought their way through a section of the palisade, causing Domnall Mac Gilla Pátraic to flee.

This time there was no turning back prematurely. The victors drove the army of Osraige south-westwards, right across their home lands and only when the entirety of Osraige was at their mercy did Diarmait's army turn for Ferns, driving cattle before them and looting as they pleased. There was no danger from Domnall Mac Gilla Pátraic's shattered army and for the Uí Chennselaig it was a glorious and triumphant hosting. Their old king was back and with him came a return to the best of times. The fact that ambitious Norman and Flemish knights were part of the army was no longer troubling, for these foreigners seemed satisfied to serve for a share of the booty and for lands that had never belonged to the Uí Chennselaig. For Maurice de Prendergast, however, this pattern of warfare was increasingly frustrating, not least because, while his Norman companions had already received lands, he and his Flemish companions had nothing but a share of booty, and that was not why he was in Ireland.

CHAPTER 4

Clashes and Reckonings

Following the second raid into Osraige, Maurice de Prendergast and his fellow Flemish soldiers, some two hundred warriors in all, decided that rewards for their efforts were insufficient; Maurice had come to Ireland to win a lordship, not to play the part of a mercenary. With no warning, he announced that his men were leaving for Wexford. Their intention was to hire ships from the port, along with navigators, and return to Wales. This was unwelcome news for Diarmait and, moreover, an insult to his newly restored authority. If such an action went unpunished, it would become evident to all that the real power in Leinster rested in the hands of the foreigners. Hurriedly, Diarmait sent messengers to Wexford with a decree that no master mariner was to assist the departure of the Flemish troops. The decree held good; no captain dared to defy Diarmait. If Diarmait thought that placing this obstacle in Maurice's path would bring the Flemish troops back to Ferns to beg forgiveness, then the king of Leinster had miscalculated.

First of all, Maurice met with the leaders of the Hiberno-Norse population of Wexford to ensure there was no threat to his men from that direction. Naturally, he was afraid of their falling upon his troops to please Diarmait. Without bothering to consult Diarmait or their supposed lord, Robert fitz Stephen, the Wexford chiefs reassured Maurice that they were no friends of Diarmait and would not risk heavy losses for the king of Leinster's favour. Then Maurice embarked on a very daring course of action. He sent messengers to Domnall Mac Gilla Pátraic, explaining that with Diarmait now his enemy, Maurice was willing to serve the king of Osraige. It was a cunning way out of Dairmait's trap and the strategy was a success.

When Maurice's messenger returned to Wexford, it was with good news. On receiving the offer from Maurice, Domnall Mac Gilla Pátraic had leapt to his feet, overcome with delight. His reply was that de Prendergast should come at once with complete confidence to St Mullins, to rendezvous with the army of Osraige on the banks of the Barrow (modern-day County Carlow). From there, they would see what opportunities presented themselves, but Maurice and his men could be reassured that whatever happened, they would receive generous and substantial payment from Osraige.

It would have been better for Diarmait if he had simply let Maurice and the Flemish army return to Wales. For when he learned of this new and very unexpected alliance, he felt his power beginning to fragment: Wexford was rebellious and there was no certainty that the other Normans with him would enter battle against Maurice. In order to attempt to intercept the Flemish army as it marched along the Barrow, Diarmait dispatched his son Domnall Cáemánach with his five hundred Uí Chennselaig cavalry. The two armies clashed, but Domnall dared not turn the encounter from skirmish to an open field battle, not in the face of the more heavily protected Flemish knights and footsoldiers. Harassed by Domnall all the way, Maurice eventually arrived at the round tower of St Mullins. There he made a stand and sent word to Domnall Mac Gilla Pátraic. The messenger returned with the promise that if Maurice held fast, the army of Osraige would be there on the third day. The king of Osraige did indeed arrive on the third day, to the cheers of the Flemish troops and the dismay of Domnall Cáemánach who now retired.

Observing the proper formalities, Maurice and his seven knights greeted the king who had so recently been their enemy. The chief men of Osraige and the Flemish knights took advantage of the fact that they were in a village which contained the altar and shrine of St Moling to swear faith to one another in the presence of the saint. In particular, Domnall Mac Gilla Pátraic swore that he would never betray Maurice and his men, so long as they were allies. Although most of his miracles favoured Leinster, St Moling was also an important saint for the people of Osraige, for it was said that, through his presence, St Moling had enfeebled an army of Leinster which had been raiding Osraige. The Leinstermen were powerless to lift a hand against the saint. All the cattle these raiders had stolen were given to St Moling, who then returned them to Osraige. It would therefore be a foolish king of Osraige who violated an oath made in the *tempall na-mbó* or The Church of the Cows and risked the saint's wrath.

Day and night, the united force now raided Uí Chennselaig territory; the men of Osraige enjoying the opportunity to revenge themselves for Diarmait's two recent incursions. As a result of being to the fore in the consequent devastation of Diarmait's lands, Maurice de Prendergast become known in Ireland as Maurice of Osraige. With the Uí Chennselaig cavalry no match for the Osraige-Flemish force, with the Hiberno-Norse army of Wexford claiming they had already provided Diarmait the annual service they owed him, and with Robert fitz Stephen reluctant and unable to chase down the faster-moving force, Diarmait had no choice but to let Domnall Mac Gilla Pátraic drive away Uí Chennselaig cattle.

The Old Alliance Reforms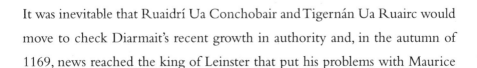

It was inevitable that Ruaidrí Ua Conchobair and Tigernán Ua Ruairc would move to check Diarmait's recent growth in authority and, in the autumn of 1169, news reached the king of Leinster that put his problems with Maurice de Prendergast and the troops of Osraige into perspective. Ruaidrí was on his way to Ferns and with him was Tigernán, Asculv from Dublin, and Diarmait Ua Máel Sechlainn of Meath. The latter had managed to regain power, having been ousted by his own people the previous year. This was the alliance that had crushed Diarmait in the past. The Hiberno-Norse army of Wexford had already made it clear that they would not fight for Diarmait again that year and the presence of Robert fitz Stephen and his men could hardly make up for the enormous disparity between the oncoming army and the small numbers of south Leinster troops, upon which Diarmait could rely. Moreover, once again most of those Irish lords who had recently sworn loyalty to Diarmait made themselves absent.

To the west of Ferns, in the valleys formed by Mount Leinster and its spurs, lay some of the most difficult terrain in the region: the woods there were dense; the open ground was of marshes fed by numerous streams. Abandoning his favoured residence once more, Diarmait retreated into this wilderness and, with fitz Stephen's help, the Uí Chennselaig army felled trees to make the forest impassable while breaking up all level ground nearby with pits and trenches, leaving only hidden and tortuous routes for their own sallies. Militarily, the position was still hopeless, but at least Ruaidrí would appreciate that it would take a considerable effort and perhaps notable losses to secure a victory over Diarmait.

On his arrival at the edge of the forest, Ruaidrí's first initiative was to try to weaken Diarmait by diplomatic means. Royal messengers were sent to Robert fitz Stephen, promising the foreigners safe conduct back to Wexford and, indeed, precious gifts, if they would depart Ireland, a country, after all, to which they had no claim. Robert, however, was not swayed. Quite apart from the fact that he took his oath to Diarmait seriously, to accept Ruaidrí's offer would be to lose his one hope of a substantial lordship: Wexford town. As Gerald de Barri put it, there was nothing for Robert and his men back home. And, Gerald continued, their claim to land and permanent roots in Ireland was one that Diarmait Mac Murchada had every right to assign to them as he pleased. Moreover, if they could weather this crisis, more of their friends would arrive and perhaps Diarmait, with their support, could become the high king of Ireland. After all, Gerald concluded, the troops they faced were a poorly-armed rabble.

Negotiators, respected by both sides, shuttled back and forth. From Ruaidrí's perspective it was not worth expending valuable warriors in wiping out the foreigners and killing Diarmait Mac Murchada. The high king's strategy – applied across the whole of Ireland – was to partition the lands of potential rivals and gain their submission and their hostages. Whether Diarmait or another, the ruler of the Uí Chennselaig needed to be integrated into Ruaidrí's authority. Peace was therefore agreed on condition that Diarmait acknowledged Ruaidrí as high king.

Tigernán Ua Ruairc was not impressed, and he insisted that the hostages extracted from Diarmait should be of the highest importance. With Énna having been blinded, it was Diarmait's son Conchobar who was heir designate and who was now sent out of the woods and across to Ruaidrí. Did he take with him a sense of impending doom? Was it any comfort that Ruaidrí treated him honourably and swore that if Diarmait acted as a true vassal, Ruaidrí would marry one of his own daughters to Conchobar? The heavy cloud that hung over Conchobar was the knowledge that his father had come to an agreement with Strongbow and that the high king would see the arrival of more Norman troops as a breach of the peace treaty. Then what would be the fate of the Uí Chennselaig hostages?

Accompanying Conchobar was his nephew, the eldest son of Domnall Cáemánach. Again, Tigernán was well aware of the importance of Domnall Cáemánach as a captain of the Uí Chennselaig cavalry and insistent that he too should yield his most precious family member as hostage. Equally important too, was a third man who made the fateful journey from the relative safety of the woods to the camp of the high king. The Uí Cáellaide, the foster family of Diarmait Mac Murchada, had stood by the king of Leinster through good times and bad. They too had to give surety for Diarmait's future actions by surrendering the eldest son of Diarmait's foster-brother, Murchad. With one additional hostage demanded at Tigernán's insistence – who was knowledgeable enough to pick out the key figures in the Mac Murchada dynasty – Ruaidrí was set to return to Connacht with very powerful leverage over Diarmait. The high king also extracted one further promise from Diarmait before agreeing to peace. In a clause that was intended to remain a secret from Robert fitz Stephen, but which soon became known to him, Diarmait agreed that no more foreigners would be invited to Ireland and that once Leinster had been pacified, those already in the country would be sent back.

All in all, the settlement looked to be a successful one from the point of view of Ruaidrí Ua Conchobair, but the high king had misjudged Diarmait. The sense of common interest that had previously prevented Irish kings from bringing Norman lords to intervene in Irish affairs was long broken in Diarmait. No matter how sincerely he acted in order to deceive the high king, the fact was that in his heart Diarmait had travelled a long way past the point of no return. Even as he agreed to peace with Ruaidrí and exchanged a last look with his departing relatives, Diarmait knew that sooner or later Strongbow would be in Ireland with his army and, on that day, there would be a new balance of power in the country, a new momentum, one that might carry Diarmait all the way to becoming high king.

Satisfied with the result of his short intervention in Leinster and with the best months of the year for campaigning nearly over, Ruaidrí returned to Connacht. There, confident in his authority over the country and mindful of how posterity might remember him, Ruaidrí decreed that every year he or his successors would give ten cows to the lector of Armagh in honour of St Patrick and in order that lectures would be given to scholars from Ireland and Scotland. In other words, Ruaidrí was endowing the first academic chair in Europe. His reign, he anticipated, would thus be remembered as one of cultural achievement as well as a model in the wielding of power.

But the high king had been deceived about Diarmait's intentions. Ruaidrí assumed that since he had left Diarmait as the king of Leinster, there was no reason for Diarmait to bring in more foreigners. Why would Diarmait jeopardise his own position by involving those notoriously rapacious Normans in Irish affairs? Would Diarmait really risk the lives of his close family members now being held hostage? By assuming the obvious answers to these questions were the correct ones, Ruaidrí was to lose the reputation he believed he held. Instead of being remembered as Ireland's greatest high king, Ruaidrí Ua Conchobair was to become known as the high king who lost half the country to the foreigners.

The Escape of Maurice de Prendergast

The withdrawal of Ruaidrí Ua Conchobair and his allies, albeit with notable Uí Chennselaig hostages, was an enormous relief to Diarmait. Once again, he had lived to fight another day and he could still hope that, with Strongbow's army, he would rise to even greater heights. For now, though, at the close of 1169, Diarmait's immediate priority was to put an end to the incursions of the Osraige-Flemish army of Domnall Mac Gilla Pátraic and Maurice de Prendergast. These unlikely partners had recently had the temerity to try to strip away Diarmait's vassals, beginning with Laigis (the northern part of modern County Laois).

One of the minor lords to have rallied early to Diarmait was Ua Mórda of Laigis but Domnall Mac Gilla Pátraic was confident that, together with his Flemish allies, he could dominate Ua Mórda. Unopposed, the army of Osraige entered Laigis and stood ready to wreak destruction on the land. They would stay their hand only if Ua Mórda transferred his allegiance from Diarmait to Domnall. This Ua Mórda was very reluctant to do. Not only did Diarmait hold Uí Mórda hostages – and Diarmait Mac Murchada was not slow to blind or decapitate his captives – but once the army of Osraige had departed, there was no doubt that retribution would follow in the form of a Uí Chennselaig raid. The lord of the Uí Mórda therefore stalled for time. He fixed a day for meeting with Domnall Mac Gilla Pátraic, a day upon which he would swear loyalty and hand over five or six hostages from the most noble men in his land.

While delaying his surrender, Ua Mórda contacted Diarmait, the messenger urging the Uí Chennselaig to come quickly: if they could do so within three days, they would save the Uí Mórda from having to yield hostages and Diarmait would have a chance of surprising the army of Osraige. This summons came at a fortuitous time for Diarmait, for only a short while earlier he had found his forces notably enhanced by the arrival of Maurice fitz Gerald. Back in 1167, when Diarmait had met Robert fitz Stephen for the first time, Robert had been accompanied by his dour half-brother Maurice fitz Gerald, who had also pledged to raise a company and sail to Ireland.

Late in 1169, with perfect timing − Ruaidrí Ua Conchobair having left Leinster and it being too late in the year for the high king to remobilise his army − Maurice fulfilled his pledge. The taciturn knight landed at Wexford with an invaluable force: ten knights, thirty mounted troops and about a hundred archers. News of Maurice's arrival was so important to Diarmait that the king of Leinster had ridden at once to Wexford to greet the Norman commander in person. 'You are very welcome, baron, you who are called Maurice fitz Gerald,' announced Diarmait's translators. Graciously blessing the 'valiant king' in reply, the newly arrived troops marched to Ferns. There they were warmly welcomed by Robert fitz Stephen, Meilyr fitz Henry and Miles fitz David. These knights were all relatives, unlike Hervey de Montmorency, who was also present and who also welcomed Maurice, if rather more coolly.

The news that Maurice de Prendergast had tried to leave Ireland but was now fighting for Osraige came as a shock to Maurice fitz Gerald. But while fitz Gerald and the other knights may have expressed their dismay at such a development in public, in their inner councils the Normans understood that de Prendergast remained one of their own and they had some sympathy for him. In fact, de Prendergast's aggressive but intelligent response to Diarmait's policies was an assistance to all the Normans. They were not in Ireland simply as mercenaries; they wanted lordships based on good land, rivers and towns. From this perspective, Maurice de Prendergast was right to chafe at Diarmait's failure to grant him a lordship and equally right in escaping Diarmait's clutches by forging an alliance with Osraige.

When the breathless messenger from Laigis arrived at Ferns, Diarmait at once summoned Robert fitz Stephen and Maurice fitz Gerald, wanting to test their response. The Normans, no fools, despite their reservations, did not hesitate. 'Get your men ready at once,' they answered the king, 'without delay. There is no time to be lost, sire.' And the Uí Chennselaig army sprang to their horses, to ride without stopping until they reached Laigis and the wide and beautiful flower meadow in which Domnall Mac Gilla Pátraic and Maurice de Prendergast were camping.

In the meantime, Maurice de Prendergast had become suspicious at the delays that Ua Mórda was introducing to what should have been a simple matter, that of swearing oaths and handing over hostages. Even as he warned Domnall Mac Gilla Pátraic to set scouts on the passes to Leinster, a spy from Ferns galloped into camp with the alarm. The Uí Chennselaig were on the march and with them were Robert fitz Stephen, Hervey de Montmorency and a newly arrived baron, Maurice fitz Gerald. Alongside the knights were some three hundred English archers and mounted soldiers.

There was no question of trying to face this incoming force and Maurice de Prendergast immediately urged a retreat to Osraige. 'Let us be off, lord King. The English are pursuing us closely and we have only a few men. Let us therefore advance in close formation, so that if they get at all close to us we shall defend ourselves well.' Domnall Mac Gilla Pátraic agreed and, empty-handed, the army of Osraige hurried south until they were safely through the mountains and could disperse in their own territory. Although close behind, the Uí Chennselaig had to move at the pace of the slower foreign troops and these, of course, had no real incentive to catch up with their friends and force a battle. Still, the prompt response by Diarmait had served its immediate purpose and, collecting more hostages from Ua Mórda, he returned to Ferns with his authority over Laigis enhanced.

For Maurice de Prendergast, however, a new crisis was developing rapidly.

The upkeep of two hundred Welsh troops and seven Flemish knights was no light burden and the aristocracy of Osraige resented that they had to divert a portion of their own revenues to the foreigners. A conspiracy developed among them to ambush Maurice and his men, and share out the captured supplies, armour and coin. It quickly gathered momentum, with the language barrier making it hard for Maurice to detect that a murderous plot was underway, even though knowledge of it was widespread among the nobles of Osraige, young and old, 'balding or hirsute'.

Later, a Norman poet imagined the scene: 'Listen to us, king, fair sire,' the conspirators are said to have told Domnall Mac Gilla Pátraic, 'we mean to kill Maurice now. We have had a very good peace: but we no longer need these men.'

'May God and his might forbid that they should ever be betrayed by me, murdered, killed, shamed or captured!' the king replied angrily. Not only had he sworn a solemn oath in the presence of St Moling, but his authority over his own people would have been undermined if the plan went ahead.

In all innocence, Maurice came before Domnall Mac Gilla Pátraic at this time and asked permission for his men to depart and take ship to Wales. They could achieve little more in Ireland, unless given a lordship and with it secure streams of revenue. At first Domnall pressed Maurice to stay: with the Flemish troops, the king of Osraige felt secure from Leinster and in his own throne from rival family members. But Maurice was adamant and Domnall yielded.

The next day Maurice and his men marched southeast, reaching Kilkenny, while the king of Osraige went to Fertagh (just over four miles northeast of Urlingford, modern County Kilkenny). At Kilkenny, Maurice and his men celebrated their impending return home with raucous drinking and great joy. But even as they did so, the nobles of Osraige were riding to surround them and occupy the key passes between Kilkenny and the southeast coast. In defiance of their own king, the warriors of Osraige had resolved to murder the foreigners and loot their coins of gold and silver, along with their valuable military equipment

Not all of the aristocracy of Osraige were part of the plot, and one of the men loyal to the king and his oath to St Moling decided to warn Maurice. In the middle of the night, a rider came to Kilkenny demanding to see de Prendergast with the greatest urgency. Once alerted to the danger he was in, Maurice woke up his seven knights and put the problem to them. There were two thousand well-armed Irish 'in a place where they can cut us off so that we cannot pass through. I am asking for advice, lord barons, as to what we should do in this matter.' They replied that they would trust whatever decision Maurice made. He had extracted them from danger in the face of an angry Diarmait Mac Murchada and they trusted him to find an answer. Maurice then told them to return to their lodgings, as if nothing was wrong. Whatever solution he came up with, it would be a mistake to mobilise the army and prepare for a fight. Even if they could defend Kilkenny, they would soon run short of supplies.

The following morning Maurice sent word to the seneschal of Domnall Mac Gilla Pátraic that his men would stay and serve Osraige for another three or six months on the same conditions as before. Naturally, Domnall was delighted with this news and replied that he would come to Kilkenny to exchange oaths once more with Maurice. When news that Maurice was staying on spread around the region, the conspirators withdrew from their ambushes and their troops dispersed. But this was the moment that Maurice had been waiting for. His offer to Domnall was a ruse. On the day before the king of Osraige arrived at Kilkenny, Maurice sent orders that everyone, knight, squire, men-at-arms and archers who wanted to see their homes again should get ready quickly for a forced march to Waterford.

Not until they arrived at the walled port, footsore after an all-day trek, were Maurice's men able to relax and their spirits revive. Every one of them had made the arduous journey. Their escape from a region of fast-moving enemies was a great achievement. The Hiberno-Norse population of Waterford were willing to take Maurice's coins in return for transporting his army back to Wales. They did not fear the anger of the king of Osraige or that of Diarmait

Mac Murchada. Their walls were strong, their axes sharp. Maurice, however, was not yet free of Ireland. While waiting to board the ships, news came to him that his knights had been taken into captivity by the Hiberno-Norse, on account of the fact that a Welsh footsoldier had come to blows with one of the citizens of the town and given the citizen a mortal wound. The Waterford people, led by two senior figures, Ragnall Mac Gilla Muire and Sitric, took the matter seriously and it required all of Maurice's diplomatic skills to calm the situation and negotiate a settlement that honoured the laws of the town.

At last, on the next tide, Maurice de Prendergast came away from the Irish shoreline, with all of his men and a great deal of experience of warfare and politics in Ireland. Their journey across the Irish Sea was an untroubled one and their joy upon landing in Wales immense. For all their difficulties in Ireland, Maurice and his men had not lost their hope of gaining a lordship there. Dispersing his army for the present, Maurice rode to Strongbow to give a thorough report on all that had happened. Both the news from Ireland and the evident competence of Maurice de Prendergast made a powerful impression on Strongbow. The problem of having to shake off the heavy hand of King Henry II still troubled Strongbow, but he promised Maurice that his army would set off soon, one way or another. In addition, Strongbow asked that de Prendergast accompany him, in return for which, the Flemish captain would be well rewarded.

Diarmait Grows in Power

Before winter brought an end to campaigning in 1169, there was still an opportunity for Diarmait Mac Murchada to make one more raid. This time he decided it would be upon Dublin, a city whose wealth, fighting force and fleet were crucial to the ambitions of any king. It was also a city where the Hiberno-Norse population had secured a relatively autonomous political position by shaking off vassalage to Diarmait and his father and placing themselves under the nominal authority of Ruaidrí Ua Conchobair. Three times, Asculv, the king of the Dubliners, had marched to Ferns with the army of the high king. But with the balance of forces changed in Leinster, the fact that Ruaidrí was on the other side of Ireland was no longer a welcome state of affairs for the Dubliners. They were vulnerable to a swift attack by the Uí Chennselaig and the Normans, and this vulnerability was not lost on Diarmait.

Newly arrived Maurice fitz Gerald and his men led the way from Ferns to Dublin, and once they were through the Wicklow mountains and in territories belonging to Diarmait's enemies the whole army took part in the slaughter of livestock, the burning of buildings and the plunder of winter stores. Diarmait's thinking was that it would be risky to storm the tall stone walls of Dublin, but that by devastating the city's hinterland, the Hiberno-Norse axemen would either come out to battle in circumstances where the Norman horsemen could play a decisive role, or they would have to sue for peace.

After watching dozens of farms burn from the walls of the city, Asculv held a council and the peace faction won the day. Grim as it was to be under Diarmait's thumb again, this was not yet the time to risk everything in battle. Ruaidrí and Tigernán would learn of Diarmait's actions – the citizens sent a rider at once – and there was a very good prospect that the following year the armies of Connacht and Bréifne would overthrow the ambitious leader of the Uí Chennselaig. The Hiberno-Norse warriors were no cowards and knew well the use of the two-handed battle axe. They were prudent and wily too. It would be much better to wait for the high king than confront the Welsh archers and Norman knights with their own forces. If it came to relying on their own strength, then it would be better to force battle after rallying support from Viking communities on the Isle of Man and the Scottish islands.

Messengers were sent to Diarmait and peace was obtained at the usual price. The citizens of Dublin recognised Diarmait as their king and swore to serve him: to send their troops and fleets as directed, to send him tribute, and give him authority in their courts and councils. Of course, they had no intention of fulfilling these promises. But equally, Diarmait was content with what he had been able to achieve on the raid. The fact that Asculv and his people had bowed their knees was a start. A proper reckoning and vengeance for all that he and his family had suffered at the hands of the Dubliners could wait until Strongbow had arrived.

Safe at Ferns for the winter, Diarmait gave Robert fitz Stephen and Maurice fitz Gerald permission to depart for Wexford. Although, with Maurice absent, the two Norman commanders had been granted lordship over the town, the title was meaningless so long as the Hiberno-Norse citizens refused to give revenues or obiedience to the Normans. Shackling the insubordinate people of Wexford to the newly arrived Normans served two purposes for Diarmait: to significantly increase his own control over the town and to provide a reward for his allies. As his dealings with Maurice de Prendergast had shown, the foreigners could not be kept satisfied with plunder. They were in Ireland for territory.

The first step in all Norman conquests was to secure any newly gained territory by building a castle, a base from which they could dominate the local region. This was Robert's plan. At Ferrycarrig, less than two miles from Wexford Town, on a rocky bank of the River Slaney, just before it broadens out as it reaches the sea, Robert and Maurice constructed the first Norman castle in Ireland.

Today, there is a very striking towered keep that stands on a rocky outcrop forming the north bank of the river Slaney, just before the river reaches Wexford. Visitors to the town, by train or car, pass right beneath the structure. Many websites and several books describe this stone structure as being Robert's castle, but in fact it is a fifteenth-century construction. The first Norman castle in Ireland was built on the hill opposite to where the keep now stands, on the south side of the river. A round tower, built in 1857 as a tribute to those who fell in the Crimean War, now covers the remains of the original fortification.

The castle built by Robert and Maurice was placed on the south side of the river, the better to threaten Wexford Town, while still being close enough to the river to be able to control the passage of ships along the Slaney. In form, the castle was based on a design very familiar to the Normans in Wales, the ringwork. The alternative model, that of a motte with a timber keep or bailey on top, would have been much more difficult to build and a waste of effort, given the defensive value of the exposed rocks of the top of the steep crag. So Robert and Maurice ordered their men to supplement the natural defences of the high terrain with a ditch and wooden palisade that ringed their residential buildings. In places where the soil was thin, the castle builders hacked out the rock itself to deepen the ditch. Although the resulting defences were not impressive – with a shallow ditch and a palisade that was relatively flimsy and reliant on sods rather than sturdy timbers – it served its purpose. A very small number of defenders could easily keep a much larger force of attackers at bay. From the castle, it was easy to ride out and ensure payment from the passing ships and carts. And the silhouette of the castle provided an excellent reminder to the Wexford population that they had new lords.

The High King Weakens

By wresting control over Dublin from the high king, there could be no doubt that Diarmait was inviting a punitive response from Ruaidrí Ua Conchobair. But Diarmait's risk was a calculated one. First of all, Strongbow was due to arrive in the spring. Secondly, even if the Norman lord failed him, Diarmait could exploit the political divisions within Ireland that meant no high king was ever able to rest. With a strategic eye to undermining Ruaidrí Ua Conchobair's plans, Diarmait had, in 1168, married his daughter Órlaith to the new king of Thomond, Domnall Mór Ua Briain. The Uí Briain of Munster had a glorious past, which they had not forgotten, even in recent times of disintegration. Although they had not recovered from the battle of Móin Mór in 1151, Domnall Ua Briain chafed at the fact that Munster was partitioned and he longed to oust Diarmait Mac Carthaig, who held the other half of Munster, from former Uí Briain territories.

Encouraged by the messages of his father-in-law and by Diarmait's defiance of Ruaidrí in marching on Dublin, Domnall decided to act and withdrew his allegiance to the high king. The reaction from Ruaidrí was immediate; the Uí Briain hostages were killed and the high king marched on Domnall's most important possession: Limerick. But equally swiftly, Diarmait Mac Murchada sent aid to his son-in-law, in the form of Robert fitz Stephen and his army. The distance from Ferns to Limerick is approximately a hundred miles, made considerably longer by the snaking paths of medieval Ireland. Nearly all of the journey was through lands held by rivals of Diarmait Mac Murchada, not least Domnall Mac Gilla Pátraic of Osraige. Yet not one of the minor Irish kings in his path dared oppose fitz Stephen.

Once joined with Domnall's force, Robert faced the Connacht invaders and his men fought on the defensive. Three hundred Welsh archers, protected by sixty ringmail-clad soldiers and a handful of knights, including the inseparable Meilyr fitz Henry and Robert de Barri, proved to be sufficient to prevent Ruaidrí from inflicting a decisive blow upon the Munster rebels. His initial attack, indeed, was repulsed and Ruaidrí, regretting he had not crushed fitz Stephen along with his master the previous year, was obliged to retreat back across the Shannon and gather a more serious force. This time, the high king returned with his fleet and was able to raid Killaloe. Situated at the southern tip of Lough Derg, Killaloe had great importance for the Uí Briain for it was the birthplace and main residence of Brian Bóruma; Ruaidrí succeeded in burning the sturdy plank bridge there. The high king also dispatched riders to burn and plunder Thomond (modern-day County Clare), but he did not risk battle with the united army of Domnall Ua Briain and Robert fitz Stephen. Ultimately, Ruaidrí was forced to withdraw, dissatisfied, without having obliged the Uí Briain to submit to him once more. It was the first check to his rule in three years and no longer could he call himself high king without opposition. Moreover, not one of the southern kings who had submitted to Ruaidrí made any move to intercept the Norman leader and his troops on their return to Uí Chennselaig.

Strongbow Makes Ready

Not until the spring of 1170 was Strongbow prepared to make his decisive move in the direction of Ireland and even then it was a perilous enterprise for him to undertake. It was not military conflict with the Irish kings that concerned Strongbow the most; the reports coming back from Hervey de Montmorency were encouraging, as was the account of his adventures by Maurice de Prendergast. Strongbow's main concern was the danger that Henry II of England would declare him a rebel. Both the act of raising an army and that of marrying Aífe required permission of his liege lord. Yet Strongbow was contemplating taking matters into his own hand all the same.

English politics in the lifetime of Henry II was more subtle than — although equally as treacherous as — the game of thrones in Ireland. Since the king wielded such disproportionate power, the rise and fall of English and Norman lordships depended on following the nuances of royal statements and those of favoured courtiers. Henry's personality was shaped by the strain of attempting to govern a huge realm and the well-founded suspicion that his leading magnates in both the church and the secular world wanted much greater autonomy than he allowed them. Those who fell from the king's grace fell hard and were not generally given opportunity to rise again. The king's notorious temper corresponded with a policy that saw him ruin many a wayward vassal. Henry was prone to ungovernable rages that caused him to discard his clothes and fling himself about, chewing on straw matting or silk garments to soften the ferocity with which he ground his teeth. Once you fell foul of the king, you were never forgiven. Moreover, it was very difficult to tell where you stood with him, for Henry was the master of the ambiguous phrase or gesture.

Balancing, as he did, the interests of hundreds of dynastic factions, Henry learned early not to bind himself to a particular course of action. He wanted the freedom to punish or reward with the advantage of hindsight. A social position at the head of a complex medieval hierarchy of restless and ambitious lords gave rise to a tendency in Henry to govern with hints and 'jests' that could be interpreted to suit his needs at a later date. This evasiveness was not always a successful strategy and it failed Henry most dramatically in the case of Thomas Becket, the archbishop of Canterbury. In the late 1160s Thomas was opposed to the king's plans for the English church. In front of his court, Henry shouted: 'what miserable drones and traitors have I nourished and promoted in my household, who let their lord be treated with such shameful contempt by a low-born clerk!' Four knights present took these words to mean that Henry would approve of the death of archbishop and they went immediately from court in Normandy to England, where, on the afternoon of 29 December 1170, they murdered Becket in Canterbury Cathedral. Much as Henry protested that this terrible deed was not the result of his words, the blame for the assassination and with it a massive backlash from the church descended upon him.

In his dealings with Strongbow, the king of England had made it clear that the former earl of Pembroke was out of favour. Strongbow lost the title of earl, lost a great deal of his inheritance (all of his Norman lands and a sizeable part of the Welsh territories), was refused permission to lead other barons in a campaign against the Welsh, and was refused all marriages worthy of his position. As a result, Strongbow had enormous debts and his financial difficulties had caused him to shed lands to the family of Henry's elderly supporter, Robert fitz Harding of Bristol. A Jewish merchant, Aaron of Lincoln, was also owed great sums by Strongbow and was pressing the king for intervention in regard to gaining some kind of recompense.

After his fateful meeting with Diarmait Mac Murchada, Strongbow was determined to come to Ireland and turn his fortunes around. But he had first to try to place both his mustering of a sizeable army and his decision to marry Aífe in a context that would not cause Henry to boil up with anger and pronounce Strongbow an outlaw. Having spent all of the previous decade in avoiding court politics, which could only harm him further, in 1167, Strongbow came forward and offered his services to the crown.

There was, in fact, a rather thankless task that Henry needed to assign to someone with a reasonable body of troops. The king of England had agreed a marriage alliance with Henry the Lion, Duke of Saxony and Bavaria. Henry's third child and eldest daughter from his marriage with Eleanor of Aquitaine, Matilda, was betrothed to the duke. But someone had to escort her safely to Germany, someone who was not required at court or in the field, and who did not resent being sent away from their own lands for several months. So Strongbow was allotted the task and from Christmas 1167 to 1 February 1168, the date of her marriage, the lord of Strigoil rode as escort to the royal princess.

On his return to the court of Henry, to report the success of his journey, Strongbow raised the matter of his bringing assistance to Diarmait Mac Murchada. If Henry would not allow for an arbitration on the estates to which Strongbow felt entitled, the king could at least give leave for Strongbow to test his mettle in lands outside the realm. Characteristically, the king of England shrugged off the request with an ambiguous response laden with irony. But for Strongbow it was enough that he had voiced the appeal before the court and it had not been refused. He returned to Chepstow satisfied he could now begin the process of raising an army and hiring the ships that would take him to Ireland.

The Battle of Baginbun

A notable trait among Norman adventurers was their appreciation of the value of good intelligence. Robert Guiscard and his brother Roger patiently explored the situation in Sicily before bringing their full force across the sea to the island. Bohemond won the principality of Antioch through his attention to the discontented voices in the city, while his nephew Tancred earned a fortune from the sack of Jerusalem by cultivating contacts with the Christians inside the besieged city. In this regard Strongbow was no different. His man, Hervey de Montmorency, was well placed at Ferns to assess events in Ireland. In the summer of 1170, as a further test of the veracity of Diarmait Mac Murchada's urgent messages, Strongbow ordered an advance force of ten knights and seventy archers to cross the Irish Sea. At the same time, Strongbow sent a messenger to Hervey, to alert him to the arrival of this small force and ask him to march to join it.

The leader of the new expedition was the young nephew of Robert fitz Stephen and Maurice fitz Gerald, Raymond, commonly known as Le Gros due to his stocky physique. Among Raymond's knights was Walter Bluet, who had been given Raglan Castle in Monmouthshire by Strongbow in return for the standard forty days military service and in consideration for the soldiers, money and arms that Walter was providing Strongbow for the expedition to Ireland. Another of the knights was William Ferrand. William had contracted leprosy and rather than slowly rot away had come to Ireland to find a more honourable death in the thick of battle. These troops departed in two ships, *La Bague* and *La Bonne*, the names of which have been preserved through the subsequent renaming of their landing place to Baginbun. At the time, however, this place was known as Dún Domnaill, a creek some eight miles to the east of Waterford town.

The main attraction of the carefully chosen landing site was that it was adjacent to a headland of some thirty acres, where the cliffs provided impassable defences to the flanks and rear. It was a cul-de-sac, but it would not be easy for anyone to conquer. The Normans were not the first people to appreciate the position, as a major ditch and bank — some seven hundred feet long by forty feet wide — had centuries earlier been constructed across the neck that connected the headland to the mainland.

The immediate task of the expeditionary force was to turn the headland into a fortress, and it must have been tempting to reinforce the existing ditch. There was a problem with the ancient defences, however, which was that they were constructed to protect a much larger force than seventy archers and a handful of knights. The newcomers would be stretched too thin if they tried to hold such a long line. The arrival of Hervey de Montmorency from Ferns did nothing to change this assessment as Hervey brought with him just three knights and a dozen footsoldiers. So Raymond selected a small spur of about two acres – ample for his troops – on the eastern side of the headland and ordered the construction of a new line of defence across the entrance to the spur. The resultant earthen defences were solid enough, although the wooden parts of the fortification – the palisade and heavy gate – left something to be desired. Once his camp was secure, Raymond sent his troops across the fields inland to round up cattle before the local population was alerted to their presence. His raiders were successful and drove a sizeable herd back to the headland. There would be no shortage of food for the expedition.

When news of the presence of the small Norman army reached Waterford, Ragnall and Sitric sent word to Máel Sechnaill Ua Fáeláin, lord of the Déise, the neighbouring Irish realm (covering modern day County Waterford and the southern part of County Tipperary), as well as to Ua Riain, lord of Uí Dróna (the border territory between Carlow and Kilkenny). The Hiberno-Norse warriors and the Irish lords agreed that they must act swiftly to destroy the foreigners before more cattle were stolen or their army reinforced. Between them, several thousand Irish and Norse troops were mustered to march on the Dún Domnaill headland.

Once his scouts reported that the Irish were coming, Raymond herded his captured cattle up the ramp and through the wooden gates of his fort. Then the Normans marched out to meet their enemies in open field, where the ten knights on horseback could hope to employ their riding and fighting skills. When the enemy army appeared, however, it was shockingly large and Raymond ordered an immediate retreat, taking up a position at the very tail of the army. Eagerly, the lightly-armoured Irish raced forward, catching the Normans just as they crossed into the supposed safety of their fort. The gates to the structure were not yet properly hung, being more of a barricade than a sturdy fortress door. Raymond himself, having dismounted among the last men through the gate, ran to defend the entrance. Drawing his sword, he impaled the first Irish warrior who had dared leap through and gave a triumphant cry to St David. The initial assault from the Irish forces was checked.

A short but bloody stalemate ensued, only to be broken by the fact that arrows flying over the palisade were striking the cattle and that, combined with the roar of battle, was causing the herd to become dangerously agitated. The Normans were forced to let the cattle run out, and the subsequent stampede obliged the Irish to part ranks. Seizing the moment, Raymond ordered his troops out again in the wake of the cattle. It was a daring and entirely effective onslaught. The Norse warriors were trained to fight as part of a shield wall, in which the round shield on your left arm covered half of your own body and half of that of the man beside you. With the shield wall broken by the cattle the Norse troops were scattered and far more vulnerable to crossbow bolts, sword edges and lance tips than when they were in formation. The Irish warriors were less troubled by the prospect of fighting independently, but their light armour did not allow them to withstand a concerted assault in the way that the Hiberno-Norse axemen could. They had to fall back and leave their Waterford allies to fend for themselves. A promising assault by the allies had turned to a catastrophic defeat and several thousand men had been scattered by less than a hundred. Nearly all of the Norman knights had survived, including William Ferrand, the leper, who had failed to find the honourable death in battle he so desired. Later that year, William founded a hospital for lepers, St Mary Magdalene in Wexford. The Norman bridgehead had held and it was certain now that there would be no local opposition to the arrival of Strongbow. Taking no chances, Raymond set to reinforcing the much larger ancient ditch, so that Strongbow would have a secure position for the landing of his army.

Some five hundred bodies were lying on the summer grass, a trail of blood marking the route back towards Waterford, while seventy of the Hiberno-Norse warriors were rounded up as prisoners. What should be done with these men? As the core fighting force of Waterford, their ransom was of considerable financial value. Politically, too, there was no doubt that the vassalage of Waterford could be obtained in return for the release of these prisoners. The Normans, however, were not in Ireland to play the game by Irish rules. They did not want the lordship of a town that would desert them as soon as the balance of forces changed.

Viking and Irish traditions were compatible in the sense that provincial and high kings treated the vassalage of Hiberno-Norse towns exactly as they would treat the vassalage of a sub-king, and thus these rulers did not demand the Hiberno-Norse towns give up their army or their practice of holding policy-making councils of the leading citizens. Those who had tried to interfere with the Viking ways of the towns, like Diarmait Mac Murchada's father, were fiercely resisted. Norman rule was far stricter than that of an Irish king. In towns ruled by Normans, the garrison was always under control of the regional overlord, and while the citizens might be allowed certain civil rights, such as their own courts or taxation systems, they most certainly would not be allowed to determine their own relations with neighbouring lords or to deploy their own army. Thus, as a first step toward the smashing of the autonomy of Waterford, the Normans decided to kill all their prisoners. A new pattern of warfare had come to Ireland, a much more remorseless and final one. If necessary, the Normans were willing to wipe out the existing populations of the key towns and replace them with immigrants from England, Wales, and further afield.

A further argument helped decide the fate of the prisoners. With seventy captives, the Normans were nearly outnumbered. If they had to fight again before Strongbow arrived, they risked a breakout by the prisoners with disastrous consequences. Those who felt uneasy about being so ruthless towards fellow-warriors were persuaded and the executions began. One terrible way to kill the captives – and send an intimidating message to their opponents for the future – was to break their limbs and throw them from the cliffs; even if they survived the fall, they would drown.

It must have come as a shock, even to warriors imbued with the fatalistic philosophy of their Viking forefathers, to realise that they were all to be executed. As the first of them had their limbs cracked across rocks and their bodies rolled over the cliff edge, a new voice spoke up, the voice of a woman. Was this a reprieve for the prisoners?

This woman was a servant, Alice of Abergavenny, who had preferred to join the enterprise to assist her master and lover than to stay behind in Wales. In the fighting outside the fortress there had been a number of losses among the Norman knights and one them was Alice's guardian. As the first of the prisoners were executed, Alice came forward, grim-faced and filled with a desire for vengeance. Hearing her request, Raymond and Hervey were only too pleased to grant it. For what she asked would further demoralise the friends of those they had vanquished by heaping shame upon them. Alice was given permission personally to kill the remaining prisoners. With an axe of tempered steel, the grieving woman hacked off the heads of the Hiberno-Norse men, one by one. Their bodies were rolled over the cliff edge in a waterfall of blood. News of the victory and that of the ignominious – from the perspective of this very masculine culture – manner of the execution of the prisoners, was sent to Diarmait Mac Murchada.

The sooner that Diarmait could march on Waterford to take advantage of the success of his Norman allies, the better. But Robert fitz Stephen was still en route back from his successful sparring with Ruaidrí Ua Conchobair. While Diarmait waited, however, Waterford was given no time to recover from the defeat at Dún Domnaill, for, at last, three years after having given his word to Diarmait, Strongbow was in Ireland.

CHAPTER 5

Strongbow in Ireland

W hen Strongbow had last gone to war, he had been a teenager, taking his father's place in the manoeuvres between King Stephen and Empress Matilda. In those heady days, the young earl had directed an army of thousands of troops, at the core of which were his vassals from the 'sixty five and a half knights' fees', which comprised his inheritance on the north side of the Channel. Riding at the head of some hundred mail-clad knights, at only eighteen years old, Strongbow could have been forgiven for dreaming that a famous military career lay ahead of him. But for nearly twenty years thereafter, Strongbow had effectively been caged. Only now, in his fortieth year, did Strongbow have the opportunity to demonstrate his abilities as a commander along with the chance to win back his birthright, and more.

At Chepstow castle, on a bright day in July, with the muster of his vassals complete, Strongbow rode for Milford Haven and the fleet that would take him to Ireland. For supporters of the Norman lord it was a stirring sight, a cavalry force a hundred strong thundering over the drawbridge, a yellow and red banner fluttering at their head. The knights were followed by the foot-soldiers, then the archers, and with them a considerable baggage train. Strongbow's commitment to the expedition was evident in the fact that among the non-combatants were his two natural daughters, both of marriageable age.

Only a bare minimum number of soldiers and servants remained behind to hold the castle.

At each notable town – Caerleon, Newport, Cardiff, Morganwg, Neath, Gower, Caermarthen, Haverford – along his journey to the port of Milford Haven, soldiers who had heard that Strongbow was on the march were waiting to join the army. Even better, there was a very welcome sight awaiting Strongbow at Haverford. The resourceful Maurice de Prendergast, with his valuable experience of warfare in Ireland, had decided to accept Strongbow's promise of land in return for service. With Maurice were his seven knights and two hundred archers, all hoping to benefit from the planned expropriation of the Irish aristocracy. Around one thousand five hundred troops were now under Strongbow's command. Of these soldiers, two hundred were heavily-armoured knights: a very significant force in Irish terms.

Just as with his Norman predecessors, Strongbow did not baulk at the difficulties of bringing an army with hundreds of horses across the sea. Strongbow planned to travel further than previous Norman adventurers; his naval enterprise was to take him over a hundred miles to the Suir estuary.

As his troops thronged the streets of Milford Haven and supplies were being loaded onto the large fleet that Strongbow had hired for the purpose – with cash and promises of favourable trading rights after the conquest of Ireland's ports – his humour must have been one of tremendous satisfaction. If so, it was a satisfaction that was utterly ruined by the sudden arrival of an exhausted rider, bringing a message from King Henry. This time there were no jests and no ambiguities. The king absolutely forbade Strongbow to sail for Ireland.

'There is a tide in the affairs of men,' says Brutus, in Shakespeare's *Julius Caesar*, 'which, taken at the flood, leads on to fortune; omitted, all the voyage of their life is bound in shallows and in miseries. On such a full sea are we now afloat, and we must take the current when it serves, or lose our ventures.' As he faced the messenger, Strongbow must have felt just such a sentiment. This was his tide, literally, and he had to take it. His decision to defy the king and embark his army, however, was filled with foreboding. Not only was he risking his own life but also the lives of his followers. The fortunes of his knights and his descendants depended not only on victory in war against Diarmait's enemies, but also on Strongbow acquiring sufficient resources to withstand reprisals by a furious king of England.

On 23 August 1170, leaving the king's messenger behind on the quayside to watch and subsequently report his act of rebellion, Strongbow brought his ships safely to Ireland. Given reports of Raymond's victory and the demoralised state of the local Irish lords, he decided it was unnecessary to waste time by using the headland secured at Dún Domnaill and disembarked his army – unopposed – at Passage, a fishing village just east of Waterford, on the estuary of the Suir. The following day was the feast of St Bartholomew the apostle, and for the Normans the celebration was made merrier by the arrival of Raymond Le Gros and his small army. With them was Hervey de Montmorency. For the first time in two years Strongbow was reunited with his uncle, who had performed admirable service for the family cause and could now bring Strongbow up to date on Irish affairs.

No one was in any doubt that the whole fate of the expedition would ultimately be determined by what happened when the expeditionary army encountered that of Ruaidrí Ua Conchobair. On this issue Hervey had encouraging news. Firstly, Ruaidrí had made a major strategic mistake the previous year in leaving Diarmait as king of Leinster when the opportunity was there to attack and overthrow him. Secondly, reinforced by Robert fitz Stephen, Domnall Mór Ua Briain of Thomond had thrown off his subservience to the high king, and half of Munster had risen in opposition to Ruaidrí.

On the morning of 25 August 1170, the united Norman army moved up to their banners, which had been raised before the walls of Waterford. To conquer the town would be no easy task, for the defences seemed very sturdy. About thirty years before the coming of the Normans, the wooden walls of Waterford, which topped a substantial bank above a wide ditch, had been replaced by even more impressive stone walls. Two towers dominated sections of the wall. One, Ragnall's Tower (or Reginald's Tower, subsequently rebuilt and today a major visitor attraction for the history of the town) at the north-eastern corner of the town, adjacent to the Suir, was the headquarters for the Hiberno-Norse commanders; the other was called Turgesius's Tower (no longer surviving, but located on Barronstrand, where it meets the quay-side along the Suir). Effectively, Waterford had state-of-the-art defences and, despite the losses at Dún Domnaill, plenty of determined warriors to man them, both Hiberno-Norse and Irish: the Déise had come too in great numbers under their king Máel Sechlainn Ua Fáeláin to help protect the town.

Twice Strongbow's army charged the walls, trying to cross the ditch and erect ladders. Twice they were thrown back by the citizenry. The Hiberno-Norse warriors were determined to preserve their freedom, and alongside them, their Irish allies were equally determined not to let the Normans secure a foothold in Ireland. The fighting in the early part of the day suggested that they might stand a chance of success against the powerful Norman army. The town, however, had expanded rapidly since its walls had been erected and overcrowding had led to the growth of suburbs that encroached upon the ditch and walls. Having carefully studied the fortifications for weak points, it was the soldiers of Raymond Le Gros who made the crucial breakthrough.

Some years before the arrival of Strongbow, a person with more of a concern for their personal comfort than the tactical needs of the town had constructed a small house by attaching it to the outside of the walls. Not only did the house lean against the town wall, but to provide even more effective support a beam had been inserted into the wall and had most of the weight of the house hanging from it. Gathering all his men at this point, Raymond's archers sent up a ferocious covering fire while his mail-clad followers ran to the house and hacked at the beam. As soon as this timber had been cut through, the house collapsed and brought down a sizeable section of the wall with it. With a great cheer, the Norman knights rushed the breach. Hand-to-hand an Irish warrior or even a Hiberno-Norse axeman had a great disadvantage faced with the much more heavily armoured Norman knight. And here were hundreds of knights clambering over the rubble into the streets of Waterford. The battle

Above: A cartoon reconstruction by Ann Bernstorff of the *Siege of Wexford* by Diarmait, in 1169.

Below: A cartoon reconstruction by Ann Bernstorff of *Battles in the Kingdom of Ossory*, depicting Diarmait's vengeful raid against his old enemies.

Above: The famous painting of the marriage of Strongbow and Aífe by Daniel Maclise (1811–1870), housed in the National Gallery of Ireland. **Below:** Reginald's Tower, Waterford.

Vol I · Pl.120

REGINALDS TOWER. Co. Waterford.

Two views of the Wicklow mountains, through which Diarmait and Strongbow marched to capture Dublin despite the nearby presence of a large army led by the High King, Ruaidrí Ua Conchobair.

Above: Lorcán Ua Tuathail, the archbishop of Dublin, depicted in stained glass in the Church of the Immaculate Conception, Wexford.

Above: A Victorian sculpture of the head of Ruaidrí Ua Conchobair, High King of Ireland, from the grounds of Cong Abbey.

Above: Trim Castle, built by Hugh de Lacy on the bank of the Boyne River in 1172, first as an earth-and-timber ringwork, then, after the destruction of the early castle by Ruaidrí Ua Conchobair, in stone.

Below: Artist's impression of Trim Castle in its heyday.

Above: Where Norman settlement took place it transformed the landscape, often creating new communities, such as that of Jerpoint. **Below:** Often described as Strongbow's Tomb, this monument in Christ Church Cathedral marks Strongbow's resting place, after a roof-fall in 1562 destroyed the original sarcophagus.

rapidly became a massacre and the gutters of the narrow curving streets of the town began to run red.

The fate of the citizens of Waterford had been foreshadowed by the executions on Dún Domnaill headland. It was not Strongbow's intention to leave the existing ruling élite of the town in place, but to extinguish them and replace them with his own people. Understanding that there was little prospect of gaining ransom for prisoners, Strongbow's soldiers rampaged through the streets without mercy. As a result, many citizens were hacked apart and it seemed inevitable that their imprisoned leaders, who had made a last stand at Ragnall's Tower, would share the same fate. Indeed, almost immediately after their capture, two of the Hiberno-Norse commanders, both called Sitric, had been executed. Another Viking leader, Ragnall, was about to face the axe alongside Máel Sechlainn Ua Fáeláin and his son, when Diarmait Mac Murchada arrived, just in time, to intervene on their behalf.

What did the king of Leinster make of the streets filled with bodies? Did the sight of an annihilated Waterford make him face up to the reality of Norman conquest and the full implications of inviting them to Ireland? The results of this battle were nothing like the earlier submission of Wexford. Together with the executions at Dún Domnaill, the Hiberno-Norse warrior élite of Waterford had been almost entirely removed from Irish political life. Henceforth the citizens of the town would pursue their business without their accustomed independence of government, without an army, without a war fleet. Not that the impact of Norman rule was an entirely negative one for the non-combatant citizens. In due course, it would emerge that Norman rule would accelerate, rather than hinder, Waterford's economic prosperity. In 1170, however, what Diarmait would have seen was the passing into history of the age of Hiberno-Norse rule of Irish coastal towns and the start of a new era. Did this disturb him at all? Hardly. The citizens of Dublin were still treading on the bones of his father, bones mixed with those of a dog. Similar scenes in that town would bring only satisfaction to the king of Leinster.

Marriage

Although he had not brought his army into Waterford, Diarmait was riding with an extended entourage, including the senior Mac Murchada nobles and more immediate members of his own family, among them his daughter Aífe. Their entry into the town in magnificent dress made quite an impression. As soon as the corpses had been cleared from inside the broken walls of Waterford and the Norman knights could exchange their armour for more genteel clothes, a ceremony took place, the significance of which was not lost on those present. Before a large crowd of notables, Richard fitz Gilbert de Clare married Aífe daughter of Mac Murchada. It was a match pledged in the depths of despair for the two families which it bound together. It was a match consummated at the outset of a campaign, the fate of which was far from certain.

Twelfth-century Norman and Irish nobles held to a shared concept of female beauty. This concept had everything to do with the fact that a true noblewoman did not perform manual work. Her form was splendid, her lineage just as radiant. Her body was smooth and white as snow, her teeth were a delight. In other words, she was physically undamaged from never having to partake in arduous labour that risked accidents; she could trace her descent back to a famous figure, such a Charlemagne or, in the Irish context, Brian Bóruma; her skin had benefited from the fact that she did not need to spend time exposed beneath the sun and her teeth from a calcium and vitamin rich diet. Aífe was, therefore, quite beautiful in Strongbow's eyes. To marry her was another act of defiance against the wishes of Strongbow's lord, King Henry II, but Strongbow would have remained a bachelor all his life if he was to wait on Henry to find him a suitable match. Now, he was marrying a princess.

For her part, back in the summer of 1166, Aífe had escaped from Ferns into exile with her father and had agreed that the only way for the family to return to its rightful position as the rulers of Leinster was to bring a Norman lord back with them to reside in Ireland. Ever since Diarmait's solemn oath in

146

Chepstow Castle, she had known and accepted her fate. Neither in Ireland nor on the continent did a twelfth-century noblewoman have much independence while subject to a male guardian: father, husband, or son. Only in the period between the death of her husband and her son's coming-of-age could a woman hope to rule autonomously, as a regent. In Ireland, however, there was a greater respect for the possessions of a wife and greater possibilities for her to leave her husband than there was in England and France.

Aífe was to prove a loyal wife to Strongbow. She familiarised herself with his world and bore him two children: Gilbert, born in 1173, who died in his teenage years, and Isabel, Strongbow's heiress. Isabel was a resourceful daughter who was to prove successful in assisting her husband William Marshall steer his way through the complexities of English court politics. Together they consolidated the family position in Leinster, and William Marshall also regained the title of Earl of Pembroke, one that had been lost to Strongbow while he was a teenager. The fact that Isabel was brought up with the skills to offer council with regard to both Irish and English affairs is proof that her mother entered the alliance with Strongbow wholeheartedly and gave her attention to Strongbow's rights and responsibilities on both sides of the Irish Sea.

In the past other Irish noblewomen had married Normans, but this was an historic moment, for it was the first time that the married couple were to reside in Ireland. Strongbow was here to stay. True to his promise, after the couple were wed, Diarmait Mac Murchada raised his husky voice to confirm that Strongbow was his designated heir as king of Leinster. In Irish terms, what this meant was that Diarmait's immediate family, most importantly his very capable son, Domnall Cáemánach, would back Strongbow in the scramble for power that would inevitably ensue upon Diarmait's death. As his subsequent career proved, Domnall Cáemánach honoured this commitment and in return, was given a leading role in Leinster by Strongbow. The marriage to Aífe would help bring more key Uí Chennselaig figures to Strongbow's faction. But more than any other Irish prince, Strongbow would still have to win the leadership of the Uí Chennselaig troops and then obtain the submission of all the other Leinster lords. Aífe was not an heiress in the Norman sense and Strongbow understood this well. But he intended to make Leinster his own, not in the Irish manner of forcing submission and holding hostages, but in the much more decisive Norman manner: that of destroying the old aristocracy and replacing them with his own vassals, who in turn would cover the country with castles and fill the fields with serfs.

No honeymoon awaited the new couple, for even to hold the wedding with proper ceremony was to waste valuable campaign time. As soon as the festivities were out of the way, Strongbow held a war council. Present with Diarmait and Strongbow were Raymond Le Gros, Meilyr fitz Henry and Maurice de Prendergast as well as many other knights. If Diarmait still felt bitter at the way Maurice had defied him the previous year, he hid his feelings well. For with a sense of common purpose, the council agreed to march on Dublin as soon as Diarmait had raised his Uí Chennselaig troops. Nominally, Dublin had already submitted to Diarmait and acknowledged him king of Leinster. But what the allies aimed at now was the same degree of control over the town as they had just established at Waterford, in other words the destruction of the leading citizens and the removal of their popular form of government.

At once, Diarmait set off for Ferns in the company of Robert fitz Stephen, sending out his summons for a hosting. On Diarmait's return, with an impressive mobilisation of Irish troops now anxious to adhere to the rising power in the region, Strongbow withdrew most of his army from Waterford. To govern the town and defend it for him, he assigned some of his own personal followers. The united army then set out for Ireland's most important town.

The Capture of Dublin

News of the fall of Waterford and of the great bloodshed that had accompanied the storming of the town had reached Dublin. There, under the leadership of Asculv, the citizens had responded with great urgency, fearing that they too would come under Norman rule, if they survived at all. Contacting the high king, the Hiberno-Norse warriors urged Ruaidrí to treat Strongbow's arrival in Ireland as a major crisis and to come at once to Dublin. The implication of their call was that Dublin would submit to Ruaidrí again, as they had in 1166 before being forced to recognise Diarmait as their overlord.

The high king did not hesitate but set out at once, mobilising his allies as he did so. First to Ruaidrí's side was Tigernán Ua Ruairc. As the army of Connacht converged upon the troops from Bréifne, Tigernán may well have mulled over the fact that, only a year earlier, Ireland could have been rid of Diarmait for good. Now, the balance of forces might be against them. Perhaps they had missed their chance. Still, with Máel Sechlainn Ua Máel Sechlainn of Meath joining them and also Murchad Ua Cerbaill and the Airgialla, it was an impressive host that came to the defence of Dublin.

The race to get to the town had been won by Ruaidrí and having set up his headquarters near the round tower at Clondalkin he was able to control the major passes between the Wicklow mountains and Dublin's hinterland. His troops began to erect defences, lashing together hedges and trees, ready for the battle that would determine the fate of the whole of the country. Yet the battle never came, not on this occasion.

There were no better experts at bringing expeditionary armies from Wicklow to Dublin than the Uí Chennselaig and once Diarmait learned that his enemies had reached the town first, he drew upon this experience. Scouts were sent out; their reports indicated that an army of tens of thousands stood guarding the main paths down from the mountains. Avoiding, therefore, the direct route and travelling east via the valley of Glendalough, on 21 September 1170, Diarmait and Strongbow drew up a careful marching order and crossed the mountains via a track that Ruaidrí had considered too inconsequential to guard. Once across the shoulder of the mountains and committed to the descent, they knew they were also committing themselves to a decisive battle should the high king attack. This could well prove to be the most important day of their lives.

In the vanguard of the Norman-Uí Chennselaig army was Miles de

Cogan, a warrior with a powerful physique. Having earned a reputation for bravery and steadfastness in the thick of hard fighting, Miles was Strongbow's favoured commander in a crisis. About a quarter of the Norman army were allocated for Miles to lead down the mountain slopes towards Dublin. With them came Uí Chennselaig veterans under their experienced commander and Diarmait's choice of leader for situations requiring hard fighting: his son, Domnall Cáemánach.

Close behind the first division came Raymond Le Gros, whose success with the advance party at Dún Domnaill had been rewarded by his being given responsibility for a much greater number of troops. Another quarter of the Norman army – around four hundred soldiers – marched with their stout commander in the second section.

Then came the core of the united army, a powerful centre, with Strongbow and Diarmait surrounded by the majority of their troops: around eight hundred Normans and several thousand Irish soldiers. It was an impressive force, but, in absolute terms, they were considerably outnumbered by the host mobilised by Ruaidrí Ua Conchobair. Looking to their west, Strongbow and Diarmait could see the huge clusters of enemy troops spreading out from a massive force at Clondalkin round tower, guarding against the army that had outflanked them. Strongbow and Diarmait had by now reached Rathfarnham and had positioned themselves to arrive at the walls of Dublin ahead of the high king. But what would Ruaidrí do? As the allied vanguard under Miles de Cogan drew up close to the town, Diarmait's scouts kept him constantly informed as to the movements of their opponents. Would Ruaidrí march upon them and force the battle that would decide the fate of Ireland?

With the heavy tread of the marching army coming to a halt and the men relaxing as much as they could in full armour, there was no sign that battle was imminent. The Irish troops of Connacht, Bréifne, Meath and Airgialla were more concentrated now, having drawn back their outlying forces. But they made no movement forward. Meanwhile, envoys came from the Hiberno-Norse people of Dublin. Asculv wished to make peace with Diarmait and was again willing to recognise him as king. This was welcome news. The worst case scenario for the allies would be if Ruaidrí attacked in force and was joined by a sortie of Hiberno-Norse axemen from the town. Faced with the most dangerous army ever to march on their town, Asculv and his people wanted to part from the high king and change their allegiance once more. Their hope might have been that given the presence of Ruaidrí's army, Diarmait would retreat with only a token submission on the part of the Hiberno-Norse. If so, it was mistaken.

The negotiations began. Lorcán Ua Tuathail, the archbishop of Dublin – and Diarmait's brother-in-law – facilitated the discussions, his mediation creating a bridge between the Dublin citizens and the army outside their walls. Maurice Regan, Diarmait's interpreter, represented the king of Leinster and demanded that thirty hostages be sent to Diarmait along with the submission of the town. This Asculv agreed to, but he asked for the surrender to take place the following day. Given that nothing good was likely to come to those who put themselves into Diarmait's hands, it would take some time and considerable coercion to round up the unfortunate hostages. Maurice returned to Diarmait with this satisfactory result; satisfactory, that is, from an Irish perspective, but not from that of the Normans.

Had matters concluded with the surrender as agreed, Strongbow would have returned to Waterford, Diarmait to Ferns, Ruaidrí to Connacht and nothing fundamental would have changed. Diarmait would have been able to demand services from the Dublin fleet and would have held a stronger authority in the town than he had previously. Not that it would have been absolute control; if Diarmait had pushed his authority too far, the Dubliners would have renounced him as they had done in the past, albeit at the cost of their hostages.

Exasperated by the possibility that Dublin might escape attack and without consulting Strongbow, Miles de Cogan gathered his men and ordered them to storm the town. There was a great roar of approval at this order from the young knights of the Norman army. Those recently elevated from the ranks of squire and those whom the heavy hand of Henry II had prevented from ever proving themselves in battle were the first to the walls.

If the Hiberno-Norse warriors had been properly on guard, the attack would have been no more successful than the first two attempts on the walls of Waterford. Dublin, too, had a deep ditch and tall well-founded stone walls. But the leaders of the Hiberno-Norse troops were at council, each arguing furiously in order to avoid becoming a hostage of Mac Murchada's. Their bickering was ended by the sound of the alarm and they ran to give battle, but it was too late. A forest of ladders were in place against the town's defences and heavily armoured Norman knights and soldiers were already on the walkways. For a short time, the fighting was intense. It was the kind of bitter and ugly exchange of heavy blows that Miles thrived upon and his men loved him for it. As the Norman troops continued to hack a path into the town, it was all too evident that the time for making a stand had passed. No martyr, Asculv ordered an evacuation of all those warriors who could reach the ships. The leader of the Dubliners had allies in the Isle of Man and in the isles west of Scotland. Better to preserve as many of his followers as possible and return with a Viking fleet than be cut down on this day.

Those too far from the ships to escape were simply slaughtered. As with Waterford, this was a new type of warfare, in which the victors were not playing for prestige or the wealth that could be generated from ransoms. Battle, for Miles and his men, was fought in order to eliminate the enemy and gain their possessions in perpetuity. There were rich pickings to be had once the fighting was over and for several hours Norman soldiers ransacked the town, grabbing what they could. They showed little discrimination. Lorcán Ua Tuathail's own residence in the precincts of Christ Church was plundered.

Much later, when calm had been restored and some soldiers were giving thanks to God in the wooden church, an archer found his attempts to donate a penny were rejected. Only after he had confessed to participating in the looting of the archbishop's home and returned what he had obtained there was his penny accepted. Some fifteen years later, when this story came to the ears of Gerald de Barri, the Norman historian and raconteur wrote that the archer had twice turned to leave the church, only to have his pennies miraculously hurled at his back by the power of the cross. The cross was the source of another miracle on that day, wrote Gerald, for the Hiberno-Norse warriors tried to wrest it from the church before they fled the town in order to carry it away with them for the value of its ornamentation, only to find the cross stuck so firmly to the church that they had to abandon it.

A far bigger prize than all the moveable goods was the town itself, with all its workshops, merchants and trading incomes. And that was now, *de facto*, in the hands of the Normans. Given that Diarmait had a policy of granting the Hiberno-Norse towns – never owned by him in the first place – to his Norman allies by way of reward, there is little doubt that the king of Leinster would have assigned Dublin to Strongbow. In Dublin, however, a quite unexpected situation had arisen. Miles de Cogan had conquered the town and he, naturally, handed it to his lord, Strongbow. Diarmait was no longer part of the equation. When he and Strongbow hastily brought their forces through the open gates of Dublin, Diarmait was treated with all due respect. But there was no question of the town being a gift from the king of Leinster to Strongbow. On entering the town, it was the Norman lord who issued the orders and it was Norman soldiers who took control of Dublin's abundant provisions.

What was the high king doing, when this major prize fell to Strongbow? The events of 21 September 1170 planted a most dangerous enemy securely in Ireland. Could it have been otherwise? Ruaidrí had watched the day's proceedings with growing dismay and anger. His own scouts had failed him and all of his preparations to block the passage of the enemy force had been wasted as a result of Diarmait's manoeuvres. Moreover, the actions of the Dubliners once the Norman-Uí Chennselaig army had descended from the mountains had been outrageous. It was Asculv who had called for the assistance of the high king, yet instead of resolutely opposing Diarmait, the Hiberno-Norse warriors had immediately opened up negotiations with their supposed enemy, leaving Ruaidrí with a difficult question. Was this the moment to put the fate of Ireland to the test?

In favour of war were those who argued that, even without the Hiberno-Norse axemen, it was a great host that Ruaidrí had managed to summon and he might never succeed in mobilising so many again. Against battle were those who knew the most about Norman arms and tactics. Although Ruaidrí had the advantage in numbers, the extra troops could well prove insufficient in the face of an enemy with vastly superior missile fire and extremely well-trained armed riders. It was a very difficult decision, and when Ruaidrí finally made his call, it was not to force battle, but to monitor the situation with caution. Initially, he brought his army a little closer to the town walls but, more importantly, closer to the fords of the Liffey, so that his line of retreat was secure. His headquarters were now at the 'Green of Ath-Cliath', modern-day Kilmainham. But once Dublin started to burn and the red and yellow flags of the de Clare's were fluttering from the towers, Ruaidrí abandoned the fickle Hiberno-Norse warriors to their fate. His sense that the Dubliners were being punished for their lack of faith was reinforced by the thunderstorm that traversed the valley of the Liffey and the lightning that flashed over the town from the dark and portentous clouds.

Diarmait Seeks Revenge

Standing on the walls of Dublin and watching Ruaidrí Ua Conchobair and his allies retreat westwards, Diarmait Mac Murchada must have felt a tremendous sense of achievement. Having once been on the brink of destruction and having experienced three humiliating surrenders, now, at the age of sixty, he was at last witnessing his old rivals fall back in fear of his strength. In the decades of see-saw rivalry with Tigernán Ua Ruairc it was Diarmait who finally had the upper hand. Not that having the upper hand was enough. Diarmait wanted Tigernán's head.

There was a lot of work to be done yet. First of all, now that the high king had departed, all of Leinster was there for the taking and a reckoning was in order for all those dynasties that had risen against Diarmait in the past. Having discussed matters with his Norman allies, Diarmait agreed that their troops would not be needed to obtain the submission of the lesser Leinster lords. Instead, the Normans would concentrate on turning their nominal lordship of the fiercely independent population of the ports into a real one. Whereas the Hiberno-Norse people of Waterford and Dublin were shocked and – for the moment – demoralised, Robert fitz Stephen was finding the challenge of becoming lord of Wexford no easy matter. Despite his newly constructed castle, Robert had major troubles in asserting his governance of Wexford and was anxious to return to the town in person.

Once his scouts reported that the high king was marching westwards and his army was dispersing, the Uí Chennselaig left Dublin on a tour of vengeance. Their first target was Kildare and the Uí Fáeláin, who had never forgotten their own claims to the kingship of Leinster and who were always the first to join in any coalition that challenged the Uí Chennselaig. Back in 1141, as part of the infamous series of ambushes organised by Dairmait against his rivals, Domnall Mac Fáeláin had been murdered by assassins. This despite promises of peace. So naturally the Uí Fáeláin had joined in the 1166 effort to kill Diarmait or drive him out of Ireland. In 1170, it was Diarmait's turn to impose exile on the leader of his rivals, Fáelán Mac Fáeláin, and the newly triumphant king of Leinster did not fail to ravage the lands of Cloncurry, Naas and Kildare.

After bringing his herds of stolen cattle to Ferns, Diarmait's army entered Osraige once more. There Domnall Mac Gilla Pátraic was unable to stand against the Uí Chennselaig. Although neither side had Norman troops, Diarmait had rallied all the fair-weather minor lords of Leinster, while the soldiers of Osraige stood isolated. With no prospect of assistance from the high king, Domnall Mac Gilla Pátraic capitulated and the price for the submission of the men of Osraige was that their king agreed to exile. Domnall Mac Gilla Pátraic set off for Connacht, while Diarmait returned to Ferns with tribute from the people who had briefly dared to claim half of Uí Chennselaig territory.

Having returned home, Diarmait was delighted at the arrival of a delegation of warriors from Meath to his house in Ferns. In 1169, Domnall Bregach Ua Máel Sechlainn had murdered his uncle Diarmait Ua Máel Sechlainn in order to come to power as king of Meath. But Domnall had then been ousted by Ruaidrí and Tigernán later in the year. Once again Meath was divided with Ruaidrí keeping the west half and Tigernán the east. Now Domnall Bregach was at Ferns, ready to make an arrangement with Diarmait to their mutual satisfaction. Domnall would recognise Diarmait as king of Leinster, raise East Meath in rebellion and assist with the fighting if Diarmait showed equal effort in backing Domnall Bregach for the kingship of East Meath against Tigernán. Confident in the arrangement, Domnall Bregach returned to East Meath and called on his followers to defy Tigernán. As soon as it became clear that he had lost control of the province, Tigernán killed the hostages from East Meath he had taken the previous year. Both sides prepared for battle.

Having allowed his army a short rest, Diarmait then took his elderly bones to the saddle once more for a far more serious enterprise than the two earlier raids. Even without the presence of the high king, Tigernán remained a formidable opponent and so Diarmait appealed to Strongbow for support in this new expedition. Nor was the appeal based solely upon strategy: Diarmait also attempted to appeal to his ally's sense of honour by reminding Strongbow of the long series of injustices that Tigernán had inflicted on Diarmait. Strongbow was willing to march against one of the most powerful figures in Ireland and the two unlikely allies marched together to battle once more. It would be their last joint enterprise.

Concentrating on the churches that were rivals to the Mac Murchada-controlled Kildare, Diarmait plundered and burned his way through Kells, Dulane, Slane and many minor parishes besides. Then the army turned northwards into Uí Ruairc territory, to Slieve Gory (modern-day County Cavan). Tigernán did not dare give battle and Diarmait's raid was a great success. Having parted from Strongbow, he drove his prisoners and plundered cattle home towards Ferns. En route, Diarmait had a further goal in mind, which was to punish Murchad Ua Brain and his son Dalbach for having deserted him. Wisely, the small forces of the Uí Brain fled, although that meant surrendering their slaves, cattle and other plunder to the man who had once raised them to power and who was now determined to crush them.

The Death of Diarmait Mac Murchada

Back in the autumn of 1169, when Ruaidrí Ua Conchobair thought he had obtained Diarmait's submission, the high king had come away from Leinster with four very valuable hostages, including Diarmait's son Conchobar. The events of 1170 meant that the lives of the hostages were forfeit. Diarmait had broken the terms of his submission, not by reasserting himself as king of Leinster, but by bringing Strongbow to Ireland and assisting the Norman in securing very valuable bases at Waterford and Dublin. Even so, Ruaidrí was reluctant to execute his Uí Chennselaig hostages: they were the last hope he had of having any leverage over Diarmait. But messengers arrived in Connacht from Bréifne. A furious Tigernán Ua Ruairc demanded that the high king kill his captives. There was no hope of compromise with Diarmait, the battle lines were drawn, and if Ruaidrí did not carry out the executions, Tigernán would no longer serve him. Worse, he would strive his utmost to unseat Ruaidrí as high king. It was a strong threat and left Ruaidrí with little choice. In any case, Tigernán was probably right, there was no prospect of taming Diarmait Mac Murchada. The axeman was sent for. In due course, Diarmait, Domnall Cáemánach and Diarmait's foster brother, all received the heads of their eldest sons.

Not long after the news of the death of the hostages came more ill-tidings from Diarmait's perspective and a further reminder that fate could turn rapidly in the struggle for dominance in Ireland, with the first defeat of Norman forces at Irish hands. The garrison of Waterford had marched out against a raid by Diarmait Mac Carthaig of Desmond. The subsequent encounter was a hard-fought battle and a number of Irish nobles fell, but the Normans were overwhelmed and those who escaped the slaughter fled back to the town. While the battle was a relatively minor one, it showed that the Normans could be beaten by Irish armies and emphasised the precariousness of their position.

Early in 1171, a further blow came to Diarmait, with the news that Sadb, daughter of Glúniairn Mac Murchada, the abbess of Kildare, had died. Diarmait's control over the important ecclesiastical centre was ended. Moreover, Tigernán Ua Ruairc was storming around the eastern borders of Bréifne, putting an end to minor rebellions against him and, in doing so, he burned the round tower at Telach Aird, despite the fact that it was full of refugees. There was no safety in churches when the princes of Ireland were competing for control of them.

The state of the church in Ireland was the main subject of a council held at Armagh at this time and, in particular, the clergy discussed the implications of the arrival of the foreigners. It was agreed that the situation was disastrous. Wars between Irish families over church appointments were deplorable and so too were wars between rival cleric dynasties. Such wars, however, were part of the landscape and had been for hundreds of years. Now the order of things was out of control and the church was likely to be taken over by the foreigners wherever they became established. It was, naturally, a result of the sins of the Irish clergy that these troubled times had come to them. God was punishing them and was right to do so. But the particular sin that the council focused on was none of the obvious ones. The fact that church appointees were often imposed by local dynasts and the fact that the clergy had children were two great sins that had been fought against, with considerable success, in continental Europe for over a hundred years. But it was not simony or Nicholaitism (marriage) that were the subjects of the self-criticism of the Irish church. Their sin was the practice of slavery.

As the Irish people had purchased English slaves indiscriminately, from merchants, robbers and pirates, the council agreed that it was divine justice that the Irish should now be enslaved by the same people. The council therefore said and publicly decreed that throughout the island all the English slaves should be freed; or so reported Gerald de Barri, our only source for this council and, as always, a source liable to mix authentic fact with self-serving invention. Here, though, Gerald was expressing an idea that was already becoming manifest. The Normans were affecting a revolution on the lands they were taking. Slaves were being made free, to the extent that they were becoming serfs. The people at the bottom of society still had arduous and backbreaking work to perform, but now at least they could keep some of the results of that work after surrendering a portion to their new lords. An Irish slave had no control over any aspect of their lives. Even the foodstuffs they were entitled to consume for their meals were determined for them. A serf on Norman lands lived as a free person, albeit under an onerous weight of obligations. If the coming of the Normans to Ireland threatened catastrophe to the lords and wealthy farmers of the country, it should not be overlooked that it also meant a welcome change for the country's slaves.

In May 1171, the person indirectly responsible for these changes in Ireland died. Diarmait Mac Murchada was in his sixty-first year. He had fought in the fiercest battles of the era, revenged the murder of his father, conducted passionate love affairs, and been a generous patron to Augustinians and Cistercians. But all across Ireland he was known for only one deed: having allowed the Normans to get a grip on the country. Outside of Leinster, the obituaries for Diarmait Mac Murchada were hostile. The annalist at Clonmacnoise wrote, 'Diarmaid Mac Murchada, king of Leinstermen and Foreigners, the disturber of Banba and destroyer of Erin, after bringing over foreigners and constantly harming Gaels, after plundering and destroying churches and boundaries, after the end of a year of insufferable illness, died through the miracles of Finnén and Columcille and the other saints whom he had plundered.' When the *Annals of the Four Masters* were written up in the seventeenth century, the author elaborated on the medieval entry to make it clear that Diarmait had gone to hell: 'Diarmaid Mac Murchadha, king of Leinster, by whom a trembling sod was made of all Ireland − after having brought over the

Saxons, after having done extensive injuries to the Irish, after plundering and burning many churches, as Kells, Clonard, etc — died before the end of a year of an insufferable and unknown disease; for he became putrid while living, through the miracle of God, Columcille and Finnén, and the other saints of Ireland, whose churches he had profaned and burned some time before; and he died at Ferns, without a will, without penance, without the body of Christ, without unction, as his evil deeds deserved.'

Naturally, Diarmait's own scribe had a rather different perspective, writing that 'Diarmait, son of Donnchad, son of Murchad, ruled for forty-six years. And he was the king of all South Erin and Meath. His natural death took place at Ferns, after the victory of extreme unction and penance, in the sixty-first year of his age.' In other words, Diarmait was destined for heaven.

Diarmait died too soon for a final reckoning with his great rival Tigernán. The feud between the two Irish lords was so deep that Diarmait had no qualms about bringing down the whole structure of Irish society through the introduction of the Normans, so long as it meant triumphing over Tigernán. By 1171, Diarmait had lived to see the recovery of all he had lost on being forced into exile and gained very much more. Even if he was now standing in the shadow of Strongbow, Diarmait could reach out with power in his fist and strike at all those who had betrayed him. It was only a matter of time before the reckoning would come that Diarmait had been anticipating for years. And there was every chance that Diarmait would get to hold the decapitated head of his arch enemy. Except that Diarmait had no time. He died having marched a great way along the path to complete revenge upon his enemies and those who had betrayed him, but too soon to see what the consequences of his strategy would be for Tigernán.

Is the satisfaction of revenge a worthy use of one's life? Diarmait had no choice but to pursue his enemies, for he was born into a culture of war, political manoeuvre, and honour. If he had accepted defeat and exile, with retirement perhaps in a monastery, Diarmait would have been branded a shameful failure by his peers and worse, by his own conscience. No one would have praised him for turning the other cheek, for refusing to seek Norman aid. Instead, he devoted all his energies to the gaining of power. Judged by that goal and in comparison with the other Irish princes who strove against him, Diarmait fared well. As a warlord, Diarmait had led the Uí Chennselaig at the pivotal battle of Móin Mór in 1151 and again, at Ardee in 1159, he brought them through the other great bloodbath of twelfth-century Irish history. As a politician he was brutal and effective, abandoning his family hostages to their fate when necessary and breaking promises of peace to assassinate rivals. Diarmait did have a sense of honour, but it was not the chivalrous one that the French and English were developing. It was honour that meant Diarmait never gave up striving to be king of Leinster, even when abandoned by all his vassals. After his comrades and veterans fell around him at Fid Dorcha, in 1166, there was nothing for it but to flee the country. Even then, Diarmait would not give up, for honour's sake. This pride would have swelled within him again in 1170, watching from the walls of Dublin, as the high king and Tigernán, his hound, retreated out of Leinster. Whatever the other annalists wrote, the fact was that Diarmait died at a time when his own sense of worth was at a height. And if he chose to overlook where the real source of his strength came from, Diarmait could easily do so, by telling himself that it was his guile and cunning that had brought the Normans to Ireland, not their own restless ambition for land.

CHAPTER 6

1171:

A Year of Crises

Having left the pugnacious Miles de Cogan in charge at Dublin, Strongbow returned to Waterford to shore up the garrison after their defeat at the hands of Mac Carthaig. There, in the spring of 1171, he faced two great challenges, both capable of bringing about his destruction. The first was an edict from King Henry II of England. Not a man to tolerate disobedience, Henry's anger grew as news from Ireland reached his court. Not only had Strongbow defied the king and set sail for Ireland, but the lord of Strigoil had also married without royal permission and, furthermore, was now master of two significant ports. Always sensitive to the danger of one of his vassals becoming over-mighty, Henry envisioned Strongbow a king in Ireland – perhaps even high king – and a symbol for all those vassals disenchanted with Henry's rule. The errant lord had to be checked. The royal decree issued by Henry in 1171 ruled that all trade from English ports destined for Ireland must cease and that all those who had left Henry's domain for Ireland must return by Easter, 4 April 1171. If they failed to do so, they would be completely disinherited and forever banished from Henry's lands.

At once, the ships from Bristol and Chester that had been serving Waterford and Dublin ceased to ply the Irish Sea. Strongbow's soldiers became anxious and the knights who had recently joined him and who owned lands in England, Wales and Normandy questioned the wisdom of staying in Ireland. While his army began to fragment, the numbers of knights who continued to arrive in Ireland from Wales seeking to join Strongbow suddenly dropped from a steady stream to a trickle. Henry had acted just in time, for it was certain that without the threat of royal sanction more and more adventurers would have looked to earn lands in Ireland.

As always in times of crisis, Strongbow held a council and listened to the advice of his closest followers, figures such as Gilbert de Boisrohard, Hervey de Montmorency and Raymond Le Gros. Between them it was agreed that defying Henry was simply not an option and thus they must attempt to appease the king. No doubt Henry's greatest concern was that Strongbow might destabilise royal authority both by deed and through example to other discontented lords. So Strongbow must reassure the king and publicly demonstrate his loyalty to the crown. The way to do this was to acknowledge that as a vassal of Henry's, all Strongbow's gains in Ireland were the king's to dispose of as Henry pleased. Giving over all his new towns and lands to the king in this way was risky. Henry could grant them out again as he liked, perhaps to court favourites. Those who had fought and established new manors on Irish soil by grant of Strongbow could, potentially, be dispossessed by the higher authority. What Strongbow's council counted on was that Henry had to take into consideration the impact of his decisions on a wider public opinion of his vassals across England, Wales and France. If he acted too harshly against Strongbow's men after they had submitted to him, the king would be seen as unreasonable and mistrust of him would grow.

Charged with the delicate task of calming Henry's fears, making the king feel as though he were in overall command of the situation while attempting to legitimise all of Strongbow's grants, was Raymond le Gros. A sturdy and talented commander on the field of battle, he now had to turn courtier and politician. Raymond sailed for Aquitaine, where the king was holding court. There, as so often was the case for figures who were out of favour, Raymond had to wait patiently, unheard, while the king prevaricated. Although this wait-and-see approach was a favoured tactic of Henry's, as it happened he had genuine cause to delay making a decision about Ireland, for Henry had been plunged into a major crisis, partly as a result of his own badly controlled temper.

Having made his displeasure with Archbishop Thomas of Canterbury abundantly clear, Henry was in a weak position to protest his innocence of the murder of the archbishop by four of his courtiers. Internationally the outcry by the church was immense and, not long after Raymond Le Gros had arrived at court, Henry hurried back to England and closed the channel ports, fearing excommunication. The point of his relocation was to ensure that no papal legate could cross over and pronounce Henry under anathema. If the king was declared an excommunicate, dangerous political turmoil would result, not least in regard to the problems arising from the fact that lords and knights would be able to legitimise any of their actions that defied Henry's authority. No one was obliged to honour an oath made to an excommunicate. Suddenly, it suited Henry to absent himself until the worst of the backlash was over and his representatives could find a means to reconcile the pope with the king. After listening to Raymond at last, Henry made declaration that would have come as a stunning and alarming shock to Strongbow's envoy: the king of England was going to come to Ireland in person.

Asculv Strives for Dublin

Although Raymond Le Gros had been delegated to deal as best he could with King Henry, soon afterwards Strongbow felt that he could spare another of his vassals for a mission to the royal court, and Maurice fitz Gerald was delegated to travel to Raymond and assist him. With his best men attempting to dissipate the dangers from England, Strongbow concentrated on the other potentially disastrous crisis of the year 1171, that arising from the death of Diarmait Mac Murchada. No sooner was Diarmait dead than the chains of authority that had bound the minor lords of Leinster to the king were broken. Only three Irish princes declared themselves for Strongbow and of them only one represented a substantial group of followers. The three were Ua Ragallaig of Tír Briúin, Amlaíb Ua Gairbíth and Domnall Cáemánach. Ua Ragallaig had been exiled from Uí Briúin Bréifne as a bitter opponent of Tigernán Ua Ruairc and so, understandably, looked to Strongbow to continue Diarmait's campaign against Tigernán. Ua Ragallaig, however, brought with him few forces. Of rather more assistance to Strongbow was Amlaíb, a minor lord from the region of modern-day Rathvilly, County Carlow, who thought it possible to work with the Normans and feared a renewed confidence among the warriors of Osraige. By far the most important, though, of these three, was Domnall Cáemánach, Diarmait's son, and the veteran commander of the Uí Chennselaig cavalry. Unlike the other Irish princes, but in common with his sister Aífe, Domnall had seen Strongbow in his castle of Strigoil and had also seen how Strongbow had fulfilled the agreement made on that portentous day in 1166 when Diarmait and Strongbow had shaken hands on their pact. The pact was effectively continued through the adherence of Diarmait's surviving children to the Norman lord, and if Domnall's decision to stand by Strongbow was based on strategy as well as personal loyalty, it was a wise one. Domnall's dynasty eventually triumphed in the region and for centuries provided the kings of Leinster.

Having Domnall as a supporter was a major asset for Strongbow. Not that this guaranteed that the Uí Chennselaig army remained allied to the Normans. Just as whenever Diarmait Mac Murchada lost authority, his brother Murchad seized power, so now, Murchad's son, Muirchertach – Domnall Cáemánach's first cousin – also claimed the leadership of the Uí Chennselaig and the crown of Leinster. Naturally, Muirchertach looked to the high king to support his claim against the foreigner and, naturally, Ruaidrí welcomed the opportunity to construct an alliance that could defeat the Normans. So as soon as Muirchertach declared himself ruler of the Uí Chennselaig, the army of Connacht was mobilised. This time there would be no return from Leinster without battle with the foreigners. Even as it seemed that all of Ireland was marching against him, Strongbow learned of yet another potentially disastrous initiative taken against the Norman force: the Hiberno-Norse exiles of Dublin had attempted a sea-born invasion to reoccupy their town.

The deposed ruler of Dublin, Asculv Mac Turcaill, had been the driving force behind the old-fashioned Viking fleet that had attempted to regain the rich town. Asculv had rallied the Norse community of the Isle of Man and the islands west of Scotland to bring a hundred longships to Dublin for its recapture. Among the Viking warriors was John the Wode, a notable commander whose name derived from a term for madness or impetuousness, a fair description of John's berserker fury in battle.

Leaving their fleet at anchor safely out in Dublin bay, the Vikings came ashore in small boats and gathered on the Steine, a strip of land on the south bank of the Liffey, just east of the town walls. As he looked out on the grim sight of the Viking army preparing for battle, messengers came to Miles de Cogan, commander of the Norman forces in Dublin. The envoys were from Mac Gilla Mo Cholmóc, lord of Cuala (modern-day south county Dublin), who sought advice from Miles. Asculv had demanded of Mac Gilla Mo Cholmóc that he and his warriors assist with the recapture of Dublin, but the lord of Cuala was related to Strongbow by marriage, for he had married Aífe's sister Derbforgaill. More importantly, he had given Strongbow hostages from the Cuala who were still in Dublin. Mac Gilla Mo Cholmóc could not stand against Asculv's army, but he did not want to risk the lives of the hostages by attacking the town.

This rather ambiguous message was hastily seized upon by Miles who understood that matters were balanced on a knife edge. The Dublin garrison of some three hundred knights suddenly looked far too weak to hold the town. There was no point attempting to insist on Mac Gilla Mo Cholmóc's participation in the battle on the side of the Normans; to threaten the hostages would most likely push him across to the side of Asculv. Instead, Miles gave a very diplomatic response.

> *Listen to me, sire.*
> *I will have your hostages handed back to you,*
> *safe and sound and their numbers intact.*
> *You will get back your hostages*
> *providing you do as I tell you:*
> *providing that you do not give any help*
> *either to us or to them,*
> *but stand to one side of us*
> *and watch the battle from the side*
> *with your men,*
> *so that you may see clearly*
> *the conflict and the fighting*
> *between us and them without any doubts.*
> *Now if God grants us*
> *that these men are defeated,*
> *then come to us with your forces to rout them completely;*
> *but if we are defeated,*
> *then help them wholeheartedly*
> *to cut us to pieces and kill us*
> *and deliver our men to slaughter.*

Happy with Miles's proposition, the lord of the Cuala drew up his army around the high mound of earth known as the Hogges, very close to the town walls and the Viking army (modern-day Suffolk Street). It was a grandstand view for Mac Gilla Mo Cholmóc.

Led by John the Wode, the Viking army came up to the town. Many of the Vikings wore chain hauberks, some, however, the rather less effective body armour of metal plates sewn onto leather; most carried round shields, painted red, whose metal rims could be used offensively as well as defensively. With a loud roar, made more ominous by the clash of their weapons against their shields, this body of Vikings gathered in a tight group, and rushed towards Dame's gate on the eastern side of Dublin. Wanting to bring his three hundred cavalry into play, Miles at first tried to engage the Vikings outside of the gates. With his crossbowmen firing as rapidly as they could, before retreating to the walls, Miles came on with his knights and drove at the front ranks of the Viking axemen. As always, the impact of a charge of Norman horse was formidable. But there were too few footsoldiers to follow up the momentum of the cavalry. The Norman horsemen faltered and, in the thick of the melée, John the Wode swung his axe with incredible ferocity, cutting through the chain links of the armour of one of the Norman knights and severing his thigh entirely at the hip.

With loud cheers at this astonishing feat by their leader, the Vikings overwhelmed the Norman horsemen. Turning to escape, with their opponents hard on their heels, Miles and his knights barely made it back through the gate. Before long heavy axe blows began to demolish the entrance to the town. Ladders were brought up and it seemed that the fall of Dublin was imminent. At that moment, however, cries of consternation from the rear of the Viking army caused John the Wode to pause and bring his best men away from the gate, perhaps thinking that Mac Gilla Mo Cholmóc had moved against the Vikings. In fact, unknown to anyone – including Miles – Richard Cogan, Miles's younger brother, had made an unobserved sortie from St Nicholas's gate on the south side of the town and, with a fierce shout, had thrown himself on the exposed flank of the Viking army. Although Richard had only a few knights with him, the surprise of their attack and the overreaction by John turned the battle. Miles seized the opportunity and urged his knights out once more. It is testimony to the loyalty of his troops for their bellicose leader that they charged out of the gate without hesitation and this time it was the Vikings who gave way.

Crying: 'Strike, renowned barons! Strike, vassals, at once! Do not spare these men!' Miles charged into the thick of the fighting. Heartened by the presence of their leader, the Norman garrison of Dublin pushed out from the city, bringing bloody slaughter to the disorganised press of Viking warriors. Rich jarls and poor bondsmen alike were cut down in the mayhem and those at the rear lost heart. They turned and ran for the ships.

Once Mac Gilla Mo Cholmóc saw the battle lines of the Vikings had been broken, he ordered his men to join the fighting. The warriors of Cuala swept down from their position to throw javelins and spears into the fleeing crowds, who tried to scatter in every direction, hoping to reach the safety of woods and hillsides. Few of them did. Miles knew how to exploit a victory and not only was he everywhere, urging his men on and on, but the Normans launched boats to intercept the small craft full of Vikings that were desperately attempting to regain the fleet. One of the few Vikings to survive the massacre was white-haired Asculv, caught on the shoreline by Richard Cogan and dragged back before he could step into a sailing boat.

As his army disintegrated, John the Wode realised his death was upon him and resolved with grim determination to take as many knights with him as he could. Nine more of Miles's vassals lost their lives to the sharp edge of John's axe before a young Norman noble, Walter of Riddlesford, killed the Viking hero. Walter was one of those knights who attended Strongbow when he sought council; he was later granted twenty fiefs in Uí Muireadaig (now southern Kildare). Surviving the frenetic battles of his youth, Walter married Amabilis fitz Henry, a sister of Meilyr fitz Henry, and lived to be over eighty years old.

Nearly two thousand Viking warriors were dead, cut down in the fields and moors around Dublin or drowned attempting to row back to their ships. About the same number escaped, but fifty percent losses is a very bloody encounter for a medieval battle and as a consequence the Hiberno-Norse era of government of Dublin was over. The survivors sailed away to their relatives in the islands, never again to attempt to recover the town. Losses had also been high among the Norman knights, but the victors took some comfort in the fact that the spoils of war were plentiful.

Back in the town, the knights gathered to celebrate their victory, but first they had a captive to deal with. The elderly Asculv, the former ruler of Dublin, did not show the slightest fear of his captors or any consternation at the outcome of his expedition. Like a Viking hero out of the legends and songs, he gave mocking and boastful speeches when the Normans were expecting contrition and desperation. Asculv knew his time was over and, careless of his fate, spoke frankly, if mistakenly, about how the Vikings would come again to Dublin and the next time they would be victorious. While the old man might have been worth a modest ransom, Miles did not care for this Viking attitude, interpreting it as arrogant rather than brave. The executioner was summoned. Taunting his enemies to the last, the white-haired head of the former leader of Dublin was struck from his shoulders by order of the new authority in the town. For the Hiberno-Norse civilians of Dublin, the execution of Asculv was deeply symbolic of their fall from power, and the symbol was reinforced by the placing of Asculv's easily recognisable head above the entrance to the town. Soon the Hiberno-Norse people would find themselves herded across the river to build new residences on the north side of the Liffey, where there was no danger of them becoming an internal enemy liable to rise up against the new owners.

The Siege of Dublin 1171

Although the Normans had survived, albeit precariously, the attempted return of Asculv, fortune was not yet smiling upon their endeavours in Ireland. As a result of Henry's intervention, the steady flow of new recruits and goods from England had been seriously curtailed. Weakened by this blockade and by knights leaving Ireland for fear of the king's wrath, Strongbow had nevertheless to deal with the revolt of the Leinster lords after the death of Diarmait Mac Murchada. Before he could attempt to force submission on these Irish princes piecemeal, the Norman lord was faced with a challenge from an enormously wide-ranging alliance under the auspices of the high king, an alliance that was cemented by the efforts of the archbishop of Dublin, Lorcán Ua Tuathail.

The archbishop of Dublin wanted the Normans out, partly because he feared the consequences if henceforth Norman candidates obtained the key positions of the Irish church, and even more so out of concern that his people, the Uí Thuathail, would lose their lands to these new arrivals. Already, Norman soldiers were seizing church property everywhere they roamed. Moreover, Lorcán had been acting as peacemaker when Miles de Cogan had stormed Dublin. The Normans had acted treacherously in the eyes of the cleric and had made him appear a fool. So Lorcán exchanged messages with Ruaidrí Ua Conchobair and the two of them co-ordinated an attack on Dublin.

One person was of particular importance if the archbishop and the high king were to succeed with their plans and so both Ruaidrí and Lorcán sent messages to Godred the Black, prince of the Isle of Man. Disaster may have befallen Asculv, but this time matters would be different. All of Ireland was mobilising against the foreigners and if Godred would bring even a small fleet to block Dublin bay, he could have all the ships he intercepted, and, in addition, Ruaidrí would give him a generous financial reward. It was not simply these material incentives, however, that led Godred to agree to assist against the Normans; the ruler of Man was also concerned about the future. If the Normans ruled both Ireland and England, it would only be a matter of time before they took over his small island too.

The high king was on the march out of Connacht. With him came a huge muster of Irish troops, determined to oust the Normans. In Leinster, Muirchertach Mac Murchada led the Uí Chennselaig to the coastline south of Dublin, near Dalkey Island. The old Leinster enemies of Diarmait Mac Murchada were keen to assist the new Uí Chennselaig leader against the Normans and with Muirchertach were Uí Fáeláin, Mac Dalbaig, and men from the archbishop's dynasty, Uí Thuathail. Joining with these south Leinster forces was the fickle Mac Gilla Mo Cholmóc. Having obtained the return of all his hostages for assisting Miles de Cogan in battle against Asculv, Mac Gilla Mo Cholmóc was free to choose sides without any restraint. And it was a strong indication of how difficult the position appeared to be for the Normans that the cagey ruler of Cuala threw in his lot with Muirchertach Mac Murchada.

Ruaidrí himself set up camp at Castleknock, on the north bank of the Liffey just west of the town. With the high king was, of course, Tigernán Ua Ruairc and the army of Bréifne; also at Castleknock was Murchad Ua Cerbaill, lord of Airgialla. Mac Duinn Shléibe of Ulster planted his banner at Clontarf, the famous battleground at which Brian Bóruma had fallen. Having made his peace with Ruaidrí, Domnall Mór Ua Briain was also at Dublin with his Munster troops, taking up position at Kilmainham. And in Dublin Bay were thirty longships, sent by Godred to complete the encirclement of the town. This encirclement of Dublin was one of the century's great mobilisations of Irish armies and it expressed both the authority of the high king and a collective determination to quash the intervention of the Normans in Ireland.

Shortly before the Irish princes arrived to set up their armies around Dublin, Strongbow had marched to the town to reinforce the garrison with the main body of his troops. With him were Maurice fitz Gerald and Raymond Le Gros, recently returned from England with their shocking news that Henry was on the way to Ireland. Only a few knights remained in Waterford, under the command of Strongbow's trusted advisor Gilbert de Boisrohard. Similarly, Robert fitz Stephen heavily depleted the garrison of his small castle at Wexford by sending thirty-six of his men to serve with Strongbow. In Robert's case, this led to disaster.

The Hiberno-Norse population of Wexford were chafing under the pressure of Robert's new castle and the revenues demanded of them. Moreover, refugees from Waterford and Dublin brought bitter tales of slaughter and of the ending of their free status. When the warriors of Wexford learned that a siege of Dublin was underway and that Robert had kept only five knights and a few archers to defend his castle, they put on their armour and marched out to confront him. Even though the Normans were few in number, they were alert and behind strong defences. It was going to be difficult to force the castle, and one knight with striking burnished armour, Wlliam Not, was particularly active in keeping the Wexford axemen at bay. But, true to their Viking roots, the Wexford soldiers were as happy to employ guile as force. They summoned various members of the Irish clergy including Malachias Ua Briain, Bishop of Kildare, and with him the Bishop of Ferns. These were the two bishops who had assisted with the negotiations over the surrender of Wexford to Robert back in 1167. Both clergymen now swore on the relics they had brought with them that Dublin had fallen to Ruaidrí Ua Conchobair and that Strongbow, Maurice fitz Gerald and Raymond Le Gros were all dead. The victorious Irish were already on their way to Wexford to put Robert's head under the axe too. How the bishops justified such a deception is unknown, perhaps believing that the saints would understand its necessity, but it was certainly an impressive piece of acting.

The bishops urged Robert fitz Stephen to surrender the castle and promised that, in return, he and his men would be escorted safely to the port and given passage to Wales. For, they said, Robert had proven himself a merciful and generous prince towards the church. The powerful performance of the two bishops won Robert over entirely and, grieving for the death of his comrades in Dublin, he opened the gates of the castle. At once the Hiberno-Norse men of Wexford rushed in, stabbing and crushing the Norman soldiers, killing all of the archers and footsoldiers and putting chains on Robert and four other knights.

Robert's plight was unknown to Strongbow in Dublin, who in any case had deep enough concerns of his own. In every direction, including the sea, Dublin was cut off and cut off, moreover, by very large armies. The Norman troops inside the town were rapidly consuming the supplies that had once seemed ample. With a very effective blockade in place, the quantity of food-stuffs in Dublin was shrinking rapidly.

June 1171 passed with no effort by the Irish to storm the walls of Dublin. Why should they? Even if Ruaidrí had the skilled engineers needed to build siege equipment, it was only playing to the Norman's strengths to engage them hand-to-hand. It was much better to take advantage of a superior mobility and control of the communications routes to starve Strongbow into submission. July 1171 came and went, corn ripening in the fields, nearly ready for harvest. Strongbow desperately needed that grain for horses and men. But there was to be no gathering of the harvest for the hungry Dublin soldiers. The cavalry of Tigernán Ua Ruairc and Murchad Ua Cerbaill rode across the lands around the town, burning all the crops.

The cruel bite of hunger was made all the sharper when Strongbow's three Irish allies slipped through the cordon of enemy armies with the help of Domnall Cáemánach's expert knowledge of the Wicklow mountains. The news that Ua Ragallaig, Amlaíb and Domnall brought was that Robert fitz Stephen was in trouble. Although not yet aware the castle had in fact fallen, Domnall had learned that the men of Wexford, assisted by the Uí Chennselaig, were besieging the Norman knight. This news was especially distressing to Robert's half-brother, Maurice fitz Gerald, who now led the faction in Strongbow's council who urged that battle should be risked.

At the end of August a crisis meeting was held. Present were Maurice fitz Gerald, Robert de Quency, Walter de Riddlesford, Maurice de Prendergast, Miles de Cogan, Meilyr fitz Henry, Miles fitz David, Richard de Marreis, Walter Bluet, and twelve others. This was Strongbow's inner council. It was a glum meeting, for they faced problems on two fronts, most aptly summed up by Maurice fitz Gerald, who pointed out that, while the Irish hated them as foreigners, they could not look to Henry for aid, for he already looked on them as Irish, despite the fact that their presence in the land had been such a brief one. Strongbow himself led the faction that favoured an attempt at a peaceful resolution of the siege, even if that did mean giving up some of the gains of the Normans thus far.

> 'Lords', said the valiant earl,
> 'may God in heaven protect us!
> 'You see, lords, our enemies

'who are besieging us here,
'and we have scarcely provisions
'for more than a fortnight …

'So, noble knights,
'let us send word to the king.

'Now, rightful lords,
'we shall, with your consent,
'send two vassals to the King of Connacht,
'and we shall send the archbishop
'to say that I am willing to do fealty to him:
'I will hold Leinster under him.'

Given such a lead by Strongbow, the advocates of peace won the argument in the council. Overcoming, therefore, his anger at the role played by the archbishop in mobilising his enemies, Strongbow asked Lorcán Ua Tuathail to act as intermediary. The terms offered by Strongbow were a sign that he considered his position to be a weak one. For by becoming a vassal of Ruaidrí's in return for Leinster, Strongbow was essentially attempting to reinvent himself as an Irish lord. Perhaps Henry's assigning of an Irish identity to these Normans was not so hasty. Although becoming Ruaidrí's man was a retreat from Strongbow's ambition to be an independent and powerful prince, with it came one possible advantage for the lord of Strigoil: it would be more difficult for the English king to dispossess Strongbow of Leinster if that meant conflict with the high king of Ireland.

The archbishop of Dublin escorted Strongbow's envoy to the camp of Ruaidrí Ua Conchobair at Castleknock. The person chosen for this delicate task was Maurice de Prendergast. Having daringly manoeuvred between Diarmait Mac Murchada and Domnall Mac Gilla Pátraic of Osraige two years earlier, and having demonstrated sound council since accompanying Strongbow to Ireland, Maurice was entrusted with the vital mission of negotiating with the high king. This was a mission that also allowed Maurice to cast an eye over the military position, and he was not impressed by the lack of vigilance in the enemy camp.

All the strategic planning and willingness of Strongbow's council to compromise was set to naught by the outright refusal of Ruaidrí to accept the Norman as ruler of Leinster. It was not that the high king was being bloody-minded, he made in return a counter-offer through de Prendergast that, under the circumstances, seemed generous. Strongbow could hold the important ports of Waterford, Wexford and Dublin, as the Hiberno-Norse warriors had done. Given that Dublin was on the verge of starvation and Ruaidrí already had committed himself to supporting Muirchertach Mac Murchada as ruler of Leinster, this counter-offer was not intended to provoke the Normans, but it did.

Once more Strongbow's barons assembled and they listened carefully to the report of Maurice and the archbishop. As soon as it was clear that Ruaidrí would rather give battle than give away Leinster to the Norman lord, Strongbow stood up and all eyes were on him. When it came to formulating policy, Strongbow was cautious and took into account the opinions of a wide body of advisors. When it came to war no one could accuse him of being hesitant, for he was as resolute and determined as any of his Norman ancestors. Raising his voice to a shout, Strongbow began issuing instructions for battle. To answering cries of approval, the barons listened to their lord call out the marching order and the plan: a desperate all-or-nothing thrust right to the centre of Ruaidrí's camp.

Late in the afternoon, Strongbow's army assembled for the enterprise. The troops were divided into three equal divisions, each of forty knights, sixty archers, and a hundred footsoldiers. First to leave Dublin and commander of the vanguard was the favourite of the army and the most battle-hardened of the Norman knights, Miles de Cogan. Next, the stalwart Raymond Le Gros commanded the second division; Strongbow himself took charge of the third division. Once out of the town, the light cavalry of Strongbow's three Irish allies rode to the head of the army to accompany Miles in the van. They were few enough to brave the tens of thousands around them. Yet a bold sortie was better than slow starvation. Moreover, Maurice de Prendergast reported that the Irish armies had done little in regard to erecting defensive fortifications and that the only vigilant troops in the vicinity of the high king were those facing Dublin.

Marching swiftly, Miles reminded his men of how they had stormed Dublin, taking the city by surprise. Soon they were at Finglas, sufficiently far to the north of Ruaidrí's position that they had passed the vanguard of the Irish army and could strike at his flank.

With the rest of Strongbow's army close behind, Miles roused his troops with war cries: 'Cogan! The Cross! Jesus!' and fell upon the Irish troops at Castleknock, his men cutting through huts and shelters, sending a great many of the Irish warriors scattering across the moors in panic. Raymond Le Gros with his war cry of 'St David' entered battle next, to cause another wave of dismay and turmoil in the Irish ranks and to duel with those who dared stay to put up a fight.

Even though the initiative was with Strongbow's army, the vast numbers of their opponents meant that every Norman soldier had to play his part to maintain the momentum of the attack in order to keep the Irish warriors from regrouping. Strongbow himself fought hard in the midst of the melée. In the opinion of Gerald de Barri the most outstanding of the Norman knights that day — proving that the reputation he had won while fighting for Diarmait Mac Murchada was entirely deserved — was Meilyr fitz Henry, whose ferocity in the battle won the acclaim of all those who witnessed his deeds. With Meilyr were Gerald and Alexander, the two sons of Maurice fitz Gerald, fighting well in their first major experience of battle.

On and on battled Strongbow's army, breaking up every attempt at organised resistance, until they reached the banks of the Liffey. There, many of the leading Irish commanders, including Ruaidrí himself, had been bathing when they were shocked to hear sounds of battle envelop them. Over a hundred Irish warriors were shot or cut down before they could escape the incoming rush of attackers. Also with Ruaidrí was the bulk of the supplies for the Irish armies, which had been shipped along the river in such abundance that the captured wheat, flour, and bacon was sufficient to feed the garrison of Dublin for a year. But there was no stopping to gather the booty at this stage. For as long as the light held, the Normans and their few Irish allies chased and killed the routing army of the high king of Ireland.

This was the day that had been looming since the arrival of Strongbow on Irish shores: the day that Ruaidrí Ua Conchobair and the Norman lord tested their strength against each other to decide who was the most powerful figure in Ireland. And it was a disaster for the high king. With losses of over fifteen hundred on the Irish side and barely a footsoldier, let alone a knight, on Strongbow's side, it was a humiliation as well as a powerful blow against Ruaidrí's ability to rally other Irish princes to his banner. Everyone fled, whether they had been in the front line against the Norman attack or not. The high king had failed the test. Strongbow and the Normans were here to stay.

As a result of his extraordinary victory against all odds, a laurel wreath was made to put atop Strongbow's banner, a tradition established by the Romans, but there was no time to rest under these laurels. Bringing the captured booty back to the town, Strongbow reorganised his army and ordered his men to be ready to march at dawn towards Wexford for the attempted rescue of Robert fitz Stephen.

Leaving the army's champion, Miles de Cogan, in charge of Dublin once more, Strongbow left with the bulk of his army and his Irish allies. The high spirits of the troops, delighted with themselves for such a famous victory, lent energy to their step, while their cause, the rescue of their comrades, was deserving enough to encourage the soldiers to go without rest intervals. The swiftness of the army was impressive, but it led Strongbow into danger.

The north-west boundary of modern county Wexford is formed by the

White Mountain, the Blackstairs, the defile of Scollagh Gap and Mount Leinster, from whence flow the waters of the Slaney, which becomes the deep river that runs through Wexford town. There was no easy route through these mountains and as Strongbow's troops made their way up to Scollagh Gap they were ambushed. Ahead of his army was a barricade of fallen trees that made the already difficult terrain next to impassable, and from which the warriors of the Uí Dróna, led by their prince, Ua Riain, poured spears and darts into the Norman ranks. It was a brave enterprise by the lord of a modest force, to attempt to best an army that had defeated the high king of Ireland and his most powerful allies. Brave and skilful too, in that this encounter was much more suited to the Irish military strengths, those based on a high mobility and raiding, rather than the open field battles in which Norman knights could ride down their enemies with lances and in which the Norman crossbow could be used to full effect.

Ua Riain's efforts, however, were ultimately checked by the sheer numbers of his enemies. The prince of the Uí Dróna died in the ambush, shot by a monk called Nicholas, who, despite his habit, picked up a crossbow and fired with precision. Once more Meilyr fitz Henry rushed to where the fight was fiercest, although this time his bravery was nearly his undoing. A stone hurled from further up the mountain slope smashed into his head and threw him to the ground, stunned. Fortunately for Meilyr, his iron helmet and the proximity of his friends saved him from death. With the Uí Dróna dispersing rapidly after the death of Ua Riain, Strongbow's route was clear to Wexford. For many years after this battle, Scollagh Gap was known as the 'Earl's pass'.

As the Norman lord approached Wexford, his enemies fled and with them were the five knights captured from Robert fitz Stephen's fort. The Hiberno-Norse warriors of Wexford knew that they could not hold the walls of their town against Strongbow, and equally they knew what would be their fate if they stayed. So, taking their warships, they rowed across the estuary to Beggerin island: an island only in that the triangle of land has the Slaney estuary as a boundary to the south and two rivers to cross running northeast and northwest. The Hiberno-Norse knew that Strongbow could not follow them without the considerable effort of making river transports. As a final act of defiance, the warriors set fire to their own town before they left, making sure that those goods for which there was no room aboard the ships would not fall into Strongbow's hands.

Frustrated by his own lack of shipping, there was nothing more Strongbow could do for Robert fitz Stephen, despite the fact that there was only a short passage of water between them. Moreover, the Wexford army sent a message to Strongbow, to warn him that any attempt to reach Beggerin island would be met by the execution of Robert and his companions. All Strongbow would gain for his efforts would be the five heads of his comrades. So in frustration, the Norman lord turned his army back inland and made for Waterford.

With just the one setback — the capture of Robert fitz Stephen — Strongbow had come through the greatest crisis he had faced since coming to Ireland. He needed now to consolidate his position in Leinster before facing another storm: the arrival of the king of England.

Divide and Conquer

On arrival at Waterford, Strongbow was reunited with his uncle, Hervey de Montmorency, who had been sent to Henry's court in order to plead Strongbow's case and keep an eye on developments there. As with Hervey's mission to Diarmait Mac Murchada, the French adventurer made an excellent ambassador for Strongbow. Hervey's advice was for Strongbow to hurry to the king before Henry crossed the Irish Sea. While the king was furious with Strongbow's insubordination, he had not yet determined to strike Strongbow down, and the offer by Strongbow to yield all his gains to his rightful lord had been effective. Although still inclined to a volatile temper, if Strongbow came in person to Henry, the king's wrath might well be assuaged. It was advice that Strongbow thought prudent and he arranged a fast ship to take him to the royal court. Before he left the country, however, it was necessary to deal with the two key threats to have emerged with the death of Diarmait Mac Murchada.

Firstly, the successful takeover of the Uí Chennselaig by Muirchertach Mac Murchada represented a grave problem for Strongbow's ability to conquer more lands in Leinster and grant them to his vassals. Secondly, there was always a threat from Osraige: whenever Leinster was divided, the warriors of Osraige would raid and plunder. As the Uí Chennselaig and Osraige were such long-standing rivals, preventing them from working together was not too great a task and Strongbow was able to deal with them piecemeal.

Targeting Domnall Mac Gilla Pátraic of Osraige first, Strongbow marched from Waterford with his army. While the Normans came up on Osraige from the south east, Strongbow had also successfully negotiated for assistance from the south west. Domnall Mór Ua Briain, king of Thomond and ruler of Limerick, had been present with Ruaidrí Ua Conchobair at the siege of Dublin when Ruaidrí's strength had been broken. But Domnall was no loyal ally of Ruaidrí's, far from it. Having married Diarmait Mac Murchada's daughter Órlaith in 1168, Domnall had been quick to try and throw off his subordination to the high king and, with the help of Robert fitz Stephen's small army, had done so in 1170, for a few months at least. Now that Strongbow had bested Ruaidrí, the Norman lord was hopeful that Domnall could be encouraged to leave the side of the high king once more. In his sealed overtures to Domnall, Strongbow was helped considerably by the fact that his wife, Aífe, was Órlaith's sister.

It was the family connection that Ua Briain cited as he came with his army to assist Strongbow against Domnall Mac Gilla Pátraic of Osraige, and the two armies joined together as a force of around two thousand soldiers that the king of Osraige could not possibly stand against. Under the pretext of claiming that Domnall Mac Gilla Pátraic had betrayed Diarmait Mac Murchada, their intention was to depose the king and replace him with a weaker figure less likely to raid either Thomond or Strongbow's lands. Having learned from experience that Maurice de Prendergast was a knight who took his oaths seriously,

Domnall Mac Gilla Pátraic offered to surrender to Strongbow and face the accusations that he was a traitor, providing that Maurice would promise the king of Osraige safe conduct.

Maurice did not blame Domnall Mac Gilla Pátraic for the conspiracy of Osraige nobles that had sought to ambush the Flemish lord in 1169, and, indeed, was grateful for the warning he had received from the king's messenger. Without hesitation Maurice offered his services as an intermediary and he went to Strongbow to confirm the terms of Domnall's surrender.

'Maurice,' replied Strongbow, 'you have no need to be apprehensive. Bring the king to me: he can leave whenever he wishes.' This was all very well, but Maurice did not trust the belligerency of the other Norman barons and, before becoming Domnall Mac Gilla Pátraic's escort, Maurice went to each of them and obtained their personal oath that there would be no violence against the king of Osraige. With their promises in hand, Maurice rode to Domnall and brought him back to Strongbow's court.

There, the Normans put it to the king of Osraige that he had acted faithlessly towards Diarmait Mac Murchada. The most vocal critic and the person who most aggressively urged a shameful punishment upon Domnall Mac Gilla Pátraic was Strongbow's new Irish ally, Domnall Mór Ua Briain. The majority of Strongbow's councillors agreed with this. Thinking the council was going his way, Ua Briain sent his men to plunder Osraige and steal herds of cattle. Maurice de Prendergast, however, considered this a breach of the surrender agreement he had vouched for personally. At once, he rallied his men to arms, and it is testament to their extraordinary faith in their lord and pride in his honour that the seven knights and two hundred footsoldiers who had twice journeyed with Maurice from Wales to Ireland now took up the cause of Domnall Mac Gilla Pátraic in the face of their compatriots.

'Barons,' shouted Maurice, 'What are you thinking of? You have broken your word to me and have perjured yourselves!' He threatened to split open the head of anyone who dared lay a hand upon the king of Osraige. This impressive defence of his own honour accorded with Strongbow's thinking.

Having cowed Domnall Mac Gilla Pátraic and accepted his submission, there was no need to jeopardise all future dealings with Osraige by breaking the surrender agreement. Instead, Strongbow handed over the king of Osraige to Maurice, who marched away with his followers to return Domnall to safety. En route they encountered Ua Briain and his Munster troops. A skirmish ensued, in which nine or ten of the Uí Briain were killed and some of the stolen cattle returned to Osraige.

Having fulfilled his oath, Maurice returned to Strongbow to find a raging Ua Briain and many of the Norman barons accusing him of disloyalty. In a gesture that showed his willingness to take the trial by combat against his accusers, Maurice folded over his gauntlet and gave it to Strongbow. Immediately, those Norman barons who admired Maurice's integrity stepped forward to act as surety for the Flemish lord. His council was divided, but Strongbow was quick to avoid any further escalation of the conflict. Heaping praise and gifts on his Irish ally, Strongbow bid farewell to the Irish army of north Munster and turned eastwards, to Ferns.

Occupying Diarmait Mac Murchada's former residence for eight days, Strongbow's troops rode out in search of Murchad Ua Brain, whom they quickly found and brought back in chains. Murchad was joined as a prisoner by one of his sons, brought in by Domnall Cáemánach Mac Murchada. Back in 1166, when Diarmait was forced into exile, one of the deepest wounds he received, politically speaking, was the defection of Murchad Ua Brain and his son Dalbach. The Uí Brain (not to be confused with the Uí Briain of Munster) had been promoted by Diarmait to act as lords of the strategic pass through the Blackstairs mountains into Uí Chennselaig territories. It was in order to force Murchad into acknowledging his obligations that Diarmait had famously disguised himself as a monk. Both Murchad and his son were shown no mercy, not least because they were hated by Strongbow's staunch Irish ally, Domnall Cáemánach, for their betrayal of his father. Side by side, Murchad and his son were executed by the axe, with the headless corpses thrown by the wayside for the dogs of Ferns to worry over.

Strongbow then turned his attention to Muirchertach Mac Murchada, but here a much less brutal approach was called for. Muirchertach, like his father, had been a bitter opponent of his uncle Diarmait Mac Murchada and had been quick to seize power in Uí Chennselaig on Diarmait's death. But Muirchertach had not carried his opposition towards the former king as far as to cause civil war. More importantly, Muirchertach had a large body of followers whom Strongbow wished to integrate into his dominion. Negotiations were instigated; three-sided negotiations, for if Strongbow was to come to an agreement with Muirchertach, it also had to be one that was acceptable to Domnall Cáemánach, whom the Norman lord could not afford to alienate.

The three factions found that, despite the tension between them, there was room for agreement. Strongbow would confirm Muirchertach as ruler of the Uí Chennselaig and Domnall would not attempt to unseat him. Nor would Strongbow supplant the Uí Chennselaig aristocracy by capturing their lands and reassigning them to his barons, as he was doing elsewhere in Leinster. In return, Muirchertach would recognise Strongbow as his overlord in the traditional Irish manner, by the surrender of hostages, and assist the Norman lord with military service. For Domnall, a new position was created, that of a kind of chief justice for all Irish people in Strongbow's dominion. Both Domnall and Muirchertach were considered of equal status and they accepted the arrangement in good faith. So long as Strongbow was alive, the Uí Chennselaig remained united and honoured their pact with him. Equally, their lands were safe from the predatory ambition of Norman lords.

With his diplomacy a success and the most dangerous threats to his rule of Leinster neutralised, Strongbow turned his full attention to the imminent arrival of Henry. The repeated missions of Strongbow's most important barons to the royal court with fair words and an insistence that all Strongbow's conquests were in Henry's name had softened the anger of the king. As Hervey de Montmorency had urged, however, it would take Strongbow's appearance in person to satisfy Henry that the lord of Strigoil was sincere in this. A messenger from the court arrived at Waterford with a summons. Strongbow was to come at once, without delay, demur, respite or postponement. It was well for Strongbow that he had acted so swiftly in dealing with Muirchertach and Domnall Mac Gilla Pátraic, for he was free now to return across the Irish Sea and brave a very different kind of danger to the military crises he had so successfully weathered in Ireland.

CHAPTER 7

King Henry II in Ireland

In the autumn of 1171 Strongbow left Ireland and, with the exception of Miles de Cogan who was given responsibility for governing Dublin and Gilbert de Boisrohard who was in charge of Waterford, brought all his closest supporters with him. He landed in Wales to find that King Henry was already in Pembroke with a large army and a fleet that was loading supplies. The king of England was within days of being ready for departure.

On being presented to the royal party, Strongbow and his barons were suitably deferential. They greeted the king in the name of Christ and called for God's blessings upon Henry. As with all who came before the king, there was never the slightest hint from their demeanour that Henry might be anything less than a model Christian ruler; this despite the fact that the king was, in effect, fleeing the possibility of an encounter with a papal legate and excommunication for the murder of Beckett.

In response to the figures kneeling before him, Henry — outwardly at least — greeted his wayward vassal pleasantly and betrayed no resentment. Inwardly, however, the king was still furious with Strongbow's disobedience and he had sounded out a number of courtiers about their willingness to become lords in Ireland and get a grip on the situation there. The most notable of the king's barons in this regard was Hugh de Lacy. Holding the lordship of Weobley, Herefordshire, on the Welsh border, de Lacy was an important tenant of the crown and his other lands, hereditary fees at Lassy and Campeaux, and a purchased honour in Le Pin-au-Haras, Argentan, made him a powerful figure on the frontiers of Normandy. In 1166, the annual military service owed by de Lacy to the crown was that of just over fifty knights. Having played a leading role at the crucial royal council at Argentan, in July 1171, de Lacy had come in full strength to join Henry on the expedition to Ireland.

While Strongbow was attending court and offering council to Henry on the state of affairs in Ireland, a delegation from the Hiberno-Norse people of Wexford arrived at Pembroke. Strongbow had last seen these men rowing away from him across the Slaney with the chained Robert fitz Stephen in one of their boats. Well informed about English affairs, the Hiberno-Norse warriors hoped to avoid the fate of Waterford and Dublin by going over Strongbow's head and appealing to the king of England. Twelve ambassadors walked into the great hall at Pembroke, hailing the king in the name of God the Almighty Father. Henry responded graciously and, the obligatory rituals of politeness out of the way, listened carefully to what these men of Wexford had to say.

'We have captured a man who is a traitor to you,' said the spokesperson for the delegation, 'Robert fitz Stephen is his name. He deceived you in the past and often committed great evil and treachery. He has often made war on you in Wales and in England. He came to Ireland with a fleet to deliver us to slaughter. He intends to lay waste our country and has repeatedly driven us from bad to worse. We have captured him in a castle and have placed him in a secure prison. We shall give him up to you, noble king.'

If the purpose of the mission was to ingratiate themselves with Henry, it appeared to have worked. After all, when Robert had been freed from prison by Rhys ap Gruffudd, he must surely have broken oaths made to the king of

England? To all appearances the king was furious with Robert, for he put on a display of rage towards the captured knight and of gratitude to the Wexford people, in taking captive this royal enemy. The men of Wexford returned to their ships, pleased that they had performed a service for the king of England and more confident for their future. Henry, however, was dissembling. He knew perfectly well that Robert had refused to turn traitor while in the prisons of the Welsh prince. Moreover, back in 1157, Robert had saved Henry's life during the unfortunate royal expedition against the Welsh. Whereas Henry had done nothing for Robert when his captor was a Welsh prince whom the king was cultivating as an ally, the Hiberno-Norse warriors of Wexford were a minor power whom the king could roll over when it proved necessary. For now, though, Henry wanted to keep Robert alive and he acted the part of the grateful monarch extremely well. There was no danger that the citizens of Wexford would put Robert under the axe while they thought they could use their prisoner to gain favour from Strongbow's liege lord.

With the Wexford issue dealt with, Strongbow and the king returned to their own affairs and, in particular, an attempt to reach an understanding on how to proceed in Ireland. This was no easy matter, but Hervey de Montmorency knew how to deal with court intrigues. With a quiet word in the right ear, with public displays of obedience by Strongbow, and, above all, with substantial concessions to the crown of conquered towns and lands, the king's anger subsided. The price of appeasing Henry, however, was a heavy one from Strongbow's point of view. Dublin, Waterford, Wexford and all the ports and castles, along with the land adjacent to Dublin, were all given to the crown. This left Strongbow and his followers the inland territories of Leinster, much of which had yet to be taken. In addition, all Normans with land in Ireland had to acknowledge that the king of England was their overlord and that they owed him service.

Was there any better settlement open to Strongbow? A number of courtiers were willing to adhere to the important principle that a knight ought to have the right to retain the land he had won by the sword. It was a fundamental tenet of the Norman world view. But so too was the belief that a vassal who owed their position to a lord should not disobey him, and this Strongbow had violated. If Strongbow nursed any bitterness towards the king, that royal authority now controlled the richest pickings of the region, he did well to hide it. After all, he could comfort himself with the thought that his lands in Leinster already made him a far greater figure than he had been at Chepstow. Moreover, there was potential for even more valuable gains to be made in Ireland.

Battles and Submissions

Satisfied with his new sources of income arising from Strongbow's acceptance of the royal demands, and armed with a secret plan to curtail the danger of Strongbow becoming the effective high king of Ireland, Henry ordered his army to prepare for departure as soon as the winds were favourable. For two weeks, however, the weather swept eastwards from the Irish Sea. Not that the wait was an idle interlude. Henry demanded that the local castellans come to meet him and when they did, Henry vented his — half-simulated — fury upon them that they had not only allowed Strongbow to embark on his adventure, but they had allowed knights and footsoldiers to leave for Strongbow's army. Many a minor marcher lord found himself having to accept the presence of a royal governor in his castle to assuage the royal temper. Once again Henry's wrath had served him well.

With fair weather at last, the royal army embarked on four hundred ships gathered at what is now Pembroke Dock at Milford Haven and made the crossing safely to Crook, near Waterford. On 17 October 1171, for the first time in history, an English king set foot on Irish soil. With the king of England was an army that in Irish terms was immensely powerful: five hundred knights and four thousand footsoldiers and archers. While the king was in Ireland he was supported by the merchants of Bristol, who brought across the Irish Sea not only large quantities of wheat, oats, beans, cheese and hogs, but also the engineering equipment needed for the construction of castles: axes, spades, shovels, pickaxes, planks, nails and timber.

It was late in the year for military activity, but news reached Waterford of a battle that had taken place while the king had been waiting for fair weather to depart Wales. Taking advantage of the absence of Strongbow, Tigernán Ua Ruairc had urged his neighbouring princes to unite and demonstrate that they did not need the high king to drive the foreigners out of Ireland. Tigernán's old ally, Murchad Ua Cerbaill, lord of Airgialla, responded to the call, as did Domnall Bregach Ua Máel Sechlainn, the ruler of East Meath who had previously fought alongside Strongbow and Diarmait Mac Murchada against Ua Ruairc in order to gain power, but who now sought to weaken the Normans before they became a threat to him.

As this allied Irish army approached Dublin, Miles de Cogan decided to lead his small force out of the town and utilise the tactical skills that the Normans had with their heavy cavalry. Miles's troops would follow him anywhere, but soon after the initial clash, it was the Normans who turned and made haste back to the protection of the town walls. Whether feigned or genuine, the Normans were masters at regrouping their fleeing riders and turning on a pursuing enemy. They practised the tactic intensively and employed it with decisive effect at some of the major battles of the era including that of Hastings in 1066. Now, with the Irish troops spreading out to chase the Norman riders who had not managed to re-enter the town, Miles and his men charged out of the city once more, directly towards the banners of Tigernán Ua Ruairc.

On the green of Ath-cliath, the cream of the Irish aristocratic fighting forces once more attempted to withstand an assault by the heavily armoured Normans and once more they failed. This time, the test of arms was much fairer than when Ruaidrí Ua Conchobair was caught off guard by the unexpected sortie of the Normans. Now the Irish princes stood with their companions in well ordered ranks and fought hard, but to no avail. Despite their significant advantage in numbers, the losses on the Irish side mounted far more rapidly than those among Miles's men. And when Aed Manach Ua Ruairc (Tigernán's own son and heir-designate) was cut down, the allies broke. In the ensuing slaughter, many noteworthy leaders of the Airgialla fell too.

The battle was another extraordinary victory for Miles de Cogan. If the Norman garrison of Dublin could successfully fight pitched battles against Viking and Irish armies with relatively few troops, how much more intimidating was the arrival of the king of England? No Irish lord even thought of conducting warfare against Henry, especially not when there was political advantage to be obtained by diplomatic means. It was obvious that Henry would not stay for any length of time in Ireland, but in the months that he was present, the Irish princes sought to submit to him: not simply to avoid being subject to an attack they could not withstand, but also to shake off their obligations to Ruaidrí Ua Conchobair and to obtain the king's protection from Strongbow and other Norman adventurers.

First to Waterford were the representatives of the Hiberno-Norse from Wexford. As agreed, they brought with them their captive Robert fitz Stephen. Filthy and in chains, fitz Stephen was harangued by the king for all to see. Henry then repeated the claims of the Wexford people: that fitz Stephen had acted treacherously against the interests of his rightful lord, the king of England. In reply, Robert folded his glove and handed it to Henry. Anyone willing to bring such charges against him would have to face Robert in a duel. Immediately, cries came from the large gathering of Normans, Flemings and French knights, that they would stand surety for Robert. At this point, it may have begun to dawn on the Hiberno-Norse delegation that, instead of being cast into a dark dungeon, Robert was likely to return to haunt them again. For the mood at the royal court was entirely on Robert's side. For the moment, however, Henry acted as though unconvinced and had fitz Stephen placed in Reginald's tower, ostentatiously chained to a companion.

Soon after this incident, Diarmait Mac Carthaig, king of Desmond, hurried to greet the king of England. In the Irish fashion Diarmait swore loyalty to Henry and offered hostages, but in the Norman fashion, he was met in response with an assessment of an annual tribute imposed upon him. As far as the head of a Norman feudal structure was concerned submissions were meaningless, even with hostages, unless there was an obligation by the vassal to provide military service or financial recompense in its stead. Mac Carthaig agreed to Henry's terms, but, as was the pattern generally with those in Ireland who became Henry's vassals, royal officials in years to come would have great difficulty in obtaining the tribute.

Having spent fifteen days in Waterford, collecting reports and hearing the messages sent by various Irish lords, Henry marched his army around the south of Ireland, via a circuitous route designed to allow him to obtain the submission of more of the Irish princes. In place of Strongbow's councillor, Gilbert de Boisrohard, Henry put his own man in charge of Waterford — Robert fitz Bernard — and moved to Lismore for two days. Decreeing that a castle should be built at Lismore, although not actually staying long enough to begin work on one, the king then moved to Cashel. The following day, on the banks of the Suir, the king met Domnall Mór Ua Briain, Strongbow's brother-in-law, the king of Thomond and ruler of Limerick. Again, Henry attempted to tie the Irish prince into his method of government, with strict oaths and another assessment of tribute.

Two other princes submitted to the king of England at this time: Domnall Mac Gilla Pátraic of Osraige and Máel Sechnaill Ua Fáeláin. Both took gifts from Henry in return for their obedience. Strongbow and his men had accompanied Henry every step of the way and had watched patiently as one after the other of the local Irish lords had transferred their submissions from the lord of Leinster to the king of England. In particular, Strongbow was obliged to witness two of his most powerful local rivals escaping his authority and instead swearing oaths to Henry. Did Domnall Mac Gilla Pátraic break into a smile as he left Henry's presence? After all, the king of England would not stay in Ireland long and that would leave Domnall with much greater independence than he had when either Ruaidrí Ua Conchobair or Strongbow was his acknowledged superior.

Throughout the royal visit, Strongbow accompanied the king with every evidence of good will. After all, he too was planning on Henry's imminent departure. At which point, the struggle to decide who would be the master of Ireland could resume. Unknown to Strongbow, however, an agreement between Henry and Hugh de Lacy, which had been conceived long ago, would soon be revealed.

Having obtained the most important Irish princes of the southeast as vassals, Henry returned briefly to Waterford. There, to popular acclaim, Robert fitz Stephen was released from prison and all accusations against him dropped. Although Robert was a free man again, his ambition to be lord of Wexford and its hinterland was curtailed, at least for the moment. The Hiberno-Norse now considered Henry their protector and overlord, while, at the same time, the king had managed to get Robert out of their hands safely and set the brave knight on his feet again. The king set out with his army once more with the intention of celebrating Christmas in Dublin.

Settling in Dublin, on 11 November 1171, in a temporary post-and-wattle palace built in the manner of local custom, Henry obtained the submission of a steady stream of Irish lords, great and small. All hoped that royal protection would allow them to remain on their lands in the face of predatory Norman lords. The most significant arrival in Dublin, to honour the king of England, was the grizzled, one-eyed warrior, Tigernán Ua Ruairc. It must have been a difficult moment for the old enemy of Diarmait Mac Murchada to walk through the assembled court, past those such as Miles de Cogan, who had fought against him and worse, had killed his eldest son only a few weeks earlier. Politics in medieval Ireland was an unsentimental business, however, and Ua Ruairc had made more drastic alterations to his allegiances in the past. This was one more pragmatic retreat. And Tigernán bent the knee as did all the princes within striking distance of Henry's mighty army.

For Ruaidrí Ua Conchobair there was no compulsion to come to Dublin: in part because it was a considerable distance away and in part because the high king of Ireland could still mobilise a force to be reckoned with. Despite his ambition in that direction, Henry could not impose vassalage on Ruaidrí.

But the king of England did send Hugh de Lacy and William fitz Adelin to the Shannon as emissaries. In response to their mission, Ruaidrí stated that he was not going to submit to Henry and he declared that the whole of Ireland was rightfully his and all the other kings of the land should be placed under his authority. The report of Hugh de Lacy on his return to Dublin angered Henry, and an expedition to Connacht was proposed for the spring of 1172. It might well have taken place but for a massive revolt against Henry that caused him to hurry away from Ireland.

First, though, the king of England celebrated Christmas 1171 in style. All his new Irish vassals were invited and those that attended were treated to an ostentatious display of Henry's wealth, with a sumptuous and plentiful feast. One of the dishes was crane, which the Irish had formerly loathed, but which they now obediently enjoyed. In part, this feast was intended to deceive the Irish participants. Although Henry's merchants were busy plying the Irish Sea, the great size of his army strained the resources of the eastern part of Ireland. Food prices began to rise. The king could not stay in Dublin indefinitely.

The Death of Tigernán Ua Ruairc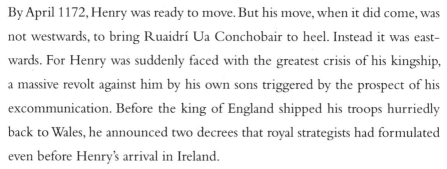

By April 1172, Henry was ready to move. But his move, when it did come, was not westwards, to bring Ruaidrí Ua Conchobair to heel. Instead it was eastwards. For Henry was suddenly faced with the greatest crisis of his kingship, a massive revolt against him by his own sons triggered by the prospect of his excommunication. Before the king of England shipped his troops hurriedly back to Wales, he announced two decrees that royal strategists had formulated even before Henry's arrival in Ireland.

Firstly, Dublin was to be governed by the ever-loyal city of Bristol, and those living in the Irish capital would have all the liberties and free customs they had at Bristol. By encouraging people from Bristol to settle in Dublin, Henry would be making up for the losses in population that had occurred with the driving out of the Hiberno-Norse leaders. Enough of the Hiberno-

Norse people remained, however, that they were considered a potential enemy within. They were forced to move to residences outside the defences of the town on the north side of the Liffey (modern-day Oxmantown, derived from the term Ostmen for these people).

Secondly, Hugh de Lacy was to be lord of Meath and constable of the Dublin garrison. Meath, by this time, was a highly fractured province, not least due to the persistent and largely successful efforts of Ruaidrí Ua Conchobair and Tigernán Ua Ruairc to divide it between east and west. Tigernán had such dominance in the province that Gerald de Barri considered him 'king of Meath'. So to clarify the nature of his grant, Henry had it stated that de Lacy, in return for the service of fifty knights, was to be lord of the province as it had been twenty years earlier. In other words, this appointment was a direct challenge to Tigernán Ua Ruairc and to Domnall Bregach Ua Máel Sechlainn, ruler of East Meath, but it was also an indirect challenge to Strongbow. It was the king's intention that, after his departure, the most powerful Norman leader in Ireland would be his favoured figure of de Lacy and not the insubordinate Strongbow. It was a clever balancing device; de Lacy was not so powerful that he could swallow up the weaker lordships and become a potential king of Ireland. But de Lacy was a firm barrier to the possibility that Strongbow would extend his lordship northwards. These decrees demonstrate how well informed Henry was about Irish politics and, of course, how very accomplished he was at controlling his ambitious barons.

Henry made his future constable, Humphrey (III) de Bohun governor of Waterford and the less exalted Philip de Briouze governor of Wexford. The king also set up a crude administrative structure for all his interests in Ireland, which, although poorly resourced, did begin the work of creating a centralised tax and legal system. Then, taking Strongbow's two best military commanders with him, Miles de Cogan and Raymond Le Gros, the king of England left Ireland. The political landscape of the country, recently so dominated by might of the royal army, was suddenly clear once more. Could those Irish lords who had bent the knee to Henry now get on with their rivalries and manoeuvres as if he had never been to Ireland?

One person who certainly thought so was Tigernán Ua Ruairc. The elderly ruler of Bréifne was intrigued by the possibility of exploiting divisions between Hugh de Lacy and Strongbow. Equally, the old war-dog was anxious about de Lacy's ambitions in Meath. An arrangement was needed to partition the province between them. So when de Lacy asked to meet with Tigernán, the one-eyed warlord willingly agreed. At the Hill of Tlachtgha (modern-day Hill of Ward, near Athboy) in Meath, the Norman and Irish lords rode towards one another to meet in conference, each with a sizeable force. At first the two armies kept out of bowshot range, with horsemen riding back and forth between them. Then, with oaths having been given on either side, Ua Ruairc and his bodyguard walked their horses forward with the intention of beginning the parley in earnest.

Once Tigernán had travelled far enough from his troops that they could not easily aid him, a group of seven Norman knights who had been pretending to be engaged in jousting practice formed up and charged. These youths were the sons of the first Norman lords to come to Ireland. They were led by Ralph, son of the recently released Robert fitz Stephen, and Griffin, a nephew of Robert's and nephew also of Maurice fitz Gerald. At the unexpected sight of this attack, Ua Ruairc turned to escape and raise the alarm with his army, but here he was met with treachery, for Domnall, son of Annad Ua Ruairc, thought the time had come when the veteran leader of Bréifne should make room for a new prince from a different faction within the dynasty. Far from assisting Tigernán, Domnall's warriors attacked him also.

It was the Norman lances that reached their target first and Tigernán fell to the ground, mortally wounded. Whatever his feelings of rage against the Norman traitors they would have been matched by fury against those of the Uí Ruairc who had turned against him. But such emotions were his last; his life was over. The man who had driven Diarmait to flee to seek aid from the Normans had reaped the whirlwind he had sown.

When Gerald de Barri came to write about the death of Tigernán, he had a problem. Having spent valuable ink and having used his powers of composition to the full in order to condemn the Irish for their treacherous habits, Gerald found it painful to acknowledge that his Norman relatives were capable of equally dishonourable deeds. Gerald did his best to turn the young Normans into heroes by rather implausibly claiming it was Tigernán who made the first gesture of attack.

The aftermath of this ambush was humiliating to the entire aristocracy of Ireland. Tigernán had been one of the greatest Irish princes of his era. His finest moment had come with the invasion of Tír Eógain in 1166. Against all the odds, Tigernán, in alliance with Donnchad Ua Cerbaill of the Airgialla, had killed the mighty high king Mac Lochlainn and in doing so completely transformed the political situation in Ireland at the time. From 1166, it was Connacht and Ua Ruairc who were dominant. Thereafter, Tigernán had the upper hand in his old rivalry with Diarmait Mac Murchada, at least until Diarmait escaped Ireland to return with the Normans. Even if Tigernán had never quite recovered his reputation after his wife had eloped with Diarmait, the ruler of Bréifne had succeeded in savaging the regions all around. People spoke of his violence, but always with a sense of respect for his power.

All power and honour left Tigernán with his last breath. The Normans had control of his body and they used that fact to send a message to every Irish prince. First they beheaded the corpse. Then the head was hung over the gates of the fortress in Dublin, 'a sore and miserable sight for the Irish', said one contemporary annalist. The torso was hung upside down elsewhere, at the north side of a place called Cell na Truan. The sorry remains of 'Erin's raider and invader' were a grim symbol of the triumph of a new order.

Strongbow in Normandy

In the summer of 1172, with an increase in the number of Norman lords in Ireland and with Henry's declaration of protection for his new vassals evidently worthless, the Irish aristocracy must all have had an anxious foreboding that Tigernán's fate might be their own. After 1066, the Normans had usurped almost all of England. The new lords from northern France had driven off the Saxon aristocracy and given themselves the means to dominate the local peasantry by erecting a dense network of castles. Ireland, a hundred years later, seemed destined to experience the same fate. Both Strongbow and de Lacy were rapidly 'sub-infeudating' those territories under their control. In other words, their own large fiefs held from Henry were now parcelled up and given to barons who in turn gave even smaller units of land to their knights. Each knight built a castle to reside in, either mottes or ringworks with wooden defences and buildings, and, having freed the Irish slaves but also having enserfed former free farmers, had begun to introduce new social relations and new farming methods.

Although Strongbow was careful to honour his oath to the Uí Chennselaig leaders and, in particular, to his brother-in-law Domnall Cáemánach, he was not so scrupulous with the minor lords of Leinster and beyond. One Irish prince who had persistently defied Strongbow's rule was Diarmait Ua Dímmussaig, prince of Uí Failge. Once kings of Leinster themselves, Uí Failge had thrown off submission to Diarmait Mac Murchada at every opportunity and were never going to accept the Norman lord as their master unless they were forced to do so. From a base at Kildare, therefore, Strongbow conducted raids through Uí Failge territory (parts of Offaly and Laois). But Diarmait Ua Dímmussaig was elusive and kept the better part of his army away from open-field encounters. Only when Strongbow was returning towards Kildare with a considerable baggage train of booty and herds of stolen cattle did Diarmait Ua Dímmussaig risk making an appearance.

Leading an army with a thousand soldiers, Strongbow was easily capable of facing any serious challenge from the front. But, skillfully utilising the Irish warrior's advantage in speed of movement, the Uí Failge swept in upon the Norman rearguard, stabbed and slashed their way through to the cattle, and hurriedly left the field before Strongbow and the vanguard could turn back and reach the battle. It was a devastating counter-raid and, in its wake, dozens of Norman soldiers lay dead, including Robert de Quency, the bearer of Strongbow's banner.

It had been Strongbow's intention to make de Quency his constable. This was the title of the office of commander of all Strongbow's forces in Ireland. The constable would take charge of these troops should Strongbow be needed elsewhere. Giving Robert his natural daughter to marry, the ceremony taking place in 1172, Strongbow also elevated de Quency by granting him Duffry, the territory that had formerly belonged to Murchad Ua Brain (the Irish lord who had betrayed Diarmait and whose body had been fed to the dogs of Ferns). It was therefore a major blow against Strongbow's rule when Uí Failge cut down Robert de Quency in 1173. The constable did not die childless, however, as a daughter Maud had been born to him only a few weeks earlier.

The question then was: who would act as regent for Maud's lands? And this question proved to be a very divisive one. One of the most effective of Strongbow's barons was Raymond Le Gros. Only Miles de Cogan could point to a better record in battle and Raymond's feat in holding Baginbun against the Hiberno-Norse fighters of Waterford had secured the foothold that Strongbow needed for his arrival in strength in Ireland. Recently taken from Ireland to fulfil his obligations to Henry II, Raymond had served his forty days and was free to rejoin the Normans in Ireland. It seemed only right that the important position of constable of Strongbow's troops should belong to Raymond, by right of his success in battle and by the popularity with which he was held. Therefore, the stout warrior asked for the hand of Strongbow's sister, Basilia, and the regency of the constable's office. Strongbow, however, demurred.

The new ruler of Leinster had other followers to whom he felt more obliged than to Raymond. In particular, his uncle, the French adventurer, Hervey, had been invaluable to Strongbow. True, Raymond had played a crucial role in battle against the Hiberno-Norse and the Irish, but Hervey had been active in the court of Diarmait Mac Murchada on Strongbow's behalf. Even more importantly, Hervey's diplomatic skills had helped Strongbow appease King

Henry, and that was just as important an achievement as the victory at Baginbun. Thus Strongbow gave the regency to Hervey.

Disgusted with this decision and frustrated by so little reward for so great an achievement as the conquest of Leinster, Raymond and his troops journeyed to Carew Castle, near Pembroke in Wales. There, Raymond's father, William fitz Gerald, was failing and it was Raymond who stood to inherit the lordship of Carew. Elevated by the prospect of this inheritance, Raymond no longer needed Strongbow's assistance to make his mark as a lord: he had gained the confidence both to demand a position commensurate with his new status and to storm off when that demand was refused. Not that Raymond was washing his hands of Ireland, far from it. His supporters in Strongbow's army began an agitation against Hervey, while Basilia made it clear that, but for Strongbow, she would gladly be Raymond's wife.

Almost as soon as he was appointed constable, Hervey was called upon to take command of Strongbow's army. For in the spring of 1173 Strongbow was summoned from Ireland to assist King Henry in Normandy. The king of England was making full use of the military service owed to him by his newly created Irish-Norman vassals in his desperate struggle with his sons, their English and French supporters, and with King Louis VII of France. Royal garrisons at Waterford and Dublin were stripped down to a skeleton force. Hard pressed, Henry was genuinely pleased to see Strongbow when the latter honoured their recent agreement in both spirit and letter, arriving in Normandy with his best knights. A testament to the trust the king now had in the de Clare lord, who had been out of favour for decades, was that Strongbow was asked to hold the strategic city of Gisors, while Henry marched west. Gisors is in the Vexin region of Normandy at the confluence of the Epte, Réveillon and Troesne. The city controlled one of the vital crossing points for a possible incursion from Paris by the king of France.

Louis did, in fact, try to invade Normandy in July 1173, but he struck north-east for Verneuil. There the French king met resistance from another Norman whose fortune now lay in Ireland: Hugh de Lacy. Hurriedly, the king of England rushed to relieve the siege of Verneuil and, on the way, he effected a junction with Strongbow. The lord of Leinster found himself in the curious situation that he was rushing to the aid of his great Meath rival. Tricked by the French king breaking a truce, Hugh had lost control of the streets of Verneuil, but he still hung on in the citadel, and Louis could not risk staying in the city and being caught between Hugh and the army of King Henry. So the French king set fire to the town before withdrawing to his own territories.

What these events in France meant for Ireland was primarily a weakening of the Norman forces on the island as, again and again, Henry called for reinforcements; they also led to the effective consolidation of Strongbow's position as the effective ruler of all of Leinster. For, impressed by Strongbow's demonstration of loyalty at a time when his supposedly faithful courtiers were abandoning him in large numbers, Henry made Strongbow commander of the troops of Waterford and Dublin (the towns themselves still being governed by merchants from Bristol under royal charter) and he awarded Strongbow the town of Wexford, along with the coastal areas from Waterford to Dublin and Wicklow Castle. In 1171, Strongbow's life and fortune had balanced on a knife edge. With almost no margin for error, he had to face down resistance to his rule from Irish lords, while risking punishment from the wrath of an angry king of England. Two years later he was clear of danger, at least from Henry.

Not that Strongbow's problems were over; they were merely lessened. For his first task on return to Ireland was to order all the remaining royal forces in Waterford, Dublin and Wexford to hurry to join Henry, and with them went several of Strongbow's own key barons, including Maurice de Prendergast and Robert fitz Stephen. It was well for the king of England that such a competent and strategic-minded commander as Maurice was with these troops, for on arrival in England they were faced with a shocking new development: the earl of Leicester and the earl of Norfolk had risen up in rebellion against Henry. Rather than follow the king's original instructions and continue on to Normandy, Maurice and Robert decided the Irish army would better serve Henry by deploying against the two rebels in England. A rapid march brought Robert fitz Stephen and Maurice to East Anglia where they joined a royal army that was enormously relieved to obtain such an unexpected accretion of strength. Although outnumbered four to one, this united army had the enthusiasm and confidence to face the forces of the two earls. In October 1173, a major battle took place at Fornham, Bury St Edmunds, and it was a stunning victory for Henry's men. The earl of Leicester was captured and the role of the Irish-based Normans was noted by contemporaries, who saw the victory as having occurred, 'through help brought from Leinster, and through the strength of the Irish.'

Soon after this battle, when the king of Scotland, William I 'The Lion', crossed over the border to take advantage of Henry's troubles, the enterprising Maurice and Robert did not hesitate but hurried north with the royal army. Again their daring and initiative brought dramatic results, as early in 1174 they captured William. Much to his astonishment, when Henry crossed the Channel to try his best to cope with what he imagined was a major crisis for his rule, he found all was in hand. It was the newly created Leinster lord, Maurice de Prendergast, along with Robert fitz Stephen, the knight that Henry had freed from the Hiberno-Norse people of Wexford, to whom he most owed this extraordinary turn in his fortunes.

The Return of Raymond Le Gros

Back in Ireland, the fact that Strongbow had reoriented himself to be a loyal royalist led to the emergence of an entirely new set of problems. Up until 1171 Strongbow had been the leader of those Norman and Welsh soldiers who were willing to risk the wrath of King Henry for the sake of gaining lands in Ireland. Now, instead of acting as a rallying centre for the interest of these troops and defying royal authority if necessary, Strongbow (along with Hugh de Lacy) had become the voice of Henry in Ireland. The poacher had become gamekeeper and immediately this led to Strongbow having to face a revolt from within his own ranks. Given that nearly all Henry's men had been withdrawn to assist the king stamp out the fires of rebellion that burned all the way from Scotland to Aquitaine, the Norman knights and footsoldiers that remained in Ireland were those adventurers with the least ties to the English crown. A policy of peace was of no use to them, yet peace in Ireland suited Henry at this time, and it suited Strongbow. Why risk arousing resistance from the demoralised Irish princes and their high king? However, just as Maurice de Prendergast had found himself frustrated by Diarmait Mac Murchada's refusal to assign him new land, so too did Strongbow's restless army begin to agitate for war. This took the form of demanding the removal of the acting constable, Hervey de Montmorency.

In the autumn of 1173 a mutiny took place. Strongbow's troops insisted that Raymond Le Gros be reinstated as their commander, so that they could be led successfully to plunder and conquer Irish-held lands. If this demand were refused, the soldiers claimed, they would desert Strongbow, or even – as Maurice de Prendergast had done in the face of opposition from Diarmait Mac Murchada – desert to the enemy. This was a threat that Strongbow had to take seriously, especially given the absence of a great number of his closest barons. With apologies to Hervey, who was compensated with Uí Bairrche on the sea (modern-day Bargy and Shelburne on the south coast of County Wexford), Strongbow sent a messenger to Raymond to come to Ireland at once. In the message, Strongbow indicated that he was now willing to allow Raymond to marry Basilia. Well informed and prepared for such news from Ireland, Raymond took sail at once and promptly arrived at Waterford.

There, Strongbow greeted Raymond warmly enough and the tensions arising from the insubordinate behaviour of his own army were dissipated for the time being. For Basilia, this was a heaven-sent moment. As sister to Strongbow she was little more than a pawn, to be played when her brother found it expedient. As such, she had spent decades with little opportunity to exercise her desire to take a lead in political affairs. By becoming Lady of Cardew and wife of the Constable of Leinster, however, she received a significant promotion. Not quite a queen, she would be the most powerful woman in Leinster after

Aífe, daughter of Mac Murchada. Basilia's enthusiasm for the marriage ensured that negotiations between Strongbow and Raymond ran smoothly and it was agreed that the ceremony would take place once a shortage of resources had been dealt with.

With these matters settled, it was time to address the demands of the army. Having surveyed the lands around them, the predatory eyes of the Norman leaders settled on the Déise in Waterford. In theory, the Déise, through their ruler Máel Sechlainn Ua Fáeláin, had become vassals of King Henry of England during the royal expedition to Ireland. But Raymond calculated that the Déise could hardly be more alienated from Strongbow's rule than they were at present, and the Normans had no scruples in bringing the hammer down upon them. In an unprovoked attack with the advantage of surprise and an overwhelming advantage in numbers, Raymond led the army west from Waterford and took vast quantities of booty, arms and horses. Not content with the copious resources now in their hands, the Norman troops then advanced on Lismore.

Again, the Normans found they could plunder and ravage to their heart's content, this time accumulating so much booty that even after filling thirteen ships – some of which had been stolen from the harbour in Lismore – Raymond still had immense quantities of goods to bring back to Waterford by the coastal route. While the army marched ahead, the ships waited for a west wind. When fair weather finally came, however, it brought with it thirty-two longships, packed with Hiberno-Norse warriors from Cork who had been alerted to the raid on Lismore and who came seeking revenge. A fierce battle ensued in which the Norman crossbow once more proved its superiority over the missile weapons available in Ireland. Despite being outnumbered, Adam of Hereford, the Norman naval commander, managed to keep his ships just out of reach of the attacking flotilla. The arrows and bolts of the Normans inflicted far more damage than did the rocks and thrown axes of the Hiberno-Norse. Once his enemies had been cut down in sufficient number, Adam turned his ships about, and victory was assured when a sturdy youth, Philip of Wales, leapt aboard the Viking flagship and slew Gilbert Mac Turger, the leader of the Cork warriors.

This extraordinary naval battle showed that the Normans had not lost any of the sailing skills of their Viking forbears. The tactics of Adam, however, seem to have reflected their land-based form of warfare in that his craft were treated as a cavalry force, drawing the enemy on and introducing disorder to their ranks, until the Normans chose to turn about and bear down as one upon the chasing longships.

When Raymond was brought news that his own ships were under attack from a Hiberno-Norse fleet, he hurried back to Lismore with the army. There, he found that Adam had successfully outmanoeuvred the enemy navy and, indeed, had increased his number of ships, his armaments, and his plunder. A new foe, however, was present. Diarmait Mac Carthaig, king of Desmond and overlord of Lismore, had arrived with a large army, just too late to assist his allies from Cork. Although considerably outnumbered by Diarmait, Raymond trusted in the superiority of the equipment and training of this army and took the initiative by launching an attack. Success against numerical disadvantage, yet again, came to Normans, who drove the Irish army off. Gathering up the four thousand cattle brought by the Irish prince, Raymond returned in glory to Waterford. His triumph was complete and the policy of war seemed to be utterly justified.

The political reaction to these events, however, was a costly one for the Normans in Ireland. Well aware that Henry's forces were temporarily depleted and concerned now that oaths made to the English king clearly gave them no protection, many Irish lords came to the conclusion that they would be better uniting in an attempt to take on the remaining Norman troops than letting such locusts descend upon their lands. From the high king down to the minor lords of the country, Ireland was astir.

One small skirmish arising from the increasing number of ambushes and raids nearly cost the Normans their bravest knight in Ireland. The diminutive but fierce Meilyr fitz Henry had been chasing down a party of raiders near

Waterford, when he found that, along with one young knightly companion, he had far outstripped the rest of his own men. In the heat of the chase, Meilyr's young companion had lost all track of the position and charged into a wood full of Irish troops, where they turned and hacked him down with their axes. Meilyr kept riding in the hope of rescuing his friend, only to find blows raining upon him from all sides and men trying to grasp him to pull him from his horse. Cutting a path out through his assailants, Meilyr emerged from the crisis unscathed, though three thrown Irish axes had hit his horse and he had caught two more on his shield.

Having stirred up the hornet's nest, Raymond Le Gros left Ireland suddenly, before he could implement the agreement with Strongbow that would have led him to marry Basilia. For William fitz Gerald, Raymond's father, had died and Raymond needed to hurry across to Carew to ensure his succession of the lordship there. Once more Hervey de Montmorency took up the office of constable. And once more, the Norman presence in Ireland looked weak enough that it could be challenged successfully. It would take a brave Irish prince to risk the consequences of war with Strongbow, but the lord of Leinster's own brother-in-law, Domnall Mór Ua Briain of Thomond, was never afraid of entrusting his fate to the outcome of war. Domnall calculated that the time had come to throw off his professed loyalty to King Henry in pursuit of a return to the glorious days when the Uí Briain dominated Irish politics. A policy of war with the Normans was also an opportunity for Domnall to establish more equitable relations between himself and Ruaidrí Ua Conchobair, and as he set out eastwards on a major raid, Domnall was supported by Conchobar Máenmaige Ua Conchobair, Ruaidrí's son.

Domnall's first target was Strongbow's new castle at Kilkenny. News of the progress of the Irish army had reached the garrison of the castle and, reckoning themselves to be far too few in number to hold the fortress, Strongbow's men fled to Waterford. As a result Domnall was able to burn the timbers of the castle and plunder the lands all around Kilkenny. It was a small victory, but it had also been a test of the Normans' ability to hold their new fortifications, and the test demonstrated that, without sufficient troops, these castles were not as intimidating as they looked. Domnall returned to Limerick pleased with the effectiveness of his raid.

From Strongbow's point of view this challenge needed to be met by a firm response or he would risk the unravelling of his control over the Leinster Irish. Summoning support from Dublin, Hervey and Strongbow set out for Limerick early in 1174 to punish Domnall and raid Munster; they camped at Cashel where they intended to meet up with reinforcements from Dublin. While in camp, however, a rider came to Strongbow with alarming news. Ruaidrí Ua Conchobair was on the march to assist Domnall and had gathered to his banner the Irish princes who owed him service. The only remaining troops available to Strongbow were the somewhat unreliable Hiberno-Norse axemen of Dublin, and these were immediately summoned to Cashel.

Normally surefooted in his strategic deployment of troops, for once Strongbow had made a mistake. Several hundred unenthusiastic Hiberno-Norse warriors, with just four knights to command them, was not a sufficiently intimidating force to march safely across contested land. Whilst hastening to join Strongbow, this small army was vulnerable and, in a daring raid on their camp at Thurles, Domnall caught the Dubliners by surprise. Four hundred of the Hiberno-Norse axemen were killed, along with all four of their Norman officers. It was another triumph for Domnall and this time with greater consequences. Hervey and Strongbow decided that they could not risk battle with Ruaidrí without reinforcements and so they broke off their attack, retreating towards the presumed safety of Waterford; but there was no safety in Ireland for Strongbow now.

All the princes of Ireland took Strongbow's retreat from Cashel for what it was, an admission that the Norman lords had been so depleted of knights for their armies that they could not hold the lands they had expropriated. When Ruaidrí led a hosting to Meath, he was joined by a dozen senior Irish princes, including major lords from Ulster who were marching against the Normans for the first time as well as those with good reason to hate the Normans, such as

Aed mac Gilla Braite Ua Ruairc, the new ruler of Bréifne, and Mac Fáeláin, the ruler of the recently plundered Uí Fáeláin. Naturally, too, Magnus Ua Máel Sechlainn of Meath, whose lands had been crumbling in the face of advances by Hugh de Lacy, rallied to the Irish high king. As the pan-Irish army advanced, they found all the newly built Norman earth-and-timber castles empty and deserted. One by one these outposts for Norman raids on Irish lands were burned to the ground.

Inside the walls of Waterford, all was not well. The Hiberno-Norse people were truculent, inspired to resist their new masters by news of revolts, the burnings of castles, and the fate of their Dublin compatriots. Yet Strongbow understood that if he remained passively within the town, it would be at the cost of losing all that he had gained in the last four years. Moreover, a messenger arrived from Hugh Tyrell with urgent news. In the absence of Hugh de Lacy, Tyrrell was the castellan at Trim and now faced the largest Irish army the Normans had ever encountered. 'Hugh Tyrell of Trim,' the messenger said, 'the old baron, sends word to you through me to give him your fullest help and come to his relief with your forces.'

No coward, nor fool enough to take any pleasure in the weakening of his strongest Norman rival, Strongbow immediately called for his commanders to mobilise their troops. The messenger was sent back to Tyrell with the promise that help was on its way. Even as the rider set out for Meath, a dozen more riders galloped out of the protection of the walls of Waterford to demand military service from Strongbow's vassals. Old and young, fair and red-haired, every last man was put under arms and marched north with Strongbow. Rapid though Strongbow's response had been, it was too late to save the castle at Trim. There, Tyrell had abandoned the defences in the face of a vast incoming army. Ruaidrí's cavalry could therefore raid with impunity, all the way up to Dublin, while his infantry burned the wooden stockade and buildings on top of the ringwork castle of Trim, before throwing the earth of the raised platform back down into its ditch. The castle was entirely demolished.

With this symbolic as well as practical act of destruction, Ruaidrí turned back to Connacht and his allies dispersed. It appeared to all that there would be no more encroachment by Norman knights on Irish-held lands in Meath, but Strongbow was close behind. The Norman army arrived at sunset, to find the glow that they had been marching towards was the smouldering remains of Trim castle. Dismounting by the river, Strongbow walked through the chaos. There was nothing left standing, not even a hut in which he could spend the night. Instead, he decided, it might still be possible to catch the stragglers of the Irish army.

Taking his cavalry, Strongbow rode hard in the fading light, following the wide trail left by the cattle Ruaidrí had plundered. And there were indeed Irish troops on the trail ahead. Unarmed, concerned with moving plunder westwards, these Irish camp followers were helpless to resist the charge of Strongbow's knights. It was some consolation to the Normans that they managed to cut down a hundred and fifty of Ruaidrí's men before turning back in darkness.

Strongbow had done as much as he could for Tyrell, who at least had the security to begin the task of rebuilding the castle now that his local enemies were intimidated by the evidence that Strongbow would come swiftly to Trim if needed. In depleting Leinster of troops, however, Strongbow stretched his own position there beyond breaking point and it was the Hiberno-Norse people of Waterford who did their utmost to exploit the Norman's weakness. While rowing the governor of the town, Fretellus, up the Suir so that he could meet with Strongbow, the crew of the boat suddenly drew weapons and struck at him. Fretellus and his companions were swiftly killed. The boat then turned about and brought rebellion to the town. Every foreigner was massacred, regardless of age or sex, and but for fact that Ragnall's Tower remained in the control of Strongbow's men the entire Norman garrison would have perished.

Faced with this disaster, Strongbow sent a message by fast ship to Raymond Le Gros: 'when you read this letter waste no time in coming to my aid with a strong force, and be assured that immediately you arrive, your wish to take my sister Basilia as your lawful wife will be fulfilled without fail.' No better incentive for a Norman lord: carnal desire and the chance of glory. Heavy-set Raymond, accompanied by his small but ferocious cousin Meilyr fitz Henry, did not delay but sailed on the first easterly wind, putting in to Wexford with thirty knights, a hundred light cavalry, and three hundred foot archers chosen from the best fighting men of Wales. It was a vital reinforcement and it arrived just in time to prevent the Hiberno-Norse of Wexford attempting a similar uprising to that of Waterford.

By this time, Strongbow was outside Waterford, but preferred the safety of Inis Teimne (modern-day Little Island) an island in the river Suir, just east of Waterford, to the dangers of attempting to resume quarters in Ragnall's tower. After Raymond's arrival, to ensure they would be travelling with sufficiently large forces to guarantee their safety in what was now hostile land, Strongbow set out with the united army to Wexford where his sister was to come from Dublin to meet them for the marriage ceremony.

Under the de Clare's yellow and red standard and the banner of all Leinster, Strongbow handed Basilia to Raymond. The public occasion, which was as much about the appointment of Raymond to the office of Constable as the wedding, was marked by Raymond swearing to the fact that these banners were to be held only until Robert de Quency's daughter Maude came of age. But at the same time and in his own right, Raymond was made lord of Fothairt Fea (the barony of Forth, County Carlow) and all Uí Dróna, the people of East and West Idrone in County Carlow whom Raymond had defeated dramatically at the battle of Baginbun, and Glascarrig, on the east coast of Wexford near Cahore point. Raymond and Basilia would not lack for land, even after Maude married.

The Storming of Limerick

Reinforced, in 1175 Strongbow set about restoring Norman authority to those parts of Ireland that he had previously conquered. Putting control of Waterford once more under his governor and placing additional troops in the town, Strongbow and Raymond then returned to Trim, where, with the additional troops of Hugh Tyrell, they were able to defeat Magnus Ua Máel Sechlainn. The Irish ruler of Meath was brought back captive to Trim where he was hanged as a traitor. Even in Norman tradition, this was a severe punishment, but Strongbow had to quell rebellion and send a clear message to potentially disobedient Irish lords as to the consequences for them if they rose again.

The worst traitor, from Strongbow's point of view, was Domnall Mór Ua Briain of Thomond. His brother-in-law had struck with bold initiative and made Strongbow's plight a far more difficult one by the slaughter of the Dublin troops. It was essential to punish Domnall, not least to prove that breaking an oath to the Norman lord had fatal consequences. A campaign against Thomond, however, need not be simply a Norman affair; there were many Irish princes who would wish to deal a blow to the ambitious ruler of Limerick. Among them, Domnall mac Donnchada Meic Gilla Pátraic, ruler of Osraige, was willing to offer support in the weakening of his western neighbour.

On the cusp of leading the expedition, Strongbow was suddenly called away to King Henry's side once more. In Raymond Le Gros, however, Strongbow had an experienced constable with the full confidence of the army. Trusting that Raymond could carry out the expedition against Domnall, Strongbow left his constable to mobilise the Leinster army, old and young, humble and great. Meath, too, supplied troops, Tyrell respecting the efforts Strongbow had gone to in his hour of crisis. Altogether Raymond commanded a hundred and twenty knights, three hundred mounted archers, and four hundred foot archers.

In preparing for the march towards Limerick, Raymond sought a meeting with Domnall mac Donnchada, whom he did not trust. The prince of Osraige presented himself to the constable and loudly declaimed that he would practise no deception or treachery. 'You have no fear about that. On the contrary, I shall guide you straight there and I will pledge my word to that.'

Of all his barons, Strongbow had taken the greatest liking to the intelligent and honourable Maurice de Prendergast, assigning lands to the Flemish lord such that Strongbow's own caput was adjacent to that of Maurice. At this time, the Norman lord felt deeply the absence of Maurice – who in 1169 had marched up and down Osraige with his men – and Robert fitz Stephen, who had previously travelled to and from Limerick, to assist Domnall Mór against Ruaidrí. Those two commanders, however, were away in the service of King Henry.

Still, the risk of undertaking a strike aimed at Limerick was lessened by the fact that Thomond had fallen out with Connacht once more. The rivalry between these two kingdoms had been persistent for hundreds of years and it flared up again now. Gaining in confidence, Domnall Mór Ua Briain had struck out, killing and blinding a number of his nearest enemies, one of whom was a relative of Ruaidrí Ua Conchobair. In retaliation, Ruaidrí mustered the Connacht host and, in a successful campaign, had driven Domnall Mór Ua Briain out of Thomond and given the kingdom to a rival branch of the Uí Briain.

Proceeding cautiously, therefore, with his troops constantly on guard, not least against the possibility of treachery from Osraige, Raymond travelled for a day and a night to the walled town of Limerick. The prince of Osraige had guided them faithfully enough and the most important town in the realm of the Uí Briain stood before them. Inside the city was a Hiberno-Norse population well used to hard fighting, but there were no local Irish forces to assist the Vikings. These had been dispersed and disorganised as a consequence of Ruaidrí's recent raid.

To attack Limerick was a challenge. The town had natural defences, being built on islands in the Shannon just before the point at which the river becomes an estuary (the modern-day English Town district of Limerick on King's Island). These natural fortifications were reinforced by stone walls and deep moats. No one could cross the water to the city without ships or constructing a bridge. Or so it seemed. There was a deep ford, but the dark waters looked extremely dangerous to both men and horses.

One of the young knights present was a nephew of Raymond's, a tall hand-some warrior called David. Impatient at the fact that the army was blocked by the fast running water and keen to make his name as a hero, David urged his horse into the river. Working a slanted course against the current and care-fully watching the crests of the rippling waves, the young knight triumphantly rode up the far bank. Crying to the other knights that the river was fordable, David finally managed to encourage a second Norman rider to test the waters. Geoffrey Judas – named in honour of the Biblical champion Judas Maccabeus – was next to attempt the crossing. And Geoffrey's fate immediately put a halt to the initiative. For although he did manage to reach the far shore, no other Norman soldiers came to join them. On the return journey, Geoffrey's horse slipped and in an instant the violence of the current swept him to a cold and miserable death.

After that horrible spectacle, the expedition seemed to be at an end, for the murmuring that spread through the army was to the effect that a crossing was impossible and it was necessary to retreat. Raymond was not in a position to counter this demoralisation, as he was with the rearguard, so it fell to another nephew of Raymond's, Meilyr fitz Henry, to give a lead. Crying 'cross over, knights! Why are you hanging back?' Meilyr plunged straight into the cold water and soon his shivering horse scrambled out of the far side.

By this time, the soldiers of Limerick, mostly axemen from the Hiberno-Norse community, had come up as close to the crossing as they could with-out falling foul of Raymond's archers. Seeing the lone knight on the banks of the Shannon, the citizens of Limerick began to bombard Meilyr with stones and arrows. Fending off the missiles with his shield, Meilyr repeatedly shouted the name of St David, appealing to the saint to give him strength and vigour. The noise of the assembled men now became a greater roar than that of the Shannon as the Normans urged on their champion and raised their own temper to the point where they dared cross. On hearing the clam-our, Raymond pushed his way through the ranks to the water's edge. There he saw his nephew holding out against a barrage of stones and arrows in such a manner that, when he came to write of the scene, Gerald de Barri barely had the words for such valor.

'Come on men, we have been shown the way ...' Raymond cried. 'We cannot let the man who has undertaken such a feat be overwhelmed through lack of support.' With that, Raymond turned his horse and plunged into the Shannon. His army followed.

Many men were pulled under by the river, but the great majority survived to storm the walls of Limerick by immediate assault. The fighting was brief and bloody, the Hiberno-Norse warriors no match for the Norman knights and their archers. Before long, the bodies were piling up in the streets and the victorious army was helping itself to the riches of the town. One of the reasons for Raymond's popularity with the army was that − after a portion was put aside for their leader − all booty was shared in common, with a just division of spoils taking place once the fighting was over. This was a system termed 'Brabantine' after the practice of the mercenaries of northern French towns. It had a tactical advantage over the 'first come, first served' policy, in that the discipline of the conquering army lasted longer: soldiers knew that they could continue fighting, without the risk that their comrades would break off in search of plunder. Once the victorious army was paid off, Raymond assigned a garrison to hold the town for the winter, under the command of his cousin Milo fitz David, and returned to Waterford.

The Death of Strongbow

In the early spring of 1176 ships arrived from England at Waterford, bringing Strongbow back to Ireland. The same ships, however, also brought unwelcome news to Raymond Le Gros. Ever cautious, ever careful to put limits on the power of rising lords, Henry II recalled Raymond to royal service in England and sent four envoys to act for the king in Ireland. These envoys were given extensive authority and understood that their role was to tighten royal control of affairs in Ireland, giving less room to figures such as Strongbow, Raymond and even Hugh de Lacy to pursue their own policies. To emphasise this, the following year one of the envoys, Robert Poer, was given custody of Waterford and its adjacent lands as far as Lismore and Wexford.

Raymond had made all of his preparations to leave and was just awaiting a favourable wind, when news came that Strongbow's brother-in-law, Domnall Mór Ua Briain, was making a bid to regain control of Limerick and had brought a substantial force to besiege the town. Since Milo's garrison had little enough by way of supplies, with winter having drained their resources, the Waterford army needed to march at once if the town were to remain in Norman hands. All the orders to mobilise were issued, but it quickly became clear that Strongbow and the royal officers had a problem. Their troops did not want to leave Waterford unless their champion and constable, Raymond, came with them. Even the king's own envoys could see that, given this crisis, it would be a mistake to insist on Raymond's departure for England, and they agreed to his remaining in Ireland. At the head of eighty knights, two hundred mounted archers, three hundred foot archers and Irish auxiliaries, Raymond raised his battle standard once more.

The campaign was another great success for the Normans, with Raymond overcoming Domnall Mór Ua Briain's forces near Cashel, where the Irish prince had made a stand behind defences of fallen trees, trenches and a barricade. Once more Meilyr fitz Henry was in the fore of the assault, helping open a route to his opponents, through which Raymond's army then charged, with great loss of life among the Thomond troops. It was the eve of Easter, 3 April 1176, and the relief of Limerick was assured.

After following up his victory with a three-way parley with Domnall Mór Ua Briain and Ruaidrí Ua Conchobair, acting in the name of King Henry, Raymond returned to Limerick with hostages. There he was approached to intervene in a conflict between Diarmait Mac Carthaig, king of Desmond, and his main rival and oldest son Cormac Liathánach. As Raymond was marching on Cork to assist Diarmait, a messenger came to the constable with an urgent and private letter from his wife. It read:

His wife Basilia desires for her most loving lord and husband Raymond the same health and happiness as for herself. Dearest, let it be known to you, my true and loving husband, that that large molar tooth, which caused me so much pain, has now fallen out. So I beg of you, if you have any thought for your own future safety or mine, return quickly and without delay.

This rather cryptic message was a reference to the death of Strongbow. The great adventure undertaken by Strongbow had come to a premature and unexpected end. On 20 April 1176, at the age of forty-six, Strongbow died of blood-poisoning. Given his active military life, there had been many moments in which a violent end could have overtaken Strongbow. The actual manner of his death, however, was a slow one and one that could have been avoided given a more sophisticated knowledge of medical matters than prevailed in northern Europe at the time. For, as a result of an unspecified accident, Strongbow's foot became infected. The wound festered and, like a septic molar tooth – which too could be a cause of death in the period – the poison began to spread. By the time the infection had taken hold of his whole body, it must have been clear to Strongbow that it was too late for amputation and that his death had crept up on him. By agreement among his closest followers, the normal public rituals accorded a dying lord were put aside. It was vital that messengers reach Raymond and the army to bring them back to Dublin, for fear that news of Strongbow's death prompt a general rising.

The Irish sources record delight at Strongbow's death. At Clonmacnoise, where the *Annals of Tigernach* were being kept, the following entry was written: 'Richard, Earl of Dublin, died. Since Turgesius [an early Viking leader] there had never come into Ireland a brigand that had wrought more ruin than him. For he ruined Conmaicne and Meath and the southern half of Erin, both church and territory; but St Brigid killed him, and he himself used to see her in front of him, killing him.' As with several of the obituaries to Diarmait Mac

Murchada, the monk writing the entry was keen to add divine disapproval to the secular condemnation of the dead prince.

On the Norman side, too, Strongbow was not greatly lamented. From King Henry's point of view, Strongbow's death created more room for royal appointments in Ireland. Although, after their reconciliation in 1171, Strongbow had served Henry faithfully, Strongbow could never be fully trusted. Not after having defied the king and sailed to Ireland in search of lands to conquer and a princess to marry. Much better was to appoint to this land courtiers whose entire lives had been demonstrations of loyalty, men who could be counted on to direct the wealth of Ireland towards the English crown and not towards establishing their own principalities.

If the king of England lacked any affection for Strongbow, perhaps it could be found instead amongst those comrades of the lord of Strigoil who had accompanied him to Ireland and fought under his banner. Certainly some, such as Maurice de Prendergast, had every reason to be grateful to the man who had raised them to positions of lordship that they could not have hoped to obtain in England and Wales. Nevertheless, from the perspective of Raymond Le Gros, Robert fitz Stephen, Meilyr fitz Henry, and their friends and relatives, Strongbow's policy of striving for peace in Ireland after 1171 was a mistaken one and they, along with the great majority of the Norman and Welsh soldiers, had become estranged from Strongbow in the years before his death. Ireland, it had seemed, was available to them in its entirety, but instead of extending the military campaign, Strongbow had followed the policy laid down for him by Henry II and held his men in check.

It is in these final years of service to Henry that Strongbow is most clearly differentiated from the Norman adventurers who preceded him. Duke William of Normandy nominally owed fealty for his duchy to the king of France, but that in no way restrained him from undertaking a most audacious attempt on the realm of England. Robert Guiscard was an entirely self-made man and owed no service to any superior. His son Bohemond defied the Byzantine Empire to rule as prince of Antioch.

Strongbow was as ambitious and as capable as the most successful of Norman lords. His military leadership was careful, thorough, but also extremely dynamic when necessary. Nor was he lacking in personal bravery. The times Strongbow lived in, however, were different to those of the earlier generations in a very significant respect. At the end of the eleventh century, even the most power-ful European king had relatively little military sway over their strongest vassals and neighbours. By contrast, in the second half of the twelfth century, Europe's kings wielded immensely greater authority than their vassals. In military terms alone, Henry II had at his disposal the service of tens of thousands of knights. Moreover, Henry had at his command a much more sophisticated govern-mental apparatus than had existed in the eleventh century. The age when a Norman hero could fight his way along a route from poverty to a crown was over, because the descendants of those who had already attained power were now jealously controlling that path. That it was under these circumstances that Strongbow dared to cross the Irish Sea in defiance of Henry II shows both the appeal of Diarmait Mac Murchada's offer and the drive that must have been smouldering in Strongbow's heart for twenty years as he laboured under the hardship of royal disfavour.

To defy the king of England and embark on the adventure that was his campaign in Ireland was to guarantee all kinds of dangers would assail him in the future, not the least being that of severe punishment at the hands of Henry II. Yet he seized his moment and, from his own perspective, if not that of the Irish aristocracy whom he forced from their lands, Strongbow's deci-sion proved to be the right one. As one near contemporary English chronicler wrote, it was a marvel that Strongbow had managed to defy the king and rise from having scarcely anything but his bare title of nobility to become cel-ebrated for his wealth in Ireland and England.

Strongbow was buried on 20 April 1176 in Christ Church Cathedral, with Lorcán Ua Tuathail, the archbishop of Dublin, performing the ceremony.

CHAPTER 8

Legacy

The stormy rivalry of Diarmait Mac Murchada and Tigernán Ua Ruairc created a whirlpool in Irish political life that drew the last of the great Norman adventurers, Strongbow, across the Irish Sea. The consequences of the introduction of this new pattern of warfare and settlement for the people of Ireland were immense, both for the particular individuals alive at the time and for generations to come.

Most of the individual Norman barons who hitched their fortunes to those of Strongbow reaped ample rewards for their participation in the expropriation of the Irish and Hiberno-Norse aristocracy. Although they had won their new lands by the sword and therefore by the ethos of their class felt entitled to it, all of them found it necessary, as Strongbow had done, to reach an understanding with the king of England in order to retain their conquests. Strongbow's uncle, Hervey de Montmorency, for example, hurried to England after the lord of Leinster's death, to appear at court and attempt to influence the custodianship of Strongbow's lands, which was given to the royal courtier, William fitz Aldelin. This custodianship was confirmed at a Council in Oxford, in May 1177, a council at which Hervey was present. Hervey owned the lands between Wexford and Waterford that had been given to him in compensation for the loss of the title of Constable to Raymond Le Gros. With the death of his lord, Hervey was temporarily relieved of the obligations – mostly military service – that came with the land, but the respite was short-lived, as at the same council King Henry reassigned the services owed on Hervey's land to the royal governor of Wexford. After a life of fortune-seeking that began in France long before he came to Ireland, Montmorency retired to make suitable arrangement for his soul and, in 1179, became a monk of Christ Church, Canterbury where he lived peacefully for another ten years, dying 12 March 1189.

Raymond Le Gros, who had married Strongbow's sister Basilia and who was extremely popular with the Norman troops in Ireland, was for a short while the main Norman authority in Ireland. After the arrival of Wiliam fitz Aldelin in Dublin, however, Raymond was obliged to hand over control of Strongbow's cities, castles and hostages to the royal official. Moreover, lands which Raymond claimed in Uí Fáeláin and near Wexford were also brought into royal control. His service to Strongbow and the crown did not go entirely unrewarded. In or around the year 1183 a castle was constructed for Raymond le Gros in Fotharta Uí Nualláin (Forth, County Carlow), by royal command. Always an important Norman lord, Raymond was nonetheless eclipsed by the growth of royal authority in Ireland and his death was unrecorded, occurring sometime before 1192.

At around the same time, Raymond's uncle, Robert fitz Stephen, died. It was Robert who had spent a great many months of his life in prison: in Wales and then in Wexford. But he had emerged from these experiences unbroken and had been at the forefront of the Norman efforts to gain territory in Ireland. Robert had also performed extraordinary service for the king of England, saving Henry's life in an early Welsh campaign and – along with Maurice de Prendergast – defeating the king's enemies in 1173. His reward for this was the grant of lands, yet to be conquered, around Cork, and Robert returned to Ireland after the Council in Oxford in the company of William fitz Aldelin. Together with a core group of Strongbow's former men, including Miles de Cogan, as well as the young knights who had killed Tigernán Ua Ruairc, Robert succeeded in making himself a lord of extensive territories.

Another of Robert's relatives to have joined in the Irish adventure was Maurice fitz Gerald. Having fought alongside Strongbow from 1171 to 1173, Maurice returned to Wales. When Strongbow granted Maurice lands in Uí Fáeláin and Wicklow between Bray and Arklow, Maurice settled in Ireland, dying in Wexford in September 1176. One of Maurice's sons, Thomas fitz Maurice Fitzgerald (*d.* *c*1213) was ancestor of the earls of Desmond.

The most pugilistic of the Norman knights to come to Ireland was Meilyr fitz Henry, nephew of Maurice fitz Gerald. In the immediate aftermath of Strongbow's death, Meilyr struggled against the new royal officials for control of the lands he had been assigned in Wicklow by Maurice. In 1181, Meilyr was permitted to exchange custody of the castle of Kildare in Uí Fáeláin for the border territory of Laigis, and his fortunes began to rise. The following year, Hugh de Lacy, lord of Meath, gave Meilyr his niece as wife and built a castle for Meilyr at Timahoe (County Laois). In 1192, Meilyr constructed another castle, at Ardnurcher (County Offaly).

By 1199, Meilyr's vigour in asserting Norman authority in borderlands was rewarded by his being appointed Justiciar, and a great extension of the territories under his control took place, courtesy of grants by King John. It was under Meilyr's direction, following royal command, that Dublin Castle was constructed in 1204. Aspiring to even more control over Norman Ireland, Meilyr entered into a number of disputes with the lord of Leinster, William Marshall, who was out of favour with the king of England. Effectively, Meilyr was attempting to surmount the fundamental division of Norman affairs in Ireland, introduced by Henry II when he made Hugh de Lacy lord of Meath to counter the position of Strongbow. But Meilyr had overreached himself and in 1208 King John came to terms with William Marshall and removed Meilyr from office. As an old man, Meilyr had to suffer the reverse of the situation he had aspired to create, when William Marshall became regent to the young Henry III. In 1219, Henry III ordered Meilyr to render the services owed for his lands to the Marshal rather than the crown and to be attentive to William Marshall as his lord. Nevertheless, it was an extraordinarily long and successful life for the young knight who had very nearly perished at the walls of Limerick.

On the whole, the Norman lords did extremely well out of their crossing of the Irish Sea to intervene in Irish politics and usurp the local aristocracy. One less fortunate among them was Hugh de Lacy. De Lacy was extremely powerful and crushed all resistance to his rule in Meath through a programme of castle building, a programme that included, from 1178, the construction of an impressive stone castle in Trim. Aspiring to even greater control over Irish affairs, following the approach taken by Strongbow, de Lacy married an Irish princess: Rose, a daughter of Ruaidrí Ua Conchobair. Through this effort to integrate himself among the Irish élite, combined with a policy of generosity towards those Irish lords who submitted to him, de Lacy obtained a period of unchallenged rule in Meath and was positioning himself to be a candidate for the high kingship of Ireland on Ua Conchobair's death.

Naturally, the ever vigilant Henry II felt threatened by these developments, and he recalled de Lacy to England in 1179 and again in 1181. From then on, although de Lacy was the main Norman power in Ireland, he had to put up with a succession of royal officials keeping a close watch on his activities. Despite all his castles, de Lacy fell, and he fell very abruptly to the blow of an axe. On 26 July 1186, de Lacy was in Durrow (County Laois), inspecting his newly erected castle there. 'There came towards him then,' says an Irish annalist, 'a youth of the men of Meath, namely Gillaganinathair Ó Miadaig of Bregmuine, having hidden an axe under his cloak, and he gave de Lacy one blow, so that he cut off his head, and de Lacy fell, both head and body, into the ditch of the castle.' The young Irish warrior then bolted for the woods and escaped to boast of his deed to In Sinnach ('the fox') Ua Ceithernaig, king of Tethba (located east of the Shannon, roughly modern-day Counties Offaly and Westmeath), whose son had been killed by de Lacy in battle eight years earlier. With the decapitation of de Lacy the final threat that Ireland would be ruled by a Norman high king came to an end. Instead, it would be the attitude of the English crown that would determine Ireland's fate.

Irish Lords after the Coming of the Normans

For each Norman soldier who earned a life-long fortune from the events of 1166–1176, there was an Irish warrior who was ruined. Diarmait Mac Murchada's involvement of Norman lords in Irish affairs was catastrophic for Ireland's aristocracy. Many dynasties of the eastern half of Ireland were displaced entirely. Even the high king, in the relative safety of his Connacht strongholds, suffered considerably. In 1166, having secured the submission of all of his major rivals, Ruaidri had been poised to become one of Ireland's greatest high kings. But the coming of the Normans not only led to a direct challenge to his authority by the new arrivals, it also led to a whole series of defections and challenges by Irish lords.

Recognition that the centre of gravity of political affairs had moved away from Ua Conchobair came with the Treaty of Windsor: this was an agreement that was concluded on 6 October 1175 between Henry II and Ruaidrí, who was represented by the archbishop of Tuam, the abbot of Clonfert, and his chancellor. The treaty recognised Henry II as overlord of Leinster and Meath, while Ruaidrí was acknowledged as high king over the rest of Ireland. Never again would an Irish king claim sovereignty over the whole of Ireland. More-over, this was not an agreement between equals: Ua Conchobair acknowl-edged Henry as his overlord and agreed to collect tribute and to punish rebels in return for miitary assistance from the English royal officials in Ireland.

Remaining in power, albeit via this curtailed form of kingship, the elderly Ruaidrí Ua Conchobair was forced into retirement as ruler of Connacht by his son, Conchobar Máenmaige. Four times Ruaidrí attempted a come-back, twice with Norman assistance, and eventually he settled for lands in Uí Fiachrach Aidne and Cenél Áeda na hEchtge in south Connacht. Ruaidrí Ua Conchobair died at Cong on 2 December 1198, aged eighty-two, and was buried at Clonmacnoise.

There were a handful of Irish lords to benefit from the coming of the Normans, the most notable being Domnall Caemanach, son of Diarmait Mac

Murchada. Domnall had travelled to Wales with his father and had been present at the fateful meeting between Diarmait and Strongbow. In the military campaigning that followed Strongbow's arrival in Ireland, Domnall had been the leader of an important body of Uí Chennselaig cavalry. In return, Strongbow, and indeed his successors, awarded most of Ui Chennselaig outside of Ferns to Domnall, who served the lord of Leinster as 'seneschal of his Irish of Leinster'. This arrangement between the Norman lords of Leinster and Domnall's successors lasted nearly two hundred years. When it did eventually break down, it was Domnall's descendant Art Mac Murchada who led a successful campaign against English royal officials in Ireland.

The fate of one other major Irish figure from these times deserves discussion: Aífe, the daughter of Mac Murchada. Another child of Diarmait's who had accompanied her father into exile, Aífe, like Domnall, honoured the agreement made with Strongbow and he in turn honoured her. While Strongbow was alive, Aífe was perhaps the most notable woman in Ireland, but with the death of her husband, difficult times lay ahead. Strongbow had left her with a son, Gilbert, who was three years old, and a daughter, Isabella, aged five. To preserve their inheritance in the face of Irish revolt and English royal demands was an enormous challenge.

As Countess of Strigoil and 'countess of Ireland', Aífe featured on English royal records as a person who was still of considerable importance. In 1183–4 Aífe was granted £20 from King Henry in order to defend herself and her lands in the Welsh marches. This indicates that Aífe was giving military direction to Strongbow's vassals and doing her best to defend her husband's lands on behalf of her young son. That she was involved in the full range of Strongbow's interests, in Ireland, Wales and England, is shown by two more documents that indicate her presence in Hertfordshire and Essex. Aífe suffered an enormous blow to her position, however, when Gilbert died while still a minor (between 1185 and 1189). This left Isabella as the heiress to Leinster and Strongbow's Welsh lands. It was far too dangerous for Henry II to allow any independence for Isabella: if some ambitious lord in Ireland were to marry the girl, a massive accretion of power would suddenly come his way. So Henry effectively took Isabella into protective custody in London, from where she was released in July 1189, when she was freed in order to marry to William Marshall.

It is in the impressive level of autonomy shown by Isabella, especially in regard to her ability to direct affairs in Ireland, that we have the strongest evidence that her mother Aífe must have prevented the support of Strongbow's vassals from disintegrating during the regency; furthermore, in alliance with her brother Domnall, Aífe must have maintained a following among the Uí Chennselaig. When William Marshall was in great danger from the anger of King John and went to England to defend himself, it was Isabella who rallied the vassals of the lord of Leinster and their Irish allies against efforts by the Justiciar to seize their lands. Isabella had her own chaplain and her own clerk. Her seal shows her standing in a dress, with pointed headdress and long cloak, and, portraying her active life and integration with the activities of her male peers, with a falcon on her left wrist.

Eight Hundred Years of Oppression?

If the coming of the Normans to Ireland had dramatic consequences for the lives of that particular generation, the events of 1166–1176 reshaped the country in a fashion that affected every subsequent generation in Ireland, perhaps all the way down to today. There is a caricature of Irish nationalist thought that states that republicans believe that with the coming of Strongbow to Ireland we see the beginning of more than eight hundred years of the oppression of Ireland at English hands. In fact, it is hard to find anyone who defends this idea, because it is too crude, and too simplistic. Strongbow's motives in launching his ships across the Irish Sea were entirely different to, say, Oliver Cromwell's decision nearly five hundred years later to pay off his army with lands in Ireland. There is no question that, at times, over the subsequent centuries English authority imposed devastating policies upon the majority of Irish people, but those policies (for example, the Penal Laws) arose from a very different motivation to the one that brought Strongbow to Ireland.

A more useful perspective from which to view the coming of the Normans to Ireland is obtained, not by running several centuries forward to the age of empires, but by moving backwards to the arrival of Vikings in Ireland from the ninth century. The Vikings robbed and plundered and did immeasurable harm to monasteries and churches, which were the main centres of sophisticated cultural activity of the era. But as they settled in coastal towns and began to trade and intermarry with the Irish population, the Vikings also brought significant innovations to Ireland that raised the overall level of culture. Their skills were primarily in boatbuilding and sailing, in knowledge of tide and navigation, so that through their presence in Ireland came a great upsurge of trade with Europe. With the Vikings, too, came Ireland's first mint and a great acceleration in the circulation of coins throughout a country that had been limited to the use of cattle and female slaves as a form of currency. The Vikings were also skilled metal workers, leather workers and masons: Ireland's first walled towns were constructed by the Vikings. A visit to Dublin's National Museum and its Viking exhibition shows a technical advance and increase in the quantity of production of crafted artefacts that took place with the settlement of Viking communities in Ireland.

The arrival of Norman settlers can be seen in a similar light. First, bloodshed and robbery, but subsequently considerable economic innovation and development. We should remind ourselves that the bloodshed and robbery was directed primarily against the Irish aristocracy. For the slaves of Ireland, who every day arduously churned away at making butter they were never allowed to eat, it was a definite improvement to be freed. Not that the Norman economic system was egalitarian: those at the very bottom of society still had to labour in the fields for their masters, and many of them were not former slaves going up in status but members of the complex hierarchy of Irish free farmers who had been pushed downwards in their social position. At least under the new system these serfs, the betaghs, kept a portion of the crop for themselves and Irish lands under Norman control improved rapidly as they and the free peasants working them had an incentive to raise productivity.

Although agriculture had been developing in Ireland in the early twelfth century, especially in the vicinity of monasteries, the Normans greatly increased the quantity of sophisticated agricultural tools in the country, tools such as the heavy plough, with its iron share and coulter, iron-bound wheels and mould-board. Norman mills, spinning and weaving techniques were – with the exception of such activities in the Cistercian monasteries – more advanced than those in Ireland. In their long strips of unfenced field, crops were rotated, with a frequent alteration of fallow fields. By reclaiming land from forest and marsh, the overall area of land given to oats and wheat greatly expanded. Before the economic and political crises of the early fourteenth century, Ireland was a food exporter, with a notable trade from Waterford with the ports of south-west France, exchanging corn for wine.

With growing agricultural prosperity in the eastern half of Ireland came increased settlement, and new towns and villages were founded by immigrants from Britain and beyond. Although their farming and agricultural activity thrived, it is clear from the expensive prices for manufactured articles, such as iron ploughs, that the iron industry did not advance significantly within Ireland. Most manufactured ironwork was imported. Pottery, however, was created on a much greater scale, with kilns proliferating in Norman regions. Wood and leather goods became more complex and were turned out in much greater quantity.

Major towns, such as Kilkenny, were established in the wake of the Normans wresting the territory from its former owners. To encourage new arrivals of farmers and artisans, villages were founded with borough status, in other words relatively favourable legal rights, such as the right to their own courts. An example of such a borough is Newtown Jerpoint in County Kilkenny, where the dramatic remains of Jerpoint Abbey still stand on the landscape nearby. An even more common form of settlement than the formation of a new village was the construction by the Normans of moated manorial centres: a few buildings surrounded by a defensive palisade and a square ditch filled with water. Then, of course, there was the castle.

The castle was the means, above all, by which the newly arrived knights secured their lands and intimidated the local population into serving them. Around five hundred earthwork castles were built in the century following the arrival of the Normans. They were often on top of mottes – tall Christmas pudding-shaped mounds of earth – but about a quarter of these castles were ringworks. Usually one castle was in sight of another, which meant the creation of a strategic chain of communication that stretched across the landscape. Within ten years of their arrival, the Normans were beginning to build their key castles in stone, such as Hugh de Lacy's headquarters at Trim. These castles were the most visible and dramatic proof that, with the coming of the Normans, the Irish landscape was fundamentally changed.

In regard to the economy, to trade and to agriculture, Norman settlement heralded a considerable growth in activity in Ireland. The picture is more ambiguous, however, in terms of their impact upon the arts. No other region in Europe had such a literary culture and respect for the poet as did Ireland before the Normans. Initially, this culture was damaged as poets were displaced from conquered lands and as Norman-led churches ceased to gather Irish literary manuscripts (including prose sagas, genealogies, etc) as had been their previous practice. After 1200, Irish poetry revived, with professional literary families taking on the role of educators in these traditions; a role that the church had previously played.

Of course, the Normans had their own literature and a major poem that was composed to honour the success of Strongbow and his followers has survived to be a crucial source for these events. On the whole, however, the transplanting of a form of French to Ireland was not a success. It is testimony to the strength and perceived value of Irish culture, at this time, that very soon after settling in Ireland, the newly arrived farmers and lords alike began to adopt Irish ways in regard to language, dress, manners and hairstyles.

In the decorative arts, the Normans were more influential, bringing new trends for architecture, sculpture and metalwork to the country, although their arrival in Ireland did not lead to the displacement of traditional Irish manu-script illumination, but rather a fusion of new and old designs.

If there was one undeniably negative result for Ireland from these events, it was in the creation of a political system of government that, for the eastern half of the island at least, was directed by the English crown. Strongbow's success had drawn Henry II to come to Ireland in person and, as a result of the decisions made there, a significant change took place in the overall political direction of the country. From this point onwards, the path of political central-isation that might have led to Ireland developing a tradition of powerful high kings with real authority over the entire country was diverted. Fragmentation of power would continue to be the rule in regions governed by Irish lords, while, more significantly, successive English kings and queens now believed they had the right to direct affairs in Ireland and to draw on the resources of the country for their own purposes.

The coming of Strongbow to Ireland does not mark the beginning of eight hundred years of oppression of Ireland by the English. Strongbow did not consider himself English and a case can be made that the overall impact of the Normans upon Ireland was not harmful but, especially in regard to agriculture, beneficial. In the intense personal battle between Diarmait Mac Murchada and Tigernán Ua Ruairc, however, we not only have a tale of kid-napping, jealousy and pride, we also can see a historical moment of much wider significance. This bitter decade was the period in which the English crown began to intervene directly in Irish affairs. Strongbow's adventure resulted in the foundation of a new relationship between England and Ireland, a relationship that was not initially oppressive, but was one that, in much later times, would indeed transform itself into that of empire and colony.

Afterword and Further Reading

In writing this book I made the decision to use the term 'Norman' to describe Strongbow and his followers. This, it has to be recognised, is problematic because Strongbow spent very little of his life in Normandy. Nor did he speak quite the same language as the Normans proper; he spoke a version of French described by modern historians as 'Anglo-Norman'. In this regard, Strongbow was typical of his generation. After 1066, England was conquered and settled by Norman knights who were very proud of their Normanitas. The sons and daughters of these conquerors also saw themselves as Norman and prioritised their Norman lands. So, for example, William the Conqueror himself bequeathed the Duchy of Normandy to his first son and the kingdom of England to his second son. By Strongbow's day, however, very few aristocratic families in England were as involved in Norman affairs as they were with English ones.

Strictly speaking, based on the language he used, which defined him and his peers, Strongbow would best be described as Anglo-Norman, although there are some who prefer Cambro-Norman to emphasise his Welsh connections and others who prefer simply 'English', with some justification, for the sources often refer to the conflicts of this decade as taking place between English and Irish. Even so, I feel it is a mistake to use a term with such potent modern overtones in a manner that would not have been intended by the medieval authors (who, on the whole, employed the term 'English', to indicate those who owed allegiance to the king of England). In any case, when Strongbow and others wanted to be absolutely clear about this matter, when they were drawing up legal and binding documents for the future, they spelled out that the terms applied to everyone, whether Welsh, English, Irish or Franci. The use of the term Franci in the charters of the newly arrived knights in Ireland is evidence they saw themselves as being of a different culture to the English or Welsh footsoldiers who accompanied them, as indeed they were, not only in terms of class but also in terms of ethnic identity.

Quite apart from being more readable when used with great frequency in the text, 'Norman' has another advantage over 'Anglo-Norman' and certainly over 'English', which is that it emphasises the essential continuity between a type of society that came into existence in Normandy towards the end of the tenth century and the world of Strongbow. In regard to the economy, military practices and political structure, Strongbow came from a society that was very different to that of Ireland — and of England before 1066 — but which shared its key features with those developed over a century earlier in Normandy. The perspective offered in this book is that Strongbow was the last of the series of great adventurers to emerge from the Norman tradition, and while 'Anglo-Norman' would be the more precise term for him and his followers, 'Norman' is much more effective in depicting the tradition in which he stood.

For further reading about the coming of the Normans in Ireland, there can be no better starting point than the two major sources for these events: Gerald of Wales's *The Conquest of Ireland* and an anonymous poetic chronicle *The Deeds of the Normans in Ireland*. Both are very well written, very entertaining and, despite nearly a thousand years having passed since they were composed, they can be read for pleasure as well as information. Gerald of Wales was a close relative of many of the knights who crossed over to Ireland and his own brother, Robert de Barri, played a prominent part in events. This means that Gerald is very well placed to recount in vivid detail the history of the period. There is a major weakness in Gerald's work, in that he was very active in promoting his relatives and the causes he believed in and was not at all hesitant about inventing material to suit his purpose. Imagining the speech of a Norman warrior before battle is acceptable artistic license and is understood as such by the reader, but making up documents and pretending they came from the papacy is another matter. Such forgeries serve to warn us be careful in following Gerald's story without corroboration. Fortunately, we do have a second major account of these events. This is *The Deeds of the Normans in Ireland*, sometimes known by a different title (the original being missing), *The Song of Dermot and the Earl*. Written in Anglo-Norman by a poet who had the opportunity to talk to Diarmait Mac Murchada's interpreter, the chronicle takes us from Diarmait's exile to the bravery of Meilyr fitz Henry before the walls of Limerick, in other words, it stops just before the death of Strongbow. Unfortunately, only one copy of this text survives in manuscript and that is incomplete. Nevertheless, what we have gives us another vivid read and a very valuable control on the material offered to us by Gerald. Both books are available in English, thanks to translations by AB Scott and FX Martin for the *The Conquest of Ireland* and Evelyn Mullally in her splendid edition of *The Deeds of the Normans in Ireland*. The translations I used here are taken from these works.

It is a great misfortune for our understanding of these events that we do not have a major source from the Irish perspective. The interested reader can, however, access the fragmentary entries of contemporary annalists, as translations from the Irish annals and chronicles are available. Perhaps the most easily viewed versions are those available thanks to CELT, the Corpus of Electronic Texts hosted by UCC at http://www.ucc.ie/celt/.

There is, of course, a considerable scholarly literature about these events, from broad surveys to local micro histories, and this extensive secondary literature is supplemented by a certain amount of archaeology. If I were to recommend just one study out of all the available material, it would be the relevant sections of Goddard Henry Orpen's *Ireland Under the Normans*. Despite being over a hundred years old (and therefore containing a number of claims that have been superseded by modern scholarship and archaeology), and despite a tendency – exaggerated by his critics – to overlook the sophistication and complexity of Irish society, it is a fabulous work of synthesis by someone steeped in knowledge of the sources.

Other Sources

Amatus of Montecassino, *History of the Normans*

Anna Comnena, *Life of Alexius Comnenus*

Annals of Clonmacnoise

Annals of Connacht

Annals of Inisfallen

Annals of Lough Cé

Annals of the Four Masters

Annals of Tigernach

Annals of Ulster

Anglo-Saxon Chronicle

Anon., *Deeds of the Franks*

Book of Llandaff

Chronicon Scotorum

Cogad Gáedel re Gallaib

Dudo of Saint-Quentin, *History of the Dukes of the Normans*

Fragmentary Annals of Ireland

Fulcher of Chartres, *A History of the Expedition to Jerusalem*

Geoffrey Malaterra, *Deeds of Count Roger and his brother Duke Robert*

Gerald of Wales, *History and Topography of Ireland*

Guy of Amiens, *Song of the Battle of Hastings*

Henry of Huntingdon, *History of the English People*

Mac Carthaigh's Book

Orderic Vitalis, *Ecclesiastical History*

Raymond of Aguilers, *The History of the Franks who Conquered Jerusalem*

Robert of Torigni, *Deeds of the Dukes of the Normans*

Snorri Sturluson, *Heimskringla*

Wace, *Roman de Rou*

William of Apulia, *Poem on the Deeds of Robert Guiscard*

William of Jumièges, *Deeds of the Dukes of the Normans*

William of Malmsbury, *Deeds of the Kings of the English*

William of Newburgh, *History of English Affairs*

William of Poitiers, *Deeds of Duke William*

Notes

Preface

Gerald of Wales, *The Conquest of Ireland* [hereafter GW].

Chapter 1

Hrólfr: Snorri Sturluson, *Heimskringla*; *History of the Earls of Orkney*.

Charles held by the ankle: Dudo of Saint-Quentin, *History of the Normans*.

'"Did you know that your wife was the thief"': Dudo of Saint-Quentin, *History of the Normans*.

Peasant rebellion: William of Jumièges, *Deeds of the Norman Dukes*.

'"Because you are younger than me"': Charter from Saint-Pierre at Préaux.

Decree on castles: *Consuetudines et Justicie*.

Tanner: Wace, *Roman de Rou*.

Jester Goles: Wace, *Roman de Rou*.

'"I am acquitting myself"': Wace, *Roman de Rou*.

'From the Cotentin came the lance': Wace, *Roman de Rou*.

Chapter 2

'The rival of London': William of Newburgh, *The History of English Affairs*.

Kidnapped for slavery: *Book of Llandaff*.

The 'three rough places': Kuno Meyer, *The Triads of Ireland*.

'Grim and wooded': GW.

'Into a man's bed': *Annals of Loch Cé*.

Diarmait's character: GW.

Irish 'treachery': Gerald of Wales, *History and Topography of Ireland*.

Battle of Móin Mór: The *Annals of Tigernach*.

Great evils of the world are brought about by women: GW.

Death of Mac Lochlainn: *Annals of Ulster*.

'Recalled to mind injustices': GW.

'Wicked king': Anon., *The Deeds of the Normans in Ireland* [hereafter *Deeds*].

'What value would Ireland be?': William of Malmesbury, *Deeds of the English Kings*.

Chapter 3

'"May God who dwell on high"': *Deeds*.

'"At my entreaties"': John of Salisbury, *Historia Pontificalis*. *Laudabiliter*: GW.

'Whose past was brighter': GW.

'The person most dearest': *Deeds*.

'A man of few words': GW.

'Traverse the island alone': *Annals of the Four Masters*.

Honour price: *Cáin Lánamna*.

'"If anyone wishes to have land"': *Deeds*.

'Fugitive from Fortune': GW.

Robert's teeth: GW.

'"Flight is out of the question"': *Deeds*.

'"As you command"': *Deeds*.

'So treacherous': *Deeds*.

Ghost army: *Deeds*; GW.

Chapter 4

Robert's response to Ruaidrí: GW.

'"You are very welcome"': *Deeds*.

'"Get your men ready at once"': *Deeds*.

'"Let us be off"': *Deeds*.

'Balding or hirsute': *Deeds*.

'"Listen to us, king"': *Deeds*.

'"What miserable drones"': Edward Grim,
   Life of St Thomas.

Chapter 5

'Sixty five and a half knights' fees': *Pipe Rolls*
   of Henry II.

Christchurch miracles: GW; Gerald of Wales,
   History and Topography of Ireland.

'Diarmaid Mac Murchada ... disturber of
   Banba': *Annals of Tigernach*.

'Diarmaid Mac Murchada ... by whom a
   trembling sod': *Annals of the Four Masters*.

'Diarmait, son of Donnchad': *Book of Leinster*.

Chapter 6

'"Listen to me, sire"': *Deeds*.

'Strike, renowned barons!': *Deeds*.

'"Lords," said the valiant earl': *Deeds*.

'"Cogan! The Cross!"': *Deeds*.

'"Maurice," replied Strongbow': *Deeds*.

'"Barons," shouted Maurice': *Deeds*.

Chapter 7

'"We have captured"': GW.

'King of Meath': GW.

'A sore and miserable sight': *Annals of Ulster*.

'Erin's raider and invader!': *Annals of Tigernach*.

'Through help brought from Leinster': *Deeds*.

   '"Hugh Tyrell of Trim"': *Deeds*.

'"When you read this letter"': GW.

'"You have no fear about that"': *Deeds*.

'"Cross over, knights!"': GW.

'"Come on men"': GW.

'"His wife Basilia"': GW.

'"A brigand"': *Annals of Tigernach*.

Chapter 8

'There came towards him': *Annals of Loch Cé*.

Index